A GARLAND FOR ASHES

World War II, the Holocaust, and
One Jewish Survivor's Long Journey to Forgiveness

Hanna Zack Miley

A Garland for Ashes
World War II, the Holocaust,
and One Jewish Survivor's Long Journey to Forgiveness
All Rights Reserved.
Copyright © 2013 Hanna Zack Miley
v4.0

Cover designer: Sheila Macho
Photographers: Thomas Cogdell, Julia Stone, Ryan Thurman

Outskirts Press, Inc.
http://www.outskirtspress.com

ISBN: 978-1-4787-1281-7

Library of Congress Control Number: 2013903752

Outskirts Press and the "OP" logo are trademarks belonging to
Outskirts Press, Inc.

PRINTED IN THE UNITED STATES OF AMERICA

outskirtspress
DENVER, COLORADO

Dedication

To George, my travel companion,
patient listener,
and caring husband,
who "keyed in" each word
as I read to him from my penciled pages.

Table of Contents

Foreword

In December 2012, a few weeks before *A Garland for Ashes* went to press, Hanna received this letter from a representative of her home town of Gemünd, Germany:

Dear Hanna,

I will try to use my best English: what I have to tell you is very wonderful!

As you know in 2013 Gemünd will celebrate its 800th birthday. There will be lots of events involving many people. It will be a very important year in the town's history. For the organizers the memory of the Jewish people is a very important part of this. We want to honor the Jews of Gemünd.

I told Manfred [the leader of the celebration's organizing group] your life story and your decision to return to Gemünd every year. The organizers want to thank you for your efforts toward reconciliation. We are thankful that you came back to Gemünd and offered us the hand of forgiveness— in this country and town where your parents and family were murdered. We want to honor the Jewish citizens of Gemünd, and we want to honor you as a Jewish citizen of Gemünd and as a woman who is seeking peace and blessing.

I have the wonderful task of asking if you would take the patronage of the celebrations in Gemünd next year. Serving as patron does not require you to carry any public duties or obligations, but you can if you would like. You can come to Gemünd whenever you want and go back to the USA whenever you want. My job is to ask if you would take this patronage. We hope you will, and we will be happy and honored if you do so.

Best wishes,

Georg Toporowsky

A few days later Hanna responded to Georg, saying that she was honored by the request and accepting his invitation. He responded that the organizers would like to have a word of greeting (*Grußwort* in German) to use on the official publications surrounding the anniversary celebrations. Hanna sent this Grußwort in reply:

Dear Friends,

Greetings from the Valley of the Sun, Phoenix, Arizona.

This year, 2013, is a significant milestone in the history of our home town. We have reached the 800th anniversary of our beginning.

When the Jewish citizens left Gemünd after Kristallnacht, I was the youngest among them. And now, 74 years later, you have invited me to be the patron of our celebration.

Why me? I believe you have given me this honor so that I may be a representative of the Jewish community. I remember some of them—their names and faces crowd my mind: Kurt Meier, my childhood friend; Gisela Teller, who gave me her sled; Ruth Meyer, who walked with me from my home on Dreibornerstrasse to the cinema. We wanted to see Snow White and the Seven Dwarfs. Above all, I think of my parents, Amalie and Markus Zack.

Many years passed before I began to visit Gemünd again. At first, reconnection with the past was a sorrowful experience. Amazingly, several citizens of Gemünd who actually remembered the small child, Hannelore

Zack were still alive. I am deeply thankful for their kindnesses. I had so few memories from my childhood, and the stories that Willi Kruff, Lisbet Ernst and Frau Schmitz shared helped me to make peace with the past. I believe that their love for a former Jewish neighbor continues in the decision you made, to remember the Jewish community during the 800th anniversary celebration.

What a beautiful thing you are doing, facing the truth about the darkness of the 1930s, by laying the Stolperstein [memorial stones commemorating Jewish citizens whose lives were lost during the Holocaust] at this time. Surely great blessing will flow out of such forthright honesty. You are seeking the good of this community.

Already in the last years there are evident signs of renewal and economic revitalization. Many visitors are coming to enjoy the beauty of the Eifel. Local young people are expressing their creativity as they connect with the history of Gemünd.

Each time my husband George and I return we experience much joy among our Gemünd friends.

Thank you for giving me this honor.

May God bless us, each one. Shalom.

Hanna Zack Miley

Preface

I remember the exact spot. Gerda and I were walking back from the Jewish cemetery on a cold, grey day toward the end of March 2008. Our friendship had begun years before, but it had been twenty-five years since we had spent time together. We were heading toward Dreibornerstrasse in the center of Gemünd, looking forward to catching up with each other over a relaxed lunch. As we crossed the bridge at the confluence of two rivers, the Urft and the Olef, where the Alte Bahnhofstrasse curves and becomes Am Plan, Gerda turned to me and said, "Why don't you write your story, Hanna?" This is where it all began.

I had always resisted the idea. What were the roots of my reluctance? I felt inadequate. Information about my family and my early years was sparse. I shrank back from the sheer slog that would be involved in such a project. But more than anything, I feared the pain of digging deep into the past.

When I look back at the events triggered by Gerda's question, I am reminded of my school days in England—I must have been about fourteen years old. Our class, dressed in ugly, green gym outfits, was attempting to run with hurdles for the first time. Everyone else seemed to take the obstacles in their stride. I couldn't. I froze before the first hurdle, no matter how many attempts I made. In the end, a couple of friends held each hand, ran with me, and pulled me up and over all the way to the end.

A Garland for Ashes began with the idea of telling "my story." As I gathered ideas, chose words, and formed sentences, sleeping memories of my parents gradually stirred to life. Newly discovered documents came into my hands, leading me to visit the places where they were born and where they died. It seems as though my book has turned into a journal recording the process of embracing my family, travelling beyond the horror and the shame of their gassing in Chelmno, Poland, on May 3, 1942, to the "Love that never ends."[1]

Like the schoolmates who guided me over the hurdles, so many have given a helping hand along the way: Hans-Dieter Arntz, Lisbet Ernst, Gisela Forbar, Ruth Holden, Annemarie and Willi Kruff, Günther Lukas, Gerda and Manfred Schaller, (who also introduced me to their editor friend, Ute Mayer, an encouragement at that early, scary stage of writing my story), Maria and Dieter Schmitz-Schumacher, Walter Volmer, Claudia and Hans Wiedenmann, and Detlef and Esther Wurst.

The names of some individuals who provided information or were a part of my story in some other way have been changed to protect their privacy; these have been marked with asterisks (*) throughout the book.

When I pick up a new book, I enjoy paying attention to the little details that indicate an author's background and attitude, so I even read the dedication. Often I take the effusive praise for an editor with a tiny pinch of salt. Now I am wiser. Like a midwife, my own editor, Kathleen Fairman, with kindness and grace, brought her prodigious skills to bear on the birthing struggle of this book. Carol Blumentritt, my gifted copy editor, told me she actually enjoyed working on the corrections, as did Cheri Beckenhauer, who brought all her administrative competence to the fine points of footnotes, bibliography, indexing, and photo scanning. And then there is Sheila Macho, creator of beauty, who discerned and expressed the heart of the book in her cover design.

Beyond this short list of names, a host of friends have prayed, and cheered me on with their acts of kindness—American, Austrian, British, Dutch, German, Polish, and Singaporean. I am grateful for each one.

PART I

Love and Hatred in the Third Reich

❧ ❧

Two statues.

I stand before the sculpture *Mother with Her Dead Son*,[1,2] and in the silence, my soul quivers.

Her silent lines penetrate the marrow like a cry of pain....

> Gerhardt Hauptmann
> Nobel laureate for literature
> writing about Käthe Kollwitz[2]

In 1993, this statue was placed in the center of the *Neue Wache* (New Guard House) Berlin. The sculptor, Käthe Kollwitz (July 8, 1867, to April 22, 1945), was one of the artists ridiculed in the Nazi exhibition *Entarte Kunst* (Degenerate Art), Munich 1937.[1]

❧ ❧

Far from Berlin, surrounded by the green hills of the Eifel, buffeted by wind and rain, I crane back my head to take in another statue, the five-meter-high *Fackelträger* (Torchbearer) planted in the grounds surrounding Vogelsang, the massive fortress that Hitler built. Today, the sculpture remains on a hill seven kilometers above Gemünd, my home town. The sculptor was Willy Meller.

The original inscription has been removed, but next to the stone statue, the full text is posted on a notice board:

> *Ihr seid die Fackelträger der Nation. Ihr tragt das Licht des Geistes voran im Kampfe für Adolf Hitler.* (You are the Torchbearers of the nation. You carry the light of the spirit forward into battle for Adolf Hitler.)[3]

In Vogelsang, young German men were taught Nazi racial philosophy. Many would graduate to lead the atrocities in the East.[4]

We have to stamp out compassion with the force of self-assertion.

Hans Dietel, Headmaster of Vogelsang
during a recorded lecture in 1937[5]

What was taught here led to the ramp at Auschwitz.

Klaus Ring, historian
describing the significance of Vogelsang[6]

1

From Köln to London

Having negotiated the stops and starts of airport security screening, I settle relaxed and grateful into my comfortable seat next to George on the Lufthansa flight. I relish the atmosphere created by the efficient yet kindly German flight attendants. I have been looking forward to this short journey from Köln (Cologne) to London for weeks. The date is November 19, 2008.

Suddenly I sit upright. It dawns on me that almost seventy years ago I travelled this same route, albeit under very different circumstances. Then, I was a little girl, scrunched into a corner of a train carriage, trying desperately to hold in my panic. Scenes from the past flicker before my eyes like an old-fashioned movie reel.

The Parting

On the evening of Monday, July 24, 1939, my parents brought me to the *Köln Hauptbahnhof* (the main train station of Cologne) to begin a journey. They could not go with me, and so they prepared me by saying I would be going on a nice trip. I was a spoiled, only child; they were attempting to "sweeten the pill." I still remember standing on the station platform and looking up at the huge, high glass and steel ceiling. The enormous 4711 sign, advertising the famous perfume "kölnischwasser," came into my view as my eyes returned to the bustle around me. The ceiling and the sign remain today.

My mother and father helped me to clamber up the steep train steps. When I turned around to wave goodbye to them, I saw that they were crying. Suddenly, a terrifying foreboding arose within me. The train was full of children, all ages, with only a few adults who were Red Cross workers. Many of the other children expressed their feelings by excitedly running up and down the aisles, shouting to each other. But I felt utterly alone; I knew no one. I have a vivid memory of an adult encouraging the children to calm down and pointing me out as an example. In reality, I was busy burrowing into myself and dealing with the trauma by stuffing my feelings. This set a pattern that would form me during the coming years.

Now, all these years later, I am following the same route on my way to attend the seventieth reunion of the *Kindertransport* in London. On that first journey, I had been oblivious to the fact that I was part of an epic endeavor—the rescue of 10,000 Jewish children from Germany, Austria, Czechoslovakia, and Poland during the nine months between December 2, 1938, and September 1, 1939. Britain had offered entry visas for children aged three months to seventeen years.[1]

The train taking me from Germany pulled out of the Köln Hauptbahnhof five short weeks before Hitler invaded Poland, and World War II broke out with all its horror. I was, of course, totally unaware of the extent of the trauma and loss I was in the process of encountering. I would never see my parents again. I would lose my *Zuhause*—my mother language, culture, family, religion, inheritance, and citizenship. My family knew no one in England. They had no idea where or with whom I would end up. The situation for Jews in Nazi Germany had become life threatening, and this brought them to the agonizing decision to put me on this train. It seemed to carry the lesser risk. I was seven years old.

Seventy years later, gratitude like the incoming tide flows over the memories, and I sit back. I am no longer alone. George, my husband and most intimate friend, is sitting next to me, and God is palpably present. Actually, He was also there on July 24, 1939, but then my perception was that I had been abandoned—cast into the unknown.

No Longer a Victim

The word "abandonment" reminds me of a day in February 2008 when thirty-five of us were together in Hotel Raitelberg, surrounded by woods, high on a hill overlooking the small town of Wüstenrot in southwestern Germany. We were an unusual combination—Israeli Arabs, Israeli Jews, Germans, one American, and myself, a Jewish-German-English woman who is at home in America. Our mutual desire to ask God about the healing of our nations had brought us together. We prayed and listened to each other's stories, and we became aware that we all shared something in common. In response to historic evils committed against us, our peoples had taken on the identity of a victim.

My thoughts drifted back to the time when I was a child cowering in the corner of the train carriage, with the fabric of my life unraveling as I sped toward the frightening unknown.

Without stirring in my chair, I returned to the present and rejoined my companions in the comfortable, quiet hotel room as we turned away from the identity of a helpless victim. Inwardly, I stretched and stood upright. I "saw" my heavenly Father. He had been with me on the train, and now, so many years later, I felt His comforting arms around me.

I do not deny or minimize the depth of evil that was done to me, my family and my people. I do not fully understand why God allowed it. Yet, I am aware of the rays of light, mysteriously penetrating the pervasive cloud of darkness, that have surrounded the Jewish people, promising future justice. And although I became an orphan at the age of seven, in the center of my being I know that I have an all-loving Father who has been with me—always.

Liverpool Street Station—Again

The seventieth reunion of the Kindertransport begins on Saturday evening, November 22, 2008, in London. Under a dark winter sky, George and I climb the steps from the Liverpool Street Railway Station platform up to what is now called Hope Square, just as the ceremony is about to begin. My eyes adjust to the bright lights, and I see the other "Kinder" already assembled with their families, bundled up in the warmest of clothing, sitting close together on metal folding chairs arranged to face the sculpture erected in Hope Square, a memorial to our arrival in England. Frank Meisler, the sculptor, himself a child of the Kindertransport, had also been rescued from Germany.

I look intently at the expressive faces of the five bronze children, one by one. I see bewilderment, anxiety, and anticipation. I focus on their suitcases, remembering my own. The suitcases represent all that is left of the tangible love of our parents. I notice the poignancy of the abrupt end of the steel railway line at the base of the sculpture, taking me back to the instrument of our sudden separation from all that was warm and familiar. So many sensations triggered in a few fleeting moments. I feel the bitter cold and gratefully take the seat offered by a gallant gentleman. His wife whispers, "He likes to show that he is still physically fit." Yes, we are all older now.

The memorial service begins. We are a cohesive group, sitting close together, each preoccupied with our own stories. We remember our parents and their fears and pain in sending us away. We sorrow for the one and a half million Jewish children who cannot join us, whose lives have been snuffed out. We are confronted with our own pain and loss in being together again at Liverpool Street Station, the place that connects us in our common history.

The ceremony combines worship with a strong call to remember—it must never happen again! We express our gratitude to Britain for the welcome we received at a time when most doors were closed to Jewish refugees. The symbols and words give meaning and purpose as we unite to mark this anniversary, perhaps the last time we will all be together.

The Hebrew words of Psalm 121 are read aloud in the hushed haven of Hope Square. Oblivious to the noise of city life flowing around us, we hear the ancient living words: "God will guard you from all evil, and protect your being. Adonai will guard your coming and going from this time forth and forever." Surely this is the reality behind the events of the Kindertransport.

But, flickering at the edge of my consciousness are other thoughts: What about the six million who did not survive? What about my parents. . . my aunts in Koblenz. . .my friend Kurt. . . ?

We pray the Kaddish as a memorial prayer for the victims of the Holocaust and conclude with the blowing of the shofar—a strident, sorrowful sound—which fills the night air and links us to our Jewish history.

My Identity

Softly falling snow surprises us as we awaken early the next day, Sunday morning. My anticipation is tempered with caution. How will this day unfold? What will be my reactions? Approaching the vast buildings and grounds of our venue, a Jewish school, we join a long line of cars. Security is tight, and I have forgotten our passes. The friendly policeman checks our names on his list and waves us through the gates. In all, 560 of us gather, including our spouses, children, and in some cases grandchildren.

As we sit, interacting with the klezmer music, I connect deeply with my roots. The musicians skillfully express the melancholy, the sorrow, the humor, and the determination of the Jewish soul. The stories we have briefly shared with each other over tables laden with kosher delicacies, the lively insightful speeches, and the music coalesce and comfort us. We all share a common history, and my own feeling of belonging to this family of survivors surprises me. For much of my life I have been separated from my roots. I embrace my Jewishness and savor my identity.

Following the Kindertransport reunion, George and I take a Lufthansa flight and return to Köln and, from there, travel on to the Eifel, the region of my roots.

2

A German-Jewish Child under the Shadow of National Socialism

The next morning, sipping a cup of coffee in our Eifel apartment, I smooth out the creased, faded copy of my birth certificate and wonder why my mother and father travelled from their home to the city of Bonn for my birth. I arrived on a Sabbath—Saturday, February 18, 1932, four days before my mother's forty-first birthday, at the University Clinic. In those days, most babies were delivered at home, attended by a midwife. Perhaps my father wanted us to have the best medical care available.

Who was Markus Zack, my father? His friends and neighbors would have observed a devout Jew, leader in the local synagogue and a successful businessman. With the tips of my fingers I carefully hold a copy of an old photograph and see three Jews—Albert Wolff, Wilhelm Teller, and Markus Zack—standing straight-backed in a line of eleven uniformed men, holding their weapons upright, butts on the ground. They are all members of the Gemünd *Schützenverein*, a shooting club. My father is at the end of the line on the far right.[1]

Membership in the Schützenverein brought social prestige. I hold a magnifying glass over the photograph, and I scrutinize my father's features, his expression, shaded by his hat. I see him savoring the honor of standing with these men. The camera must have captured a moment in time before the first months of 1933, when the three Jews were ejected from the Schützenverein.[2] It is the only photograph of my father that I possess.

The Gemünder Schützenverein in 1929 or 1930. My father stands at the end of the row on the right. The barrel of each rifle holds a flower.

Gemünd was a popular *Kurort* (spa), situated west of the Rhine at the confluence of two rivers, the Urft and the Olef. The healthy air and the beauty of the rolling pasturelands and thick forests of the northern Eifel region drew many visitors.

My joyful parents brought me to their lovely home on the *Dreibornerstrasse*, the street running through the center of town. I was welcomed into the large, comfortable apartment above my father's *Kaufhaus* (store). His antique business was housed in a structure behind the main building. Customers would look over the goods displayed behind two large glass windows, climb the steps between the windows, open the door, and step inside to the clang of a bell attached to the door.

Adolf Hitler Emerges

At the beginning of the 1930s, anyone with the ability to stand back and objectively consider the worldwide economic situation must have turned away, filled with apprehension. Our country, Germany, was especially troubled. The Versailles Treaty—the peace settlement signed on June 28, 1919, following Germany's surrender at the end of World War I— imposed ruinous, vengeful reparations, fueling bitterness, shame, and resentment. The German *Volk* (people) struggled with unemployment and rampant inflation. By the mid-1920s, the government, the Weimar Republic, had become weak and ineffectual. The country was disintegrating and chaos reigned, providing fertile ground for the gospel of National Socialism. Adolf Hitler emerged, preaching deliverance from this unconscionable burden. He promised jobs, order, and the return to greatness. "Germania" would rise again. The people listened eagerly, swallowing National Socialism intact.

On January 30, 1933, when I was eleven months old, Hitler and the National Socialists seized control of the country, bringing my parents with all their hopes and dreams for their little family twinges of uncertainty and anxiety.

Fresh Snippets of Information

My father was born on September 24, 1878, in Strasburg, West Prussia, now the town of Brodnica, Poland, south of Gdansk. I know he was part of a large family because in 1972 I received a letter from a cousin I had never met, Helmut Zack, living in Skokie, Illinois. He shared the details he knew about the Zack family. He wrote, "Your father was known as Max, and he had seven siblings: Minna, Sara, Aaron, Tobias, Georg, Doris, and Saul. According to Uncle Saul your father was very wealthy."

I have seen my father's birth certificate, and the letter "X" my paternal grandfather used to sign his name. Why did my father leave his home as a young man and move so far west to Gemünd? At that time, both places were part of West Prussia.

My mother, Amalie Schneider, was born on February 22, 1891, in Heddesheim/Kreuznach (today Guldental), a village just south of Bingen in the Nahe wine region of Germany.

Most of the snippets of information, and the pitifully few family photographs that I now possess, have come to light in recent years as I have experienced a process of gradual inner healing and gained courage to begin to face the reality of the horror of my past. Significant insights have surfaced for me through unplanned encounters with eyewitnesses, fellow Jewish survivors, former German neighbors, new German friends, and journeys to the places of my parents' origins.

For many years my hidden, inner hurt was so great that I did not want to know about my past. How does a child, or even an adult, cope with overwhelming emotional pain? Large areas of my being simply shut down in self-defense.

I have found a similarity between my own experiences and those of many Germans. After years of being unaware, or in denial, more recently there has developed openness and courage among many Germans to look honestly at the past. This change has released a flood of information.

Think of a phrase, one loaded with connotations, such as "Jews under National Socialism." Type the phrase into Google. Click the arrow, and pages of details appear. Begin to follow the trail until it becomes unbearable. Then, the books—so many books. Hans-Dieter Arntz's careful research and scholarly arrangement of facts in *Judenverfolgung und Fluchthilfe im deutsch-belgischen Grenzgebiet* (Persecution and flight of Jews in the German-Belgian border region) was a milestone along the journey to my past. On page 352 he wrote:

> *Things were also going well in the house of the Jewish businessman Markus Zack (1878-Holocaust) on Dreibornerstrasse 174. Born in Strasburg, West Prussia, he was the proprietor of a furniture business and a general store. He introduced the business of payment by installment in Gemünd, and developed a large customer base by offering favorable terms of payment. The records show that in the year 1937 he was still the owner of 23 plots of land, meadows and fields. He was among the well-to-do citizens of the town, a member of the Gemünd rifle club along with his Jewish friends Albert Wolff and Wilhelm Teller, and served from time to time as one of the representatives of the synagogue community. He married relatively late in life. His wife, Amalie Schneider Zack (1891-Holocaust), like him, was not born in the Eifel, but came from Heddesheim in the Kreuznach district. In the large and elegantly furnished house on Dreibornerstrasse the little Hannelore (Johanna Flora) Zack, born on February 18, 1932, had a very good life. She was adored both by her parents and her father's customers. Markus Zack was very devoted to his child, and it was obvious that financial considerations need not prevent him from securing for her an escape out of the country.[3]*

My father's first wife, Martha Wolff, died in 1928. The gravestone he erected for her still stands in the Jewish cemetery in Gemünd. This stone is the only material object that I can touch and physically connect with him—with his creativity and life experience. Markus and Martha had no children, and after her death, in his loneliness, he looked for a wife through a Jewish matchmaker! (Gisela, a fellow Jewish survivor from Gemünd and some years older, told me that story.) So Amalie, from the Nahe region near the Rhine, came to Gemünd and joined Markus.

Like Amalie, Markus had been an outsider. Some years earlier he had left his family in the East to settle in this small town near the western border of Prussian territory. She brought light and love into his empty home above the store at Dreibornerstrasse 174.

The Live-in Maid

Lisbet Ernst re-entered my life in the summer of 1992. George and I were in Gemünd, attending a reunion of Jewish survivors from the area. There were eight of us. I was the youngest. George and I were guests of Frau Huber,* a widow much younger than her husband. She remembered how he had talked about my father. Our room on the top floor faced Dreibornerstrasse, and when we opened the window and looked out we saw, across the street, the shop and apartments built on the bombed foundation of the former Zack family home and business.

One morning over breakfast, as I lifted the spoon to scoop out my boiled egg, Frau Huber casually asked, "Hanna, can you remember that your family had a live-in maid?" "No, I have no memory of such a person," I replied. "This woman still lives in Gemünd. Would you like to meet her?" At the edge of my consciousness I had a half-formed thought: "This is going to be big—way beyond my expectations for this trip." Exactly at 3 p.m. the doorbell rang, and Frau Huber opened the door.

Looking back now, I see a generous bunch of summer flowers, held in the strong hands of a seventy-six-year-old, white-haired woman, her eyes alight with anticipation. It is Lisbet, our former live-in maid. Frau Huber invites us to follow her to the back of the house. We walk behind her tall,

We meet again: Lisbet and I in 1992. Photograph by George Miley.

Our friendship continues: Lisbet in her home several years later. Photograph by George Miley.

graceful stride, through French doors, down wide stone steps, and across the classical landscape to a round glass garden house. Porcelain, silver, coffee, and cake are laid out on the lace-covered table. There, in that elegant setting, Lisbet flings open the door, takes my hand, and leads me back to the past. She is about to satisfy my longing to know something of my parents' way of life, their idiosyncrasies, their personalities. I listen intently, straining to understand, aware that I am hearing stories colored by Lisbet's perceptions from a time when she was a teenager. Her words are vivid and unembellished, her voice is passionate, and I trust her memory.

Passover

In the spacious apartment above the Kaufhaus at 174 Dreibornerstrasse, we kept a kosher household. My father was very religious, so during the seven days of Passover, we did not buy or eat anything containing yeast. Like the other Jewish families, we would prepare for the festival by thoroughly cleaning our home, making sure there was not a crumb left, even in the most obscure corner.

But there were exceptions to these rules. Even during Passover, Lisbet, a Gentile, was permitted to have her own special cupboard in our kitchen and to keep a loaf of hearty rye bread behind the closed cupboard door.

Lisbet leans in closer and continues in a confidential tone: "Occasionally during the days of Passover, your father was away visiting the surrounding villages with his horse and cart, delivering furniture that the farmers had ordered from Kaufhaus M. Zack. Your mother would say to me, 'Come, Lisbet, let's do something nice for ourselves!' I would open my cupboard, place the loaf on a wooden board, and slice two pieces of rye bread. We would each bring a chair to the kitchen table, sit, spread the butter on the bread, and enjoy." I relish Lisbet's revelation of my mother's personality and her genuine friendship with our live-in maid.

Lisbet has other stories, sad stories, reflecting the menace encroaching on our daily lives. She speaks of the time when Gentiles were no longer allowed to work for Jews. Indeed, any social contact was forbidden. She describes the young SS officers guarding the front entry to our store, just in case any German would dare to break the law by entering a Jewish business. Lisbet loved my mother and was determined to visit her. She knew the back way into our home. She tells me of their final poignant encounter: my mother holding me, a tiny child in her arms, moving toward Lisbet and saying over and over, "*Sie ist kein jüdisches Kind … sie ist kein jüdisches Kind … sie ist kein jüdisches Kind*" (she is not a Jewish child).

Lisbet repeats my mother's words to me and then she says, again and again, "Why did she say that? Why did she say that? I could not take you." It was as though she had carried the burden of my mother's words ever since they were first uttered.

When our former live-in maid returned home from this risky visit, her father pleaded with her not to endanger the family by entering a Jewish home again. They already had one black mark against them, and he feared another forbidden visit would bring severe punishment on the whole family. She never saw my mother again.

I think our meeting, the two of us, so many years later, both comforted and lifted a burden of guilt from her. As for me, a part of my mother was restored. She had really lived, and I could connect with her joys and heart-rending pain.

Berries

The Schmitz family had lived in their home on Dreibornerstrasse for several generations. They were our next-door neighbors.

In 1992, Frau Schmitz invited George and me for *Abendessen* (supper). Her husband was elderly and frail. Frau Schmitz, gracious and dignified, made us feel at home. Six of us sat together at the large family table: Herr and Frau Schmitz, their daughter Maria, her husband Dieter, George, and I. The elderly couple had both endured and survived the bombings and deprivations of the 1940s.

Over supper, Frau Schmitz shared her memory of a day when she heard loud wails coming from the garden at the back of the Zack home. The cries were coming from the small Hannelore, who had been plucking and eating so many of the luscious, ripe berries straight from the bushes that her stomach ached. Frau Schmitz remembered my father coming, comforting me, gathering more berries, tucking them into my pocket, and saying, "These are for you to eat tomorrow."

Frau Schmitz and I after Abendessen, in 1992.
Photograph by George Miley.

As we were about to leave, Frau Schmitz said, "Would you like to see something from your childhood?" She led us to the garden at the side of the house and pointed to a large apple tree with branches hanging over the fence into what would have been the Zack yard. She said, "This apple tree is all that was left standing after the bombing." I plucked two leaves.

Hilde

Almost ninety years old in 2003, still bright, energetic, and artistic, Hilde Reiniger* stands on the steps of the Kurpark Hotel and pries open the lid covering the past, pulling up memories that rarely saw the light. She tells of her young brother, delivered back to the family after being in SS custody, no longer recognizable. She speaks of her own breakdown after being selected to bear a child for Hitler.[4] Despite her age, George and I recognize traces of the Aryan beauty of her youth. She tells us that her emotional collapse delivered her from the dreadful consequences of racial selection.

Casually, she adds as an afterthought, "You know, I never met your father. I was young and we lived in nearby Kall. But I heard the name Markus Zack and remember the word on the street: 'He is an upright businessman.'"

Willi Remembers

George and I are sitting with Willi and Annemarie Kruff around the coffee table in their comfortable, tranquil home. It is the summer of 2001. Willi's skill as a member of the Schützenverein is displayed on three of the walls—so many deer heads—small, medium, and large—neatly and symmetrically arranged. The windowsills are filled with a thriving variety of colorful plants. Outwardly, we are enjoying *Kaffee und Kuchen* (coffee and cake), passing the plates, pouring the cream. Inwardly, both Willi and I are overwhelmed by the significance of this encounter.

Annemarie and Willi welcome us into their home, 7 August, 2001.
Photograph by Willi Kruff.

Willi remembers crossing Dreibornerstrasse with his mother, "*das neugeborene Kindchen besichtigen*" (to visit the newborn child). The eleven-year-old Willi was a little bored. Years later he wrote in the journal he was preparing as a gift for his grown children, "She lay in the Kinderwagen (pram) howling loudly."

Willi delights to reminisce. His mind is crystal clear and holds a treasure trove of stories. I ask him, "Willi, do you have any stories about my father?" And so Willi takes us back to the Gemünd of the 1920s:[5]

> *My first unforgettable encounter with Herr Zack came when I was 4½ years old. At that time, in 1925, we still lived in the large house belonging to the Huber family, and our kitchen faced the street.*

*Right across from the kitchen window was the entrance to the Zacks'
courtyard.*

*It was my mother's washday, and she was out in the garden hanging
the colorful washing on a line and laying the bed linen on the grass
to bleach. The 4½ year old Willi was playing in the kitchen with
wooden blocks, leftover pieces from the ladder factory Poensgen &
Scheibler where my Uncle Peter worked.*

*When a child is alone, as everyone knows, it has plenty of time to look
around and thoroughly investigate its surroundings. And what could
be more interesting, in an unguarded moment, than a stove and fire,
from which one is usually warned to stay away. My eyes fell on the
place near the kitchen stove where the long wooden tapers used for
lighting my father's pipe were kept.[6] I had often noticed with great
interest how he shoved one of the thin, long, wooden pieces through
the small hole in the stove ring, and then pulled it out with a small
flame on it in order to light his pipe.*

*What came after that was even more interesting for me: the small
flame was not blown out like a candle on a Christmas tree—I
had been allowed to do that under supervision. My father waved
the wooden taper rapidly back and forth through the air and out
went the flame. The resulting sparks, which made such wonderful
bright lines in the air with the waving of the wooden taper, were
unforgettable to me.*

*I wanted to do that too—"because it was so easy"! So I climbed up
on the chair on one side of the kitchen stove, took one of the thin
wooden tapers, climbed up on the chair on the other side of the stove
and successfully stuck the wooden taper through the stove ring. The
small flame must have already gone out by the time I climbed down
from the chair, but the wished for brightly glowing end of the taper
remained. I swung it back and forth, delighted by the bright lines
and sparks it now and then created.*

Then I saw Mr. Zack standing in front of his gate across the street, and I had to show him my fireworks. So I ran to the window and pushed the old net curtains to the side with the glowing taper still in my hand. In a flash the curtains burst into flames all the way to the top.

I only know that I screamed and that Herr Zack was immediately at our door, pulling hard on the bell cord. My mother came running in from the garden, and Herr Zack used a bucket of water to douse the blazing curtains with a slosh from below.

In our kitchen, we always had a bucket of water for daily use because there was no permanent water supply....

Naturally, I was punished. My mother consigned me to the dark cellar. I will never forget how I stood on the cellar steps, banged on the door, and cried out over and over again, "Mama, take me out, I will never do it again!" I don't believe my mother left me to cry like that more than a couple of minutes, but my shock was great.

That was my first unforgettable memory of our neighbor Herr Zack.

Following our visit, Willi wrote: "After 61 years, to be able to greet my little, blonde neighbor as an American [*sic*] and as Frau Miley, to greet her once again in Gemünd, it was the most moving greeting of my life except the greeting of my parents in 1946 when I came back from my Russian imprisonment."

Lisbet, Frau Schmitz, Hilde, Willi—each one has died since I began to write this book. We were companions along this healing journey for brief moments in time. They were eyewitnesses, and I treasure the gifts they brought to me from the past.

My Own Fogbound Memoryscape[7]

Those encounters and stories, gifts from the past, have caused a few of my own memories to emerge, fogbound, into the light.

My earliest awareness is suffused with the tenderness of my mother. Was I two years old? I was lying in my cot placed against the wall of my parents' bedroom. It was afternoon nap time. I was conscious of the light filtering through the curtains, playing on the white and pastel colors around me. I clearly remember crying stridently and loudly. I did not want to go to sleep. My mother's face appeared over the rails of the cot. Imprinted deeply in my being is her expression, gracious and kind, reflected toward her squalling child.

I picture another scene. My mother is sitting, bending over her circular knitting needles, her hands moving without effort, smoothly, rhythmically. The striped skirt of the dirndl dress she is creating for me spreads across her lap. The bodice is red, tomato red. I can still remember the tiny stitches, neat, knobby, and perfectly regular. I believe the stitch is called "moss stitch" in English. The edging of the bodice echoes the colors of the striped skirt and holds a drawstring ending with two fluffy pom-poms. If I close my eyes I can see her shadowed shape, suffused by a glow of light. Am I embellishing the memory or was she really sitting by the window on a sunny day?

Another time, *Mutti* (Mama) and I are standing close together at the same window, silently watching lightning pierce the darkening sky and listening to the startling thunderclaps. She whispers softly, "God is angry."

It must have been during the seven days of Passover. My father and I, just the two of us, are sitting together at the kitchen table—maybe on the same chairs that my mother and Lisbet had drawn to the table in order to enjoy the bread of their conspiracy. I know it was Passover time because my father was breaking the crisp matzos into little pieces, dropping them into his big, steaming cup of coffee and cream and topping off the treat

There really was a dirndl dress. I was five years old, with my
wooden scooter in our back garden.

with spoonfuls of sugar. A small cup with lots of cream and a little coffee is placed before me. I try to copy my father. He helps me snap the matzos into uniform pieces, not crumbs but small enough for my cup. I can still taste the sweetness, the exotic textures and flavors, the broken bits of matzos, both crisp and soggy. More than the combination of tastes on my tongue and the aroma of the grown-up coffee under my nostrils, I relish sitting close to *Vati* (Papa), being with him, sharing with him our Passover ritual.

Such small, daily incidents in our family life—how many more have I forgotten? Only recently have I recognized the potency of my parents' love during those first seven years.

In their secret, unexpressed, fearful thoughts, my mother and father could never have imagined what was to come.

3

Poisonous Seeds
Sown in Darkness
Begin to Sprout

Mountains, shrubs, and grasses—the subtlety of the colors, the variety of shapes and textures—surround me as I amble along a dusty path in the high, dry desert of southern Arizona. Blue sky and halcyon winter sun above, solitude and silence around, far from the usual noise and distraction, in the quiet I hear an appeal for my attention: "Remember the past."

For so long I have kept the past at arms' length. The enormity of the disaster surrounding my childhood, when the morality of a nation's whole way of life unraveled, was too great a burden for me to bear.

If my little part in the German drama of the 1930s was to be portrayed on a stage, I would play my role facing a darkened audience, unaware of the scenery, the backdrop, or the action around me. I think my parents did their best to shelter me from the contempt of anti-Semitism. And yet, the intimidation and fear my mother and father were experiencing entered my soul, as if by osmosis.

Hitler Visits Gemünd

I remember the atmosphere in our room upstairs, facing the street. I was five years old, a curious, precocious child. My nose was pressed to the large window pane. What were my Mutti and Vati doing? Both of them cowered on the sofa against the wall at the other end of the room. Standing on a chair close to the window, I watched beautiful young girls with long, blond, braided hair; dressed in colorful dirndls; dancing and throwing flowers. Creeping slowly along Dreibornerstrasse came an open car. Hitler stood, stiff and upright, with his arm stretched out in the *Heil Hitler* salute. Our familiar street was filled with people offering adulation to their *Führer*.

He must have been gratified by their exuberant welcome, but his visit had a greater purpose than the adoration offered by the citizens of a small, backwater town.

On Thursday, April 29, 1937, Hitler's train arrived at the Gemünd railway station. The carriage door opened, and he stepped down onto the single platform. Probably, he was greeted by a crowd of local Nazi officials. An open car waited to take him on the short journey through Gemünd, continuing on for seven kilometers up the hill to Vogelsang.[1]

Vogelsang was built to endure. Most of the buildings are still standing today. George and I visited the *Ordensburg Vogelsang* (Castle of the Order) in 2002, when the Belgian army occupied the site. As we were leaving the original castle cinema after watching a film on the dark history of the Nazi period, I glanced down and saw a bundle of stapled handouts lying on a worn table. I asked permission from the Belgian officer in charge of our tour to take one. Written in English, with the title "History of Burg Vogelsang," the undated handout begins with a description of the orders given by Hitler to Dr. Robert Ley, the Reich Leader of the NSDAP (Nazi) Organization, for the castle's construction. Dr. Ley is quoted as saying:

Before the castles appeared, there was nothing besides wilderness. I did not want to start in some existing castle, because it is my conviction that the new, mighty ideal of Adolf Hitler may not be preached and learned in old, muddy and dusty castles. The places where these world-changing thoughts are proclaimed to mankind must be as new as the ideas themselves.[2]

Vogelsang, one of three castles conceived by Hitler, sprouted out of the verdant pastures seven kilometers above Gemünd. "The main buildings that were required for schooling were built in record time. . .two years."[3]

Who were the students and what did they study in these massive, intimidating, dark, grey buildings? The *Junker* (cadets) were selected according to seven criteria:

1. Excellent health
2. A member of the Nazi party; the *Hitlerjugend* (Hitler Youth); the *Sturmabteilung* (Brownshirts, also known as the "SA," an early Nazi paramilitary organization); or the *Schutztaffel* (also known as the "SS," literally translated "Protection Squadron")
3. No hereditary taint
4. Pure Aryan blooded
5. Able to prove racial origin
6. At least 1.60 meters (5.25 feet) tall
7. Age between 23 and 26[4]

Their studies? Rigorous physical training for their bodies and racial philosophy for their minds. "Racism was the centerpiece of Nazi ideology. Extermination and racial improvement were the two inseparable components."[5] Their education completed, these virile young men would have been elevated to the position of *Gauleiter* (governor). They were needed to rule the conquered eastern territories on behalf of Hitler and the party.[6] In their limited free time, they would have made their way down the hill to relax in Gemünd, their ears ringing with the poisonous philosophy that was their meat and drink day after day.

Das Schwimbad

It must have been around the time of the 1936 Olympics. I was walking with my parents along a hilly path overlooking the Gemünd Kurpark. I walked between them, and they each held a hand. I was wearing tiny orthopedic boots for correcting my tendency to be "pin-toed" (walking with toes pointed inward). I looked with mounting excitement at the great body of water below us, glistening in the sun. I could see children and whole families and watched their joyous movements as they swam and splashed and ran around the new community swimming pool. Their shouts and laughter floated up to us on the hilly path. All over Germany, new swimming pools were being built to celebrate the Olympics in Berlin.

I heard myself saying, "I want to go there and play in the water." A long silence followed, and then came my father's strange, sad words: "Jews are not allowed."

Das Kino

Another walk, this time closer to home. Our family friend, Ruth Holden, was taking me to the *Kino* (cinema) to see *Snow White and the Seven Dwarfs*. Disney's cartoon version of the old folk tale had just been released, a milestone in cinema history.

I was excited, anticipating this magical event. It seemed to me that the way was long; we walked and walked. The miniscule Kino is still there today, showing films in a back alley off Dreibornerstrasse, just 100 meters away from where our home used to be. Ruth and I rounded the corner into the alley, and I saw the sudden change in her expression. Alarmed, I asked, "What's the matter?" She was eleven years older than I and spelled out for me the large, black letters on the prominently displayed new notice: "No Jews allowed."

Early School Days

All of us Jewish children attended the *evangelische Schule* (Lutheran school) on the Bahnhofstrasse in Gemünd, across the street from the *evangelische Kirche* (church).

I remember the smell of new leather as I traced with my finger the embossed pattern on my satchel and relished the importance of carrying it on my back. I can see the slate with squares for doing arithmetic on one side. I can hear the loud screeching sound I could make with my slate pencil, with its pretty paper wrapping. I can feel the texture of the little cotton square with its long crocheted tail that was tied to a hole in the slate's wooden frame, used for wiping out my earliest numbers and letters.

My father engaged a Hebrew tutor, who scared me a little. When he entered our home I hid under the table, resisting this extra learning.

Back at the regular school, I noticed the changes in our arithmetic books. The pages were filled with pictures, but now we added and subtracted images of colorful tanks, helmets, guns, and soldiers.

The crisis came one playtime. I became aware that our little group of Jewish children was in the middle of a circle, surrounded by all the other children who were dancing round us, holding hands and singing anti-Semitic songs. Why did they despise us? They were children. Where had they learned to look on us with such contempt? I don't remember the words they sang, but I can still see the looks of hatred on their faces and feel the rhymes beating on our heads like acid rain. That was the last day we attended the evangelische Schule. I was six years old.

On Tuesday, November 15, 1938, the Reich Minister of Education issued a decree excluding all Jewish children from attending German schools.[7] Our new school was in nearby Kall, and we travelled there by train. We joined other Jewish children in a one-room schoolhouse. There our teacher, Moses Lauterbach,* provided a place of refuge.

The Man Downstairs

A nationwide boycott of Jewish businesses had taken place on April 1, 1933, three months after the Nazis took the reins of power in

Germany. The action lasted for only one day, but a wall of restraint had been breached, and from then on thoughts and words of hatred and discrimination increasingly took the form of malevolent deeds. Jewish businesses began to be "Aryanized," purchased by non-Jewish Germans at bargain prices fixed by the Nazis.[8]

I do not remember when it happened, but my life has been marked by a sudden moment of abuse. At the time, my father no longer ran his business. The spacious ground-floor shop, with its large double windows, was now occupied by a non-Jewish man. I cannot recall his name or the nature of his business.

My father stood on the landing, his back to our apartment door. I was close by his side, drinking in the sudden drama as it unfolded. The two of us looked down toward the bottom of the stairs where the man stood glaring up at us. His body was leaning forward in a threatening stance, his face distorted with hostility and wrath. Like sewage pouring out of an open pipe, a stream of curses and contempt spewed out of his mouth, aimed at my father.

I felt my father's silence as if I were fused to his side. He absorbed it all without one word of response. Internally, I had the feeling that I needed to protect my father—how incongruous the thoughts of a small child.

For years I carried an impression of my father as a weak, powerless, and ineffectual man. However, when I read Hans-Dieter Arntz's documented description of him as a successful businessman and leader in the synagogue,[9] and I heard Willi's stories, and I listened to Hilde say, "I never met your father, but even in Kall we knew that Markus Zack was an upright businessman," I then began to form a true picture of my loving Vati.

Years later, when I finally connected with my story, I realized he would have placed himself and his family in jeopardy if he had defended himself or rebuked the anti-Semitic tirade. I now recognize the wisdom of his restraint.

Under the Shadow of the Hakenkreuz

A dark shadow in the form of a *Hakenkreuz* (swastika) spread over Germany and infiltrated the Eifel. I must have noticed the powerful, black, jagged shape imposed on a white circle, surrounded by a blood-red frame. Flags emblazoned with the symbol fluttered high above. Or, frighteningly nearby, across the narrow street, the image came toward me, wrapped around the arm of an important person. Neighbors walked in the street, raising their right arms in stiff, straight salutes, and saying in clipped words, "Heil Hitler" instead of their usual "Guten Morgen," their left hands holding a walking stick, a shopping basket, or a dog leash. On a day when I was still attending the German school, looking up from my desk, I saw a picture of Hitler in the prominent place at the front of our classroom where the cross had always hung.[10]

How was I affected when I saw the new, intrusive emblem? When I try to recall my feelings, I draw a blank.

Despite my parents' attempts to shelter me, I was deeply affected by the legislation of hatred and exclusion being woven into the fabric of the society in which we lived day by day.

Calendar of Events and Decrees: 1932-1938[11-15]

February 18, 1932. Johanna Flora (Hannelore) Zack is born in Bonn. The Zack family lives at Dreibornerstrasse 174, Gemünd.

January 30, 1933. President von Hindenburg appoints Hitler as Chancellor.

February 27, 1933. The Reichstag, Berlin (the government building), is set on fire, leading the Nazis to demand sweeping powers, laying the foundation for a police state.

April 1, 1933. During a one-day boycott of Jewish shops and businesses, Hitler's Brownshirts paint slogans and yellow stars of David on Jewish shop windows. The process of Aryanization (the transfer of Jewish businesses to non-Jewish Germans with prices officially fixed below market value) begins.

September 22, 1934. The foundation stone is laid for Burg Vogelsang, accompanied by large-scale celebrations.

September 15, 1935. The Nuremberg Laws are announced, institutionalizing racial theories already prevalent in Nazi ideology. A partial list includes the following:

• Jews are excluded from Reich citizenship.
• A Jew is defined as anyone having three or four Jewish grandparents.
• Jews can no longer employ German females younger than 45 years of age in their households. The law takes effect on January 1, 1936. Goodbye, Lisbet.

November 9-10, 1938. Kristallnacht (commonly translated as "Night of Broken Glass"), a coordinated destruction of synagogues and attacks on Jewish businesses, rages throughout Germany and Austria.

November 15, 1938. All Jewish children are expelled from public schools. Jews are barred from cinemas and sport facilities.

How Can I Break Free from the Bondage of Hatred and Revenge?

I have been travelling along the road leading to forgiveness and liberation from the trauma of the past for a long time. There have been many stops and starts. My preferred way of coping with the wounds so deeply penetrating my being was to suppress—to block out the memories. Years went by before I could face the past and say, "Yes, those things really happened to me."

My healing journey has taken me along two parallel tracks. On one track, I have been learning how to forgive those who did evil acts. Some were ideologically inflamed perpetrators; others fearfully acquiesced and did nothing. The villainy was real and specific, whether expressed in attitude or in deed. My people, my family, and I experienced the murderous abuse in our bodies and souls.

On the second track, I have been asking God's forgiveness for my own wrongful, destructive responses to the evil done to us—for my bitterness, hatred, contempt, and self-pity.

I have come to experience freedom from the captivity of the curses and contemptuous words that were thrown over us like a toxic garment. The poison had seeped into my soul, but during the ensuing years, my inner being has been washed and renewed.

I am reminded of a time thirty years ago when I was invited to a natural swimming pool in a mountainous region of the Philippines. The sun, suspended in bright blueness, warmed our skin. The pool was constantly fed and emptied by springs as they flowed down the rock formation. To plunge into that pool of cold, crystal clear, flowing water was an indescribable experience. I emerged like a new person, refreshed, clean— my body quivering with life. To forgive, and to be forgiven, is to know similar sensations in the heart, the mind, the soul.

Fortified by my flashback to that open-air swimming pool, I now return to the story of my fragile childhood in Gemünd.

4

Reichskristallnacht: The Night That Saved My Life

S ome of the Jews fleeing the Roman persecution in the Holy Land in AD 70 chose to settle along the Rhine River in cities such as Köln (Cologne), and later in smaller villages westward, taking root in the idyllic, hilly landscape of the Eifel.

During their long history in the land that first became a united Germany in 1871, they experienced periodic accusations, persecutions, pogroms, and death. However, by the early nineteenth century, Jewish citizens began to feel more secure.[1]

At the beginning of the twentieth century, members of the Jewish community in Gemünd enjoyed taking part in the life of their little town. My father and two other Jewish businessmen were enthusiastic members of the Schützenverein. Willi Kruff's mother sometimes crossed the street and visited our home. He wrote in a letter dated June 27, 2003:

> *Frau Zack was, among other things, an excellent seamstress. My mother had wonderful training in the running of a household, especially in food preparation. But she received further help from Frau Zack in sewing aprons and shirts and trousers for the children. In the economic hardships of the 1920s, this played an important role in helping our household money go further. My brother and I went through many pairs of trousers during those years. Herr Zack had material in his shop that lasted a long time under heavy use.*

Our Synagogue

Our synagogue in Gemünd was dedicated on February 27, 1874. The small, sturdy, stone building, with ninety seats on the ground floor and thirty in the balcony, served the seventy-five Jewish families who worshipped there.

Holding my father's hand, walking along *Mühlengasse* on *Shabbat* (Saturday) morning, I remember looking down at the cobblestones under our feet. Inside the synagogue, I can picture my legs swinging as I sat beside him in the front row downstairs, even though the place for women was upstairs. I remember a vague sense of reverence as I looked up and listened to the Hebrew words read from the Torah and watched the light glistening on the shiny pointer moving from right to left. I can feel again the joyful atmosphere in the synagogue when we celebrated Purim, the feast of Esther. All of us children scrambled for sweets landing around us—ping, crackle, and pop—coming down in handfuls from the balcony.

Ideas Beget Action

From 1933 to 1938, the plans against our people had been bubbling in the cauldron of poisonous ideas, spilling over in sporadic, scattered acts of violence. The Aryan population had been exposed to continuous, anti-Semitic propaganda for five years. Fires of hatred had been deliberately stoked by inflammatory legislation, speeches, books, and newspaper articles. Now, during the night of November 9-10, 1938, a pre-arranged plot burst into reality throughout Germany and Austria—wherever Jewish citizens lived.

The catalyst for this coordinated action was an event that took place in Paris on November 7: Herschel Grynszpan, a seventeen-year-old citizen of Hannover, shot Ernst vom Rath, the counselor to the German embassy in France. Grynszpan's crime was committed in response to a cruel deportation. On October 28, thousands of Polish Jews living in Germany were rounded up, transported to Poland, and left without food or shelter just beyond the border. His parents were part of the deportation.

Vom Rath died on November 9, 1938. On the evening of the same day, a carefully planned and prepared nationwide operation, now known as *Reichskristallnacht*, was unleashed, masterminded by Joseph Goebbels.[2-4]

Was I Afraid?

I was there in Gemünd, but I have no personal memory of the dramatic events that took place during that night in November. In my imagination, I see a six-year-old child asleep in the comfort and warmth of the well-appointed apartment above the Zack family store. Was I protected by my terrified parents? Did they hold me in their arms? Or, have I blocked out the fears of that night? I don't know.

Laying down my pencil, I stop writing, squeeze my eyes shut, and attempt to bring the past into the present. Can I sniff the faintest whiff of smoke? I am walking between my parents, holding their protective hands, listening as they talk above my head. Did we always walk so close to each other? Or, were we responding to the climate of danger? Their voices low, they speak about the rock thrown through the front window of our neighbor's house. The large rock landed on a shelf above the bed, miraculously saving my friend Kurt and his grandmother from injury as they cowered under the blankets.

What Really Happened in Gemünd?

For most of my life, I carried the illusion that nothing happened to our property that night. I assumed no windows were smashed because my father had already rented his shop to a non-Jewish citizen. But when I read *Reichskristallnacht* by Hans-Dieter Arntz, which includes a careful collection of testimonies given by men who were present and witnessed what took place, I learned the truth.[5]

Clusters of men gathered under the cover of darkness along narrow Mühlengasse. Secretly, and in haste, they entered the synagogue and gathered its sacred objects into a sack. Bundles of straw were carried from the barns of neighboring houses and stuffed into the stone building, which had been emptied of its treasures. *Benzin* (gasoline) was at hand . . . the straw was soaked . . . the fire was lit. As the blaze intensified, the fire wagon stood by. The firemen watched without intervening, forbidden to pour water on the flames until the moment when the neighboring houses were threatened.[6]

Intoxicated by the taste of violence, the men rampaged through the main street—our street—Dreibornerstrasse. Smashing Jewish windows along the way, they stormed into our *Hof* (courtyard). They broke open the *Stall* (shed) door and stole my father's antiques.[7]

Why are those dramatic hours erased from my memory? Probably, I was sleeping between my parents in their bed. Surely the uproar outside our bedroom window must have startled me awake. It was about 3 a.m.

Did I intuit my mother and father's fear? Did we hear the loud, harsh voices, the smashing of the Stall door, and the receding sounds of the continuing assault along the street below?

Daylight revealed the ruins of burned out synagogues, the ashes of desecrated holy books, and shards of glass strewn on pavements outside Jewish stores and houses all over Germany and Austria. In one night, 1,574 synagogues were damaged; 267 synagogues destroyed; 2,500 businesses vandalized; 91 Jewish men killed; and 30,000 Jews arrested. A penalty of one billion *Reichmarks* (about 400 million U.S. dollars at 1938 rates) was imposed on the Jewish community to be paid to the Reich for the cost of the damage.[8]

On November 11, 1938, all Jewish males in Gemünd who were eighteen years or older were rounded up and prepared for a transport to the city of Aachen, located about 60 kilometers northwest of our hometown.[9] The report of their arrest has given me the background for a partial memory that has stayed with me over the years. I am eating at the table in the kitchen of my friend Kurt's house. I am being called: "Hannelore, go home quickly. Your father has returned." I have no recollection of his leaving. How far did he travel? All the way to Aachen? Or, was he released at the railway station in Gemünd? I don't know. According to the report in *Reichskristallnacht*, he was seriously ill.

What were my father's thoughts and feelings as he returned home and slowly climbed the stairs leading to our apartment? Was he full of despair as he looked back on five years of increasing abuse: the systematic dismantling of everything he had built materially, the loss of his role as a leading *Bürger* (citizen), the robbing of his goods without redress or justice, the torching of his community's house of worship? Did he blame himself for ignoring the signs? Or, was he galvanized to action?

Another Gemünd memory surfaces. The time is late evening, and I am awakened by the murmur of voices. I creep out of bed and quietly enter the empty sitting room. People are talking in our doorway. The door is half closed. I am alone in the room. I look at the pretty red lines left in the wine glasses, the crumbs scattered on the plates. I reach out, grasp a wine glass from the low table, bring it to my lips, and drink the sour dregs. I have forgotten what happened when my parents turned and found me. Was the group that had just left our home discussing a move to Köln?

Saying Goodbye to Gemünd

I am not sure if we left Gemünd for Köln under duress or voluntarily, looking for anonymity in a big city. Once my father returned from the roundup, I think we must have pulled up our withered roots without delay. I don't remember our departure from Gemünd or making the journey to our new home in Köln. Did my father say goodbye to his friends? Did he still have any friends? Were our neighbors aware that we were leaving? Or did we just slip away that winter of 1938? Were we shivering with cold, sorrow, and fear as we stood on the platform of the Gemünd railway station, just by the Jewish cemetery? Were we travelling with other Jewish families? What were my parents' thoughts as the train clattered out of the Eifel hills into the level land approaching Köln? Was my father regretting his decision to stay in Germany when our friends, the Tellers, had asked us to join them in their flight to Palestine three years earlier? Was my mother grieving the loss of her German friends? Or, was she anxious about her three sisters in Koblenz and Berlin?

The drama of Kristallnacht has faded over the years. Is it possible to know who did what and when they did it? I am grateful for the courageous researchers—the truth-tellers—who have sifted and displayed the fragments from the past. They have connected me with reality.

Historical records; copies of orders and pictures; testimonies of onlookers, perhaps shaded by defensiveness; and my own subjective, fractured memories combine like so many brush strokes to create a vivid, impressionistic painting. As I reflect on the past, the intolerable burden of judgment, blame, and revenge has been lifted. I give it all—the facts, the suppositions, the pain—to the Judge who is just.

Meanwhile in London

Aroused to action by the events of Kristallnacht, leaders of the Jewish community in England approached the British Parliament. They were granted permission to bring Jewish children to safety in England. Ten thousand children were rescued; I was number 8814.

The costly decision to send me away . . . did such a thought first enter my parents' minds during the violent night of November 9?

5

Horst-Wessel Platz 14

I left Köln with a round, cardboard identification label hung around my neck. Today, it stands on my bookshelf, sandwiched between two small pieces of glass. On the back, written in pencil, the word "Horst" has been crossed out and replaced by "Köln." I carried no family photographs in my luggage, but I still have the two postcards my parents and aunt tucked into my suitcase. They wanted to be reassured. Had I arrived safely? Was I "welcomed into the arms of strangers"?[1] The postcards were pre-stamped, ready to be mailed. My aunt's address in Koblenz was clearly typed on one card, and my parents' address, Horst-Wessel Platz 14 II, was on the other. I never sent them.

When I began researching what happened to my parents after we separated, I would sometimes ask German friends, "Where can I find Horst-Wessel Platz 14, our home in Köln after we left Gemünd?" They would answer uncomfortably, "Oh, that street no longer exists." Then a certain unease entered the atmosphere, and I became aware of my own ambivalence between curiosity and a reluctance to engage.

I had lived with my parents in Köln for seven or eight short months. Yet over the years, the word "Köln" sounded cold and inhospitable to my ears, and our address resonated menace. Who was Horst Wessel? Why was he memorialized in a street name?

Horst Ludwig Wessel joined the Nazi party in 1926 at the age of nineteen and was made a posthumous hero of the movement following his violent death in 1930. He became well known for writing the lyrics of the song, *Die Fahne Hoch* (Raise high the flag), usually known as the Horst Wessel

Lied.[2] A sample line reads, "Already nations are looking to the swastika, full of hope." From 1933 to 1945, his song became Germany's official co-national anthem with *Deutschland über Alles* (Germany Above All). In those days, if you had taken part in a typical Sunday service at the local Lutheran Evangelical Church (the larger wing of the church also known as "The German Christians," who were aligned with the Nazi state), you most likely would have opened your new hymnbook and joined the congregation in singing the Horst Wessel Lied.[3]

A reader of the January 2, 1934, edition of the Nazi journal *Der Brunnen für deutsche Lebensart* (The fountain for the German way of life) would have come across this eulogy: "How high Horst Wessel towers over that Jesus of Nazareth—that Jesus who pleaded that the bitter cup be taken from him. How unattainably high all Horst Wessels stand above Jesus!"[4-7]

Rathenauplatz 14

How can I be reconciled with the city of my past? Perhaps a good beginning would be to visit the street where we lived.

George and I make an early start and drive to Köln during the first week of April 2009, a few days after we have discovered the current name of my family's old street. We slowly edge through the morning city traffic, find a place to park the car, walk soberly around the corner, stand on the pavement, and look up at Rathenauplatz (formerly Horst-Wessel Platz) 14. I am on the street where we lived! I feel pain and anticipation simultaneously. At that moment, a car stops next to us. The driver's door opens, and a tall young woman steps out. She notices us standing there and asks, "Are you looking for something? Can I help you?"

We talk. I share my childhood connections to this address. She lives in the ground floor apartment of Rathenauplatz 14. Her name is Anke. She takes us through double doors into the *Hof* (courtyard) and confirms that this green, angular, utilitarian apartment building was constructed after World War II on the foundation of the building in which we lived. However, the building next door, with its elegant façade, survived the bombing. I stare at the carved stonework towering above us and feel a stirring in my memory. Anke leads us to the owner of the property, Herr Wolfgang Knips,* who lives on the second floor. We begin our conversation as George and I stand just inside the entrance, and Herr Knips leans over the stairway. It takes only a few moments before he invites us into his home.

Herr Knips is only a few years younger than I, and he has inherited the building from his parents. We follow him into his charming front room, and I approach the large windows. I look out across the little park to the restored and imposing Roon Street Synagogue. Suddenly, in that moment, I am a seven-year-old child again, looking out of the front windows of our second floor apartment, seeing the same scene. The surprise of it all, and a certain reticence, prevent me from asking him about his parents, and what they might have told him about the neighbors. What was the mood in our home back in the spring of 1939? Were there undercurrents of fear, premonitions of doom?

Our second floor surroundings must have been elegant. I remember the novelty of using an elevator to go up and down between our apartment and the large entry doors. The size of the bathroom sink must have impressed me. I have a quaint memory of climbing up the pedestal, lying in the large bowl, turning on the water, and attempting to take a bath.

A New School

I have forgotten the name of my new school. Documents recording the dates when Köln Jewish schools were closed and consolidated into one school, the Jawne, are inconclusive. I would like to have found reliable confirmation of my disconnected but vivid memories. My school adventures in Köln seem to float in space, with no place to dock. Objective facts would help in reclaiming my past. I have gradually surrendered my vigorous but unsuccessful pursuit of accuracy in finding the name of the actual school I attended in Köln. Strangely, I have experienced an enlargement of soul living with the incompleteness, the imperfection. The vignettes I write are stored in my memory without concrete names and addresses.

The contrast between the simple one-room Jewish school in Kall that I had abruptly left and my new Jewish school, with its imposing architecture and large playground, could not have been greater. As a newcomer, I entered a stream that had been flowing for some time. Everything was unfamiliar: the other children, the teachers, the physical surroundings, and the "way things are done." How did I cope with all the sudden changes?

It is the first day in my new school. I am sitting and watching two teachers at the front of the classroom. They are standing and talking earnestly with each other while making notes on the blackboard. One has red hair, the other black. To my recollection, one is handing the class over to the other, since he is to leave for Palestine. I wonder what ultimately happened to each—one going and one staying behind?

Another day I am walking home from school among a group of other pupils. They run off and leave me. I feel very small under the gigantic apartment buildings towering over me on both sides of the narrow street. I am lost and alone and begin to bawl loudly. A kindly woman hears my cries, invites me into her home, and contacts my father. Is she Jewish? He comes. As I tell this painful little story, I can still feel his arms gathering me into the safety of his presence. Yet, the preceding moments of panic, the awareness of being totally alone, that the world is a dangerous place, become portents for what will follow.

From the vantage point of age, I wonder what I said or did that caused those children to flee and leave me alone?

Our Last Passover Together

The details of our Seder celebration in 1939 are hazy, and yet remnants of the event lie in my memory like broken pieces of matzo, left on the plate at the end of the meal.[8]

A good number of people are seated around the large, festive table in our apartment. I see a room flooded with light. Am I remembering the brilliance shining from many candles or the atmosphere created by the gathered group? We are animated and familiar, yet solemn and formal as the ceremony begins. I am a seven-year-old child, and the significance of our ancient practice, celebrated by centuries of Jews to remember God's intervention and deliverance from Egypt, is quite beyond my grasp. As the youngest child, I am involved in the series of questions at the core of the service. The key question of the ritual, "Why is this night different from all other nights?" resonates for me even today.

At that 1939 Seder, as we celebrate behind the closed doors of Horst-Wessel Platz 14, second floor, and the adults hear the familiar words being recited, what are their thoughts? When Psalm 137:4 is quoted—"How shall we sing the Lord's song in a strange land?"—are they connecting the cruel bondage of our people in past generations with the present reality of our lives in Nazi Germany? Does anyone have a premonition that this will be the last time we observe the Seder together?

Das israelitische Krankenhaus

On a summer night around July 18, 1939, I wake my parents from their sleep with loud cries of pain and shame at soiling the bed. Like a movie, the next scene fills the screen. I am lying in another bed, a hospital bed in room 154. A woman sits by my bed, a soft pillowy presence. She tells me gently, "You must lie very still and not move." It is night. I don't know if it is the same night I cried out in pain or the following night. When I ask for water, she explains I need to wait awhile before drinking and eating.

She suggests we spend the waiting time with me telling her the things I would like to eat and drink, while she writes a list ready for me to enjoy all my favorite tastes in the coming days. I find pleasure in naming nuts, berries, gherkin, Shabat potato kuchen . . . and imagining their taste. I am a patient in *Das israelitische Krankenhaus* (the Jewish hospital), Köln-Ehrenfeld, Ottostrasse 85. My appendix has been removed by a skilled Jewish surgeon, and I think my father has hired a private nurse to sit with me through the night.

The room is crowded. My parents, with others, have come to visit me. I lie in bed reading a few lines from a selection of *Grimm's Fairy Tales,* a little book they have brought as a gift. I still see the beautiful painted pictures and the spiky letters. I hear their praise and delight at my reading skill, probably filled with relief at my recovery.

At school I was learning to read and write the *Sütterlinschrift* (Sütterlin script), known to most German children at the time but banned by the Nazi government in 1941.[9,10] The sharp, pointy letters and intricate loops

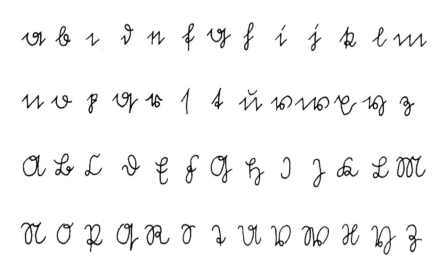

My attempt to copy the old alphabet.

still intrigue me today, all these years later. As I write this chapter, I search for an example of the script I was reading in my hospital bed. I discover an old alphabet page used for practicing penmanship, tightly grasp a pen, touch the paper . . . and I am transported back to the classroom in Gemünd. Once again, I am holding a thin slate pencil between my thumb and fingers, muscles tense, eyes focused, attempting to copy the alphabet in Sütterlinschrift. I feel the old anxiety—the task is so difficult and I must get it right. . . .

Another hospital scene: I am walking along winding paths surrounded by an expanse of green grass, basking in the warmth of inclusion among important grown-ups. I am walking in the company of doctors. Perhaps I have returned to the hospital for the removal of the stitches.

In 2009, I found two photographs dated 1908 and 1912 in the book *Das jüdische Krankenhaus in Köln*.[11] Das israelitische Krankenhaus was very large. A number of double-story buildings were set in extensive grounds. The carefully tended plants and trees, the verdant lawns, all those curving paths, had really existed. They were not figments of my imagination. Das israelitische Krankenhaus opened on January 12, 1869, and from the beginning, patients from all confessions were welcomed. The hospital's reputation drew patients from Köln, the Rhineland, and Westfalen.

How could it be that busy hospital doctors and surgeons, in their white coats, had time for a stroll in the gardens with one small patient? By July 1939, when I was a patient, the hospital was functioning under intense pressure. The effects of the anti-Semitic racial laws enacted in 1933 and 1935 were gathering momentum—reimbursements to Jewish doctors from public health insurance funds were restricted; Jews were dismissed from government service; and in some parts of Germany, Jewish doctors and hospitals were banned from providing medical care for Aryan patients.[12] Perhaps some of these Jewish surgeons and doctors swelled the ranks of the healers at Das israelitische Krankenhaus, and certainly the hospital was treating fewer patients.

Translation: My dear, precious "mouse," I was so glad to receive your greetings. Soon you will be well again. I will soon be with you and will give you many kisses. It is good that your operation is over. Write to me what I should bring you. Is Aunt Hanna with you? Tell her to write to me quickly. Have you had many visitors? Greet everyone and for you many, many kisses from your Aunt Lisbet.

My aunt Elisabeth (Lisbet) mailed a postcard to my hospital room on 18 July, 1939, from Berlin. Who removed the postage stamp, and why?

Jews could no longer receive medical care in an Aryan setting.[13] I wonder if my parents could have found a nearby hospital willing to give emergency treatment to a Jew if we had still been living in Gemünd in July 1939?

My Life Hangs on a Frayed Thread

As I look back and try to journal my memories of our last week together as a family, I remember the moment when my life was hanging on a thin thread, although I did not know it at the time.

Home from the hospital, I am lying in my own bed again, overhearing the conversation in the next room. My mother is speaking loudly. To this day, I can hear her saying, "She is not sufficiently recovered from the operation to leave." The critical timing of my operation and recovery is confirmed by a postcard. I still have the card that my aunt Elisabeth sent from Berlin on July 18, 1939. I can read my name and the address: Room 154, Das israelitsche Krankenhaus, Köln. My return home must have been only a few days before the Kindertransport train left Köln Hauptbahnhof.

My father insists, "She must go." In that pivotal moment his voice prevails. My heart weeps with my Mutti's agony; at the same time, I am filled with gratitude. The fragile thread did not break, and I received the gift of life.

Maud, the Eyewitness Who Survived

In 2002, I received a letter from South Africa, written by Maud, the stepdaughter of my father's brother, Georg Zack. Her own father, a Gentile, divorced her Jewish mother in 1937 under National Socialist pressure. Her mother, Emilie, married Georg Zack. They both died in Auschwitz via the Theresienstadt ghetto. Maud writes that the delay in the deportation of *Mischlinge ersten grades* (people of mixed blood of the first grade)[14] saved her half-Jewish husband and herself. "Our fortune was that the war ended when it did, because they started to deport half-Jewish people also." In the same letter, she describes my last evening in Germany:

> *I will start with the last time I saw you and your dear mother. . . .*
> *In the evening, prior to your departure with the Kindertransport,*
> *my mother and I came to say goodbye to you. If I remember right,*
> *you just had your appendix operation. Your mother had washed your*
> *hair, and you were lying in the double bed, your head covered with a*
> *towel. Your mother was so brave. I don't remember seeing your father*
> *at the time. We consoled your mother. I must have been 17 years old.*
> *We said, "What a blessing for you, to have the chance to get away!"*
> *From Gemünd I remember you all well. You liked a little boy, Kurt*
> *Meier, called him your friend.*

Goodbye, Kurt

Kurt Meier had been our neighbor in Gemünd and also moved with his parents to Köln. Both of us were the only children of our parents. He was three years older. We were two among a handful of Jewish children living in Gemünd. From 1933 onward, the isolation of the Jewish community gradually increased until all social contact between Germans and Jews was forbidden.

Kurt and I were like brother and sister. We often played together in the fields near our homes on Dreibornerstrasse. One time we brought back strange news. We told our parents, "We saw groups of men digging and burying 'things' in the ground." What were these things? Armaments?

I remember Kurt coming to our Köln apartment to say goodbye. I still have the creased little picture he gave me. It looks just like a passport photograph. I focus on his face—his open guileless expression and his sad eyes. I turn the picture over. In his own handwriting, he has written his name and address. It is in Sütterlin script. In my imagination, our heads

Kurt, was this your visa picture?

My German visa issued 20 July, 1939.

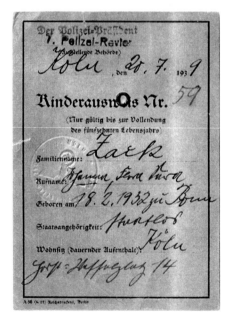

The handwritten word *"Staatslos"* (stateless) is written after the printed
word *"Staatsangehörigkeit"* (citizenship).

are close together, and we are using one finger at a time, pressing the keys of my father's typewriter. Underneath Kurt's spiky handwriting, I read the typed words: "Kurt Meier, Köln, Lochnerstr. 11, 1 Etage." Lochner Strasse was just around the corner from Horst-Wessel Platz 14.

Maud, Kurt, and I—all three of us—lived close to each other in Köln. In Maud's letter, she wrote about her family: "After having to leave Gemünd, we stayed at the Rubensstrasse . . . not very far from where you had to move to." Were we living in a Jewish ghetto? I remember only our comfortable surroundings.

I see myself standing at the open door of our apartment, watching as the door of the elevator clangs shut and Kurt disappears.

Ruth, another Jewish survivor from Gemünd—the same Ruth who had taken me on our painful walk to the Kino—later told me that Kurt's parents had turned down an opportunity to send him away with the Kindertransport. They were unable to release their son into the unknown. Today, his name is carved on the family stone in the Jewish cemetery in Gemünd: Kurt Meier, *Deportiert* (deported) 1942.

In April 2009, George and I visited the Erich Klibansky Platz, Köln. A large memorial fountain, the *Lowenbrunnen* (the lion fountain), dominated the small square. A stone lion towered over us, rising out of a tall pillar at the center of the fountain. We bent down, kneeling on the cobblestones, to search systematically among the 1,100 names etched on eight bronze plates attached to the base of the stone fountain. The names belonged to the 1,100 children deported from Köln. Finding the name "Kurt Meier" publicly and permanently engraved on the brass plate shocked me out of the self-protective distance I had created around Holocaust statistics. We stayed awhile at the Lowenbrunnen. Each of these children had been a living soul who loved and was loved. Each had been created by God to reflect His image.

My name was not among them.

Three years after my train slowly pulled out of the Hauptbahnhof on July 24, 1939, carrying me west, a train left Köln on July 27, 1942, deporting Kurt and his family to the East. At thirteen years of age, Kurt was old enough to be aware of impending doom when the train stopped at Auschwitz. He emerged from the cattle car and was directed to the right by the Nazi guards, part of the group shuffling straight to the gas chambers. He was not yet old enough to qualify for the line to the left, those selected for slave labor with a very slight chance of survival.

Recently, a copy of Kurt's official records came into my hands.

Kurt Meier
Born Euskirchen 16.06.1929
Deported 27.07.1942 to Theresienstadt.
Died in Auschwitz.

How Did My Father Do It?

I have no idea how my father obtained the priceless permission for my travel to England with the Kindertransport. Did he experience fearful, humiliating encounters with Nazi officials? Or, was my place secured through the heroic rescue efforts of Erich Klibansky, headmaster of the Jawne School? Between January and July 1939, approximately 130 children connected to the Jawne School escaped by train to England.

To finance the rescue of his teenage students, the headmaster invited parents of children who were too young to attend the Jawne to send their children to England with the Kindertransport. The children had to be at least six years of age, and their parents had to pay for a place. "For with every paid place the Jawne could have a place free."[15] I was seven years old. Did my father buy a place for me?

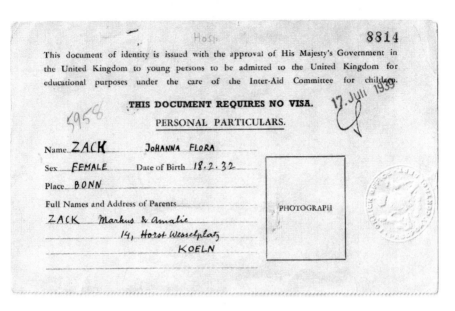

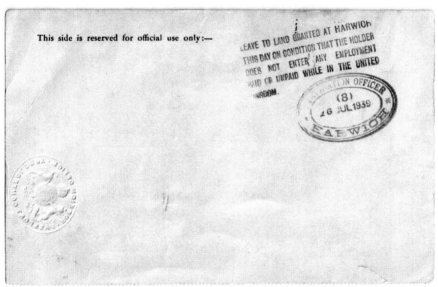

Travel document number 8814, issued by His Majesty's Government on 17 July, 1939. Note the abbreviation "Hosp," written in pencil and floating uncertainly in the middle of the heading space.

The identification label that my parents hung around my neck. The string is still attached.

Erich Klibansky worked closely with the Kindertransport organizers.[16] A replica of the *Anhängeschild* (identity label) worn by each child travelling with the Jawne group is reproduced on page 178 of *Die Jawne zu Köln* (The Jews of Köln), a book written by historian Dieter Corbach in remembrance of Erich Klibansky and the school.[17] I wore an identical round, white card displaying my number, 8814, all the way to England, and the same words, *"Kindertransport des Hilfsvereins der Juden in Deutschland e.V.,"* curved around a printed circle in the card's center. My parents had hung the label around my neck at the Hauptbahnhof in Köln. I have seen old pictures of Kindertransport children arriving in England, wearing plain, brown, cardboard squares around their necks showing a handwritten number, nothing else. Could the more elaborate card on page 178 be another clue to the means of my escape on July 24, 1939?

Erich Klibansky, his wife Meta, and their three sons—Hans Raffael, fourteen years of age; Alexander, eleven; and Michael, seven—did not escape. They left Köln July 20, 1942, on a train carrying 1,160 Jews; 315 of them were children. Their destination: the Theresienstadt ghetto, or so they believed. As they travelled east, members of *Einsatzgruppe* (mobile killing unit) B were digging large pits in a forest twenty kilometers outside Minsk, the capital of German-occupied Belorussia. Their train was diverted. In the early morning of July 24, 1942, all 1,160 left the train to stand in the forest at the rim of the pits. They were shot.[18,19]

Hasty Preparations

I remember nothing of the frantic shopping and open suitcases lying in the rooms of Horst-Wessel Platz 14, second floor, waiting for the piles of neatly folded clothes. I still have the letter, sent by my aunt Johanna on August 2, 1939, addressed to the unknown English family who would take me in. She expressed her gratitude to them for opening their home and referred to the frenzy of the last days in Köln before the leave taking. Why is there no letter from my mother? My aunt Johanna was a successful businesswoman. Was she the designated correspondent? Was my Mutti undone in her grief?

Wrenched Asunder

It is the evening of July 24, 1939. My parents lock the door of our apartment on the second floor of Horst-Wessel Platz 14. The three of us enter the elevator, press the down button, open the front door, step into the street, and head toward our appointment at the Hauptbahnhof. I have no awareness that each step we take brings us nearer to our forever parting. Are my parents silent in their bitter anguish? Or, do they swallow their own pain and give me encouraging words describing an exciting journey ahead?

6

What Happened to My Parents?

We could not anticipate the horror of reality.

Hatred backed by power always meant catastrophe.

Eli Wiesel in his memoir
All Rivers Run to the Sea

❧ ☙

Good is always getting better and bad is always getting worse . . . the possibilities of even apparent neutrality are always diminishing.

C. S. Lewis
That Hideous Strength

❧ ☙

What happened to Markus and Amalie Zack after they watched my train disappear into the night? Were they left with an inconsolable emptiness, standing together under the lights of the Köln Hauptbahnhof platform among a throng of grieving mothers and fathers on that July evening? Was the severing like the amputation of a limb before the discovery of anesthesia? Contrary to normal medical practice, the purpose of this surgery was to save the limb, while the body would gradually succumb to the virulent plague of anti-Semitism.

I was born eleven months before Hitler and the National Socialists seized power. In the ensuing years, signs and portents of the encroaching darkness steadily penetrated Jewish life in Germany. My parents tried to shield me but in my experience, our hostile environment was normal life. The protective cocoon was shattered the instant the train wheels began to turn, and I shut the door of my heart. Only in recent years have I begun to hunger for my Mutti and Vati, to be with them in the reality of their lives after they put me on that train.

To Know Who You Are, You Must Remember

"To know who you are, to whom you belong, and where you are headed, you must remember."[1]

In the quest for identity, I have explored the social context of Jews in twentieth-century Europe. Like a collector of artifacts, I have mounted a selection of my discoveries on the walls of my mind.

1922. "Once I really am in power, my first and foremost task will be the annihilation of the Jews. . . . Once the hatred and the battle against the Jews have been really stirred up, their resistance will necessarily crumble in the shortest possible time. They are totally defenseless, and no one will stand up to protect them." Josef Hell, a retired major and a journalist, reported that Hitler had used these words in a private conversation in 1922.[2]

1928. "*Die Juden sind unser Unglück*" (The Jews are our misfortune): On March 27, 2009, when I visited the EL-DE-Haus museum in Köln, I saw a photograph with this phrase spanning a huge banner, hung high on a four-story building, part of the permanent exhibit, "The history of Köln under National Socialism." The two words "Jews" and "misfortune" were extra large and bold and could not be missed by the citizens. The building was the Nazi party headquarters, located at Hohenzollernring 81.[3]

January 30, 1933. The Nazi party takes power in Germany. Adolph Hitler becomes chancellor, or prime minister, of Germany.

April 1, 1933. The first boycott of Jewish businesses takes place. From April through October 1933, Jews who were civil servants, doctors, or lawyers were dismissed from employment.[4,5]

August 2, 1934. Hitler combines the positions of chancellor and president to become "Führer," or "Leader of Germany."[6]

September 15, 1935. The Nuremberg Laws are announced at the annual Nazi Party rally in Nuremberg: "the law for the protection of German blood and honor" and "the Reich citizenship law." These laws stripped away the civil rights of Jews and defined who was a Jew and who was not, thus legalizing future repressive measures that would be systematically applied.[7]

May 23, 1936. Dr. Chaim Weizmann (who was to be elected Israel's first president in 1948) is quoted in the *Manchester Guardian*, a UK newspaper: "The world seemed to be divided into two parts—those places where the Jews could not live and those where they could not enter."[8]

March 12, 1938. The 8th Army of the German Wehrmacht crosses the German-Austrian border. The Austrian Army offers no resistance; German troops are greeted by cheering Austrians with Hitler salutes, Nazi flags, and flowers.[9]

July 6-15, 1938. At the initiative of U.S. president Franklin D. Roosevelt, a conference is convened at the Hotel Royal in Evian-Les-Bains, France, on Lake Geneva to discuss the future of stateless Jewish refugees fleeing Nazi persecution. Thirty-two countries and twenty-four volunteer organizations are represented. Delegates rise to express sympathy, but only the Dominican Republic offers a place of refuge. A committee is created with little authority and virtually no funds. "Nobody wants them," was the summarizing statement published in the German newspaper *Völkischer Beobachter.*[10]

October 5, 1938. After this date, at the request of Swiss immigration officials, the passports of all Jews in the German Reich are stamped with a large "J" to "[make] it easier to refuse Jewish refugees."[11]

November 9-10, 1938. Kristallnacht. Shortly after this event, we move to Köln.

July 24, 1939. I leave Köln.

September 1, 1939. Germany invades Poland.

September 3, 1939. World War II begins, bringing drastic new restrictions for the German-Jewish community, such as strict curfews and general food rationing. (For Jews, the allowance is meager and obtainable at only a few designated shops.)[12]

May 10, 1940. Sections of the German Western Army gather near Köln before invading the Netherlands, Belgium, and France. For the first time in the history of aerial warfare, assault gliders are launched to storm the Belgian fortifications. They take off from an airfield on the outskirts of Köln.[13,14]

May 12, 1940. Köln becomes a target of Allied bombing. Between May 1940 and March 1945, Köln suffers 262 separate air raids. On March 13-14, 1942, 135 Royal Air Force bombers pound the city, and on May 30-31, 1942, "Operation Millennium," approximately 1,000 planes, bomb Köln for 90 minutes.[15]

June 22, 1941. The German invasion of Russia begins.

July 31, 1941. Hermann Göring orders Reinhard Heydrich to make "all necessary preparations . . . for a total solution of the Jewish question in German-occupied Europe."[16]

September 1941. Jews in Germany are forced to wear a yellow star to facilitate identification for their deportation to the East and are banned from using public transportation.[17]

October 30, 1941. My parents leave Köln for the East.

Two Years, Three Months, and Seven Sorrowful Days in Köln: From Monday, July 24, 1939, to Thursday, October 30, 1941

As the train carried me away, my parents left the Hauptbahnhof next to the tall, twin spires of the *Dom* (cathedral) in the city center and made their way through the dark July night back to Horst-Wessel Platz 14, opposite the rubble that once had been the Roon Street Synagogue.

How did they survive the desolation, the privations? Cruel constrictions steadily increased during their remaining time in Köln. Certainly, they knew the pangs of hunger. I remember the strange story that Frau Schmitz, our former next door neighbor in Gemünd, told George and me when we were together in 1992. She remembered hearing a knock on the back door and was surprised to see my father standing on the step with a knapsack on his back asking for food. How had he managed to travel from Köln to Gemünd?

Were my parents afraid when they stepped into the street, wearing the yellow stars sewn on their coats? Would they be viewed with contempt, hear curses, feel the thud of stones . . . or be rounded up? They endured isolation: no telephone, no radio, and no news of their child. They were under curfew, imprisoned in their Jewish building. How did they deal with the rumors circulating in the Jewish community? What were their feelings when they heard the wail of a siren signaling a bombing raid and listened for the whine of a descending bomb? Did they hold their breath waiting for the shattering boom? When they tried to lie down and sleep at night and then awoke to another oppressive day, how did they cope? They brought their life experiences, personalities, inherited traits . . . their uniqueness to ever-increasing encounters of expanding horror. How did they relate to each other? What changes took place in their perceptions, values, faith?

EL-DE-Haus

On March 27, 2009, a cool, grey morning, George and I stand before a tall, grim, old building, Appelhof Platz 23-25, Köln. What will I discover here in the EL-DE-Haus, a museum dedicated to the history of Köln under National Socialism? We are punctual for our appointment with Dr. Barbara Becker-Jakli, a historian and research specialist. We open the front door and enter a tiny lobby. We wait for directions. The time-worn, drab interior is a mute testimony to former days; I feel as though I am at the threshold of a long, dank tunnel that will lead me into a wasteland of darkest evil. But I must forge ahead.

Dr. Becker-Jakli's greeting is warm and kind as she welcomes us into her small office. Her red jacket, clear bright eyes, and gracious demeanor reassure us in the harsh, stark interior of the EL-DE-Haus. We sit together, surrounded by papers, books, computers—evidence of hours and hours of patient, focused research, attempting to unveil what really happened in Köln during the Nazi years. Below us in the basement, the former Gestapo interrogation chambers have been preserved as a warning for the thousands of visitors, many of them schoolchildren. We are being received with gentleness and respect in the building that between 1935 and 1945 evoked terror—the Köln Gestapo headquarters. After so many years, will I receive further information about my parents from Dr. Becker-Jakli?

A Letter on the Mat

When I was thirteen years old in 1945, living at 167 Coventry Road, Exhall, England, a little crack appeared in the hard shell of indifference protecting me from news of my parents. It was peacetime; the war was over. I heard the metal flap on the front door wrenched open. There was a soft thud followed by the closing clank. A letter lay on the mat. It was addressed to Johanna Flora Zack from the Red Cross. I opened the envelope and reluctantly read the black letters on the official white paper. My parents had been taken to Lodz and my mother had died in Riga. I did not want to know. I closed my heart to this confirmation of my hopeless view of life.

My past, that integral part of my existence, lay undisturbed for many years. Slowly, so slowly, over the years the protective shell has been melting. Now, in 2009, George and I are in the EL-DE-Haus, whose walls are saturated with vile acts and bitter suffering. Dr. Becker-Jakli gently offers us a printout fresh from her computer.

Markus Zack

Born: 24.September.1878

Date deported to Litzmannstadt (Lodz): 30.Oktober.1941

Date of death in Kulmhof (Chelmno): 3.May.1942

Amalie Zack

Born: 22.February.1891

Date deported to Litzmannstadt (Lodz): 30.Oktober.1941

Date of death in Kulmhof (Chelmno): 3.May.1942

She assures us that we can trust the facts in this latest research more than previous reports.

I feel weary and raw with the disturbance of the story I had so reluctantly accepted when I was thirteen years old: that my mother had died in Riga and that a mystery surrounded my father's end. Shock and sorrow mingle as I now learn that they both endured six months in the Lodz ghetto. And what happened in Chelmno? I had never heard of such a place. Now as I write, three months have passed since I received this more accurate information, and I see a new openness within me to face the past and grieve for my parents in the reality of their ordeals. How can I honor and authenticate them in their inexorable ending? Is it possible to dig up, like an archeologist, something of how they lived out their daily lives while hidden plans for their death moved systematically to their consummation?

A Lovely, Refined, Happy Couple

In my belated desire to connect with my mother and father, I am faced with the deprivation of my ignorance. Looking for rare seeds among the stubble of the harvested past, I try to glean among the stories recounted by others and the faint images of my own memories. I cautiously hold the glimpses of their personhood lightly, knowing all our stories are colored by our own perceptions and experiences. And, what about all the untold tales that could round out the picture?

How did my parents see themselves? Years earlier, my father had undertaken the long journey to Gemünd, far to the west of his birthplace, leaving behind his home and family in the Prussian East. He had established himself as a successful entrepreneur. In a very small town, he had risen to an honored place and was a respected leader among the Jewish families that called Gemünd home.

The evidence of his social success in the wider community was confirmed by his membership in the Schützenverein. Belonging to the Schützenverein brought honor and respect from the citizens of Gemünd. I look closely at the photograph of the line-up of the Schützenverein in their uniforms, the only picture I have of my father. I wonder, what was he thinking? What was going through the minds of the other two Jewish Bürgers in that row? Were they reflecting with amazement at how far they had advanced? Did they feel satisfied with the good life they were experiencing, accepted in measure as part of the "in-group"?

I re-read the letter Maud wrote in 2002, searching for insights. Maud, the stepdaughter of my father's brother, Georg, survived because her own father was a Gentile. I am touched by the kindly, honoring way she writes and her desire to give me a good gift. Her P.S. grabs my attention: "I do remember your dear parents as a lovely, refined, happy couple. They adored you. Your dear Mother, I think was not from the Eifel, spoke with a different dialect, like from the Rhineland somewhere. She used to roll the 'R' in Hannelore."

I mull over her choice of words: "lovely, refined, happy couple." "Refined" sets off a train of thought that may follow a firm track to reality but could well be an ephemeral journey to the world of my imagination. Having buried my parents and my past at the moment that the train, full of children, pulled out of Köln Hauptbahnhof, and only arriving at the place of mourning and honoring them in my later years, I think it is all too easy to hold an idealized picture of their personalities. That word "refinement" is like a net that I dip into the pool of memories and catch scraps of conversations, suggestions, innuendos.

Gisela, another survivor from Gemünd, tells the story of walking from her home over the bridge and up Dreibornerstrasse to our house with her mother, Frau Teller, bringing her beloved sled—the one she had outgrown—as a gift for me. Did this take place in 1935 when they were packing up to leave for Palestine? I have a flashback to the exhilaration I felt, sitting in my father's lap, skimming down a vast, snowy slope. Sledding was very popular in Gemünd, when the snowy winters clothed the undulating fields in white. My response to Gisela's generous gift? I stood in the doorway at the back of our house, next to my mother, raised my hand toward the garden, and said, "Put it in the shed!" Where did this imperious sense of entitlement come from? I have always thought my reaction was that of a selfish, spoiled child. Perhaps this is only partially true?

More stories stir faintly in my memory. I can see myself in a small group of Jewish children, talking and laughing together, walking under trees, their leaves filtering the sun as it glittered on a briskly flowing stream. There on the narrow path between the trees and the water, the other

My mother sent this picture to the Teller family and wrote on the back "Hannelore Zack, 4 Jahre Alt."

Eric Hertz, the young boy at the end of the bench, gave me this photograph. I am sitting on the far left. He wrote on the back: "Circa 1936, taken in the garden of the Zack family." I think the adults and the other little girl must have been his relatives.

children threatened to throw me in the river. Was this a case of the older asserting power over the younger? Or, was there more to the story? Could it be that this tiny, fearful girl communicated superiority? Was there a sliver of resentment toward the "refined" Zacks?

Then, later in Köln, when the children abandoned me as we were walking home from school, is there a connection between their running away and my misty recollection of being in the playground recounting how my father was helping a poor family whose children were right there playing among us?

Had I first absorbed in my own home this sense of self-importance that I so naïvely expressed?

Is Maud gently alluding to that aspect of our family identity when she uses the word "refinement"? I have heard faint whispers of some estrangement between my father and his brother Georg, Maud's stepfather, having to do with my father's strict view of Jewish practices. Our Sabbath walks together to the synagogue were an expression of his beliefs. Did he find sustenance in the realities behind these practices when all he had built and all he had become were dismantled piece by piece? And then, finally, when he stood at the door of the abyss?

In the only likeness that I have of my mother, she stands facing the camera. Her left hand, with a ring on its third finger, firmly grips the rope of the swing. Her right hand is hidden behind my back as I sit, my feet crossed in little black boots and dressed in a white sundress and flowered headband, secure in the shelter of her presence. Her elegant pointed shoe is peeping out from under her long, fashionable dress. George has enlarged the tiny black and white photo so that I can study the details. It is a sunny day, and our garden is filled with a careless abundance of shrubs, trees, and plants. Is that a rhubarb patch behind the post? Her hair is white. Written on the back of the photograph in faded ink is the date, 29 August, 1936; she is forty-five years old. Her eyes seem to reveal a large soul engaged with reality, a woman it would be rewarding

The words on the back of the photograph, "29 August, 1936, Hannelore Zack mit mutter," were probably written by my mother. She sent the picture to the Teller family in Israel, and Gisela returned it to me.

to know. Her smile is gentle and kindly. I imagine Amalie and Markus complemented each other well.

My mother expressed her love of beauty and color in the garments she knitted, sewed, and embroidered. The dresses and doll's clothes that she sent with me to England were an embodiment of her creativity. The stories that Lisbet told me—Lisbet, who had known her intimately as our live-in maid—reveal her lightness, spontaneity, and joy. She liked to "color outside the lines."

I think of my father as more reserved, creative in business, loving to hike in the countryside. I remember the little shields nailed down the length of his walking stick, a record of the many places touched by his feet. He was consistent and disciplined in the way he followed the Jewish traditions. The times my mother greeted us with a smiling face, my father and I, as we returned from the synagogue, confirm for me the atmosphere of peace and contentment I believe we enjoyed in our home.

"God is angry." I still hear her words as the two of us watched the thunder and lightning from our upstairs window in Gemünd. I sense my mother struggled with fear, remembering her dread the night before I left. Like a burr that attaches to my socks as I tramp through the desert scrub, unnoticed until I feel a sharp prick, so I think I caught the ancestral thorn of fear in the few years we had together.

A Lasting Legacy

How well they nurtured me. More than the abundance of beautiful things they showered on me were their enduring gifts: the attentive kindness in their eyes as they turned their faces toward me, their physical closeness, tenderness, approval, and affirmation. They placed my small, pin-toed feet on a firm foundation before the shattering of all their carefully tended security.

They saved my life.

7

Endlösung: The Final Solution

I stop, make the decision to enter, and push down on the handle. There is no lock on the iron door. It is only a simulation. Inside, George, Thomas, Cynthia, and I respond without words. Disoriented in the darkness, our eyes gradually adjust and follow the thin shaft of light to the small open slit above, beyond reach. Faint sounds from outside seep into the silence. What if we can't find the door? What if it will not open? It is only a simulation. Cold, barren, sharp-angled concrete surrounds us, sucking us into the void. We are stripped, isolated, abandoned, forgotten. Hopelessness seeps through the membrane of our defenses. It is only a simulation. We are inside the seventy-nine-foot-tall silo, the Holocaust Tower, at the Berlin Jewish Museum in the year 2010. It is only a simulation.

Die Tatsachen der Vergangenheit ans Licht Bringen
(Bringing the facts of the past into the light)

On June 27, 1999, George and I are seated at a long table in a London hotel, eating a kosher lunch. The word "Köln" is clearly printed on a prominent sign. We are experiencing our first Kindertransport Anniversary Reunion—the sixtieth. The buzz of voices reverberates around us. The ballroom is filled with tables labeled "Berlin," "Vienna,". . .

At the Köln table, we are all chasing our memories. In the midst of the hubbub a tall, thin, grey-haired woman quietly stands and begins to speak softly. A pile of thick, heavy books is stacked on the table before her. She is Irene Corbach, a book publisher from Köln. The new books are the tangible evidence of her late husband Dieter Corbach's tireless labor to bring to light the fate of the Jews in Köln under National Socialism. He died on July 17, 1994, and Irene brought his research manuscripts to completion and published *6.00 Uhr ab Messe Köln-Deutz Deportationen 1938-1945* (Departure: 6 a.m. Messe Köln-Deutz deportations 1938-1945), in 1999.

George and I pull a copy of the 805-page book toward us. At the top of page 383, under the heading "II Transport: Litzmannstadt 30.10.41," we find number 964, Zack, Markus I (Israel) and number 965, Zack, Amalie S (Sara).

We buy the book and carry it back to our home in Phoenix, Arizona. For the next seven or eight years, Dieter and Irene Corbach's book remains on the shelf unopened, ignored. Snail-like, I arrive at the moment when I feel a flickering desire to open my arms to my parents. I take up the book and begin to turn the pages. On page 5, I notice Hebrew letters centered for maximum impact. The translation underneath reads:

> *He will swallow up death forever;*
> *and the Lord GOD will wipe away tears from all faces,*
> *and the reproach of his people he will take away from all the earth,*
> *for the LORD has spoken.*
>
> Isaiah 25:8

I re-read the words before I take the plunge and begin to face the reality of my parents' final years, months, days, hours, minutes, seconds. . . . My guides are Irene and Dieter Corbach, the text, their collection of documents and eyewitness accounts.

Evakuiert nach Litzmannstadt
The Second Transport from Köln

The Gestapo required the Köln Jewish community to take much of the administrative responsibility for travel to the East. For example, when the order came for 1,500 pure Jews of middle age to leave for Litzmannstadt (Lodz) on October 30, 1941, the selection had to be made by a Jewish leader. My parents' names were typed on the list for that day. The office of the Jewish community was also charged with sending out the sixteen-page questionnaire that each traveller had to complete, listing his/her entire property in unbelievable detail only days before the transport left.

On the day prior to evacuation, the deportees reported at 6 a.m. to the Trade Fair Center Köln-Deutz. They were given a number to hang around their necks. All luggage was searched. Each Jew had to confess in writing that they had engaged in Communist activity, by which their entire property was confiscated "legally." Barriers and guards made escape impossible.

According to the eyewitness account of Helmut Lohn, written in 1945:

> *Just before dawn we heard the sound of marching feet, a squadron of SS marched into the exhibition hall . . . singing, 'Comrades, soldiers, put these Jewish scoundrels against the wall.' With loaded rifles, these were the assigned escorts.[1] . . . A siding under the Köln-Deutz Bahnhof leads almost to the Trade Fair Center. Out of public sight and under guard, with beatings and insults, the Jews were taken to platform 5. The human cargo was quickly crammed into old passenger carriages, ten or more in each 6 seat compartment. The carriage doors were locked from the outside.[2]*

How long did these thirsty, hungry, constricted, grieving, fearful, pure Jews of middle age endure these conditions? Today, travelling by car, the distance of 1,037 kilometers from Köln to Lodz takes approximately 11 hours, 21 minutes, according to Google maps. The old passenger train, leaving Köln on October 30, 1941, with many stops and starts, could have taken days before arriving at *Radegast/Radogoszcz Bahnhof*, Lodz.

The report made by the captain of the security police in Lodz, dated November 13, 1941,[3] describes in bureaucratic detail the arrival of the transport in Lodz during the exact period when my parents stepped out of the train and placed their feet on that hard, uncaring ground:

> *The unloading was done so that in each case the Jews from six railway carriages made up one group and were escorted to the ghetto gate by two security policemen. . . . Despite the unfavorable weather and the difficulties arising from the fact that a large number of the railway carriages had only two doors and the corridors as well as the exits were frequently blocked by luggage, the unloading and the transportation of the Jews to the ghetto was accomplished smoothly in a very short space of time.*

In the twenty days between October 16 and November 4, 1941, approximately 25,000 human beings—Jews and Gypsies—were forcibly moved to Litzmannstadt (Lodz) from within the German borders.[4]

Was my father thinking about the irony of his return? Lodz was only 167 kilometers from his place of birth—Strasburg, West Prussia. Perhaps he passed through Lodz all those years before when as a young man he left home to travel west. Now he was back with his bride . . . all that was left of his successful life in Germany.

By the time my parents entered the Lodz ghetto, the hunger, cold, epidemics, and persecution there had already killed approximately 43,500 people. "Further transports caused even more disastrous conditions in the ghetto."[5] The compact area, four kilometers square, formerly a slum, had been cordoned off from the city of Lodz on April 30, 1940. With the overcrowding, lack of running water, and poor sewage, "the area soon became filthy and the air fetid . . . with long lines at the toilet . . . 60 Jews died every day." The leading cause of death was heart disease, the result of the overwhelming pressure and suffering of ghetto life.[6]

Past and Present Collide

When George and I fly back to Germany from Phoenix in 2009, I am continuing to gather material for this memoir, so we carry Corbach's book and other heavy research volumes in our luggage. I sit in our Eifel home, reading the vivid descriptions of life in the Lodz ghetto, and it dawns on me—I could have been there with my parents in that noisome pit. I place a bookmark between the pages of the book I am reading, close the book, and step into a relaxing bath. Our apartment is under the roof, and I look out at the tidy charm of the old houses and the beautiful soothing landscape as I luxuriate in the abundant, warm, cleansing water. Eifel water is so pure that the Romans built aqueducts through hills and valleys to carry this prized water to the city of Köln in AD 80. Today, centuries later, you can still find remnants of their achievement, such as the portion of a small stone channel lying exposed by the side of a street in Gemünd.

Past and present collide. The unutterable sadness of my soul is touched by the sweetness of the gift of life that I have received.

Chelmno/Kulmhof: The Valley of the Shadow of Death

On July 16, 1941, when my parents were still enduring life in hostile Köln, a Nazi official overseeing the region of Poland that included the Lodz ghetto sent a letter to SS-*Obersturmbannführer* (Lieutenant Colonel) Adolf Eichmann. He wrote that one solution for the coming winter food shortage would be to eliminate the Jews by some fast-acting poison.[7] Unknown to its inhabitants, the ghetto in Lodz, like other ghettos, "was only a stage in their eventual extermination."[8]

A venomous spider was spinning a vast web completely covering the territory of the Third Reich. Hatred fueled the monstrous scurrying black creature, weaving its sticky thread. The systematic, precise, efficient extermination process developed in rapacious response to opportunity. Zyklon B gas was already being used for delousing to control typhus in the Auschwitz/Birkenau concentration camp. The first experiment with Zyklon B gas as a killing agent took place there on September 3, 1941.[9]

In the autumn of 1941, secret preparations for mass murder began in Chelmno/Kulmhof, a small village about seventy kilometers west of Lodz. A large stone building, a dilapidated manor house known as "the castle," was encircled by a high, wooden fence. About three kilometers away, in a forest clearing, four separate large holes were dug and fenced off.[10]

In a lengthy report spanning the years from 1941 to 1944, Heinrich May, the German *Forstmeister* (master forester) responsible for the surrounding forest, reveals a soul unprepared for an encounter with starkest evil. He begins his report with a conversation that took place in the autumn of 1941. He was strolling through the woods in the Kulmhof-Kolo area with the *Landrat* (district administrator). Pointing his finger at May, the Landrat said, "*Bald werden Ihre Bäume besser wachsen.*" (Soon your trees will grow better.) The forester asked the meaning of this enigmatic phrase. And, the answer came, "*Die Juden geben einen guten Dung.*" (The Jews will make good fertilizer.)[11]

As I read May's account of his growing awareness of the Nazis' plans and his own lack of resistance, I am challenged to question my own fear of God. Would I be ready for such a test?

Because the practice of killing by mass shooting on the Russian front was beginning to negatively affect the morale of the *Einsatzgruppen* (mobile killing units), experiments took place using exhaust fumes from motor vehicles as an alternative. Mental patients near Minsk were the first offerings in September 1941.[12]

In Kulmhof, two (later joined by a third) new, medium-weight Renault trucks arrived, the outsides painted grey and the insides lined with zinc sheets. Between the metal floor and a covering of wooden slats lay a pipe, pierced with holes.[13] On December 8, 1941, Kulmhof became operational.[14]

By the beginning of April 1942, a constant flow of trains had carried 44,056 persons from Lodz to Kulmhof. After transport number 40 on April 2, 1942, there was a pause. Why? The Gestapo feared unrest, even spontaneous rebellion, in the ghetto. Rumors circulated despite the intense secrecy covering the purpose of the transports. A high Gestapo official arrived with an assignment to spin a story. There was, supposedly, a place thirteen kilometers from Lodz, near Kolo, large enough to hold 100,000 Jews, with furnished barracks, sufficient food, and work opportunities. Thirty thousand already lived there![15]

Summoned for the Journey

My parents were summoned for their journey out of the Lodz ghetto on a harrowing day at the beginning of May 1942 by the *Judenrat* (the Jewish council). Once again the depraved strategy implicated the Jewish leaders of the community in the deaths of their own.

Mordecai Chaim Rumkowski, the "Eldest of the Jews" in the Lodz ghetto, assigned scholarly Jewish writers to chronicle daily events. Their records from 1941 to 1944 survived, and the first paragraph of the lengthy introduction contains enigmatic words: "for reasons known only to itself . . . on May 1, a German medical commission stamped letters on the chests of 1,200 people."[16]

My parents bared their chests to receive the stamped letters.

On May 4, 1942, the first transport of the new wave of deportations left the Lodz ghetto. The chronicles continue:

> *On Monday, [May 4, 1942], around eight in the morning, the first transport of deportees left from the platform next to the Radogoszcz*

Station, made up of western European Jews, who had been brought into the ghetto a half year earlier. For the first time, with the departure of the first transport, crucial details connected with it became clear: all the travellers (the transport was made up of a thousand people) had their suitcases, backpacks and hand luggage taken from them. This news blanketed the entire ghetto with a depressing atmosphere.[17]

Slight differences in dating among surviving Holocaust records cast a shadow of uncertainty. The document from *jüdische Bevölkerung* (Jewish population) #12681 gives the date of my parents' death in Kulmhof as May 3, 1942, while the *Chronicles of the Lodz Ghetto* records the date of the first transport leaving Lodz after the month-long interruption as May 4, 1942.

Without doubt, my parents left the misery of the ghetto in the first week of May 1942.

Did my parents believe the "spin"? A furnished place near Kolo? With sufficient food? There was no alternative but to join the stream of 1,000 carrying their pitifully few belongings, trudging toward the appointed gathering place, Marysin, in the northern quarter of the ghetto. Their train was scheduled to leave Radegast/Radogószcz Bahnhof at 8 a.m. Sixty-seven years later as I accompany them in spirit, I see them closing the door of their tiny hovel, walking the ugly street, heads down, watching their steps, probably in the dark before dawn. Intense terror gripped the human mass as they stood and waited . . . and waited . . . and then came the sudden command, "Proceed to the Radegast/Radogószcz Bahnhof." When their suitcases, backpacks, and hand luggage were taken from them, were they also bereft of their last faint hope of survival?

This time there was no place to sit. They were herded into freight cars like cattle. No, animals would have been given more consideration. To reach their destination, Kulmhof—only seventy kilometers from Lodz— took many hours, as there was no direct rail link between the two places. They travelled to Kolo in the gloom of the closed freight car. Contrary to the propaganda that had been used to deceive them, Kolo was not their final destination. Reaching Kolo, they were transferred to a narrow-gauge track, packed into open freight cars and transported to the Powierce railway station, five kilometers northwest of Kulmhof. Two kilometers from the Powierce station stood a disused mill in the village of Zawadki. Here they were kept overnight. The following morning, crammed into open trucks, they reached the end of their journey—Kulmhof.[18]

What Awaited My Parents in Chelmno/Kulmhof?

Where can I find the truth about their deaths? I search among the reams of evidence left from the post-World War II trials. The German city, Nuremberg, is forever associated with the international trial of nineteen war criminals, from November 24, 1945, to August 31, 1946. I read the relevant transcripts from the trial of Adolf Eichmann, in Jerusalem, from April 11, 1961, to May 29, 1962. There were other courts in smaller places trying criminals lower down the ladder of the Nazi hierarchy.

The "Kulmhof Guard Trials" took place in the city of Bonn between 1962 and 1963.[19] Court records reveal the eyewitness accounts of perpetrators, observers, and a few surviving victims, supplemented by documents dating from the period when Kulmhof was functioning as an extermination center.

I pick up the book *Nazi Mass Murder: A Documentary History of the Use of Poison Gas*. Schmuel Krakowski is the author of chapter five, titled "The Stationary Gas Vans at Kulmhof." He is a survivor of the Lodz ghetto, Auschwitz, Buchenwald, and Theresienstadt, and was the director of Yad Vashem archives in Jerusalem from 1978 to 1993.[20] I learn the stark, unadorned facts through the scholarly research of Dr. Krakowski. I read the detailed testimonies given under oath at the guard trials. The words batter my soul like the pounding of a hammer. At the same time, I know that my own hardness of heart will soften when I accept the reality of what happened to my parents.

"The Delivery of the Victims"[21]

The open truck, packed with fear, stops before a high wooden fence, and the gate opens.[22] The vehicle enters the compound. The gate closes. Those who are packed into the back of the truck stumble out into the courtyard of the large, stone building. They line up.

A man dressed in a doctor's white coat addresses the bedraggled Jews:[23] "You are being sent to work in Germany, but first you will take a bath, and your clothes will be disinfected here in Kulmhof. Any valuables are to be handed over for registration."[24] At the witness stand in Bonn, Kurt Möbius, a former guard, reveals the reasoning behind the deceptive words: "We told the Jews this so they would not know what fate awaited them and to encourage them to obey calmly the instructions they were given."[25]

Men, women, and children are led into the ground floor of the castle, pushed along a corridor that leads to two connecting rooms where their valuables are collected in baskets held by Polish workers who record their names. When they have undressed, they are ordered down the stairs lit by gas lamps into the cellar. Signs reading "To the baths" hang on the staircase walls. From there the naked people in groups of thirty-five or forty leave the building by a rear door and are forced up a wooden ramp, protected from view on both sides by 2.5-meter high boards. The only opening leads into the rear of the grey van, parked with its double doors open.[26]

Möbius elaborates: "The Polish workers accompanied them. They carried leather whips with which they struck obstinate Jews who had become mistrustful and who hesitated to go further."[27]

90 More Minutes at the Most

Walter Burmeister, a former SS *Hauptscharführer* (technical sergeant), testifies: "From the time the people got out of the transport truck in front of the castle courtyard to the time they were loaded into the gas vans, a little less than an hour, at most one and a half hours, had passed. It depended on how long it took the old people to undress and hand over their valuables. It all happened without undue haste, quite calmly, so as not to arouse suspicion."[28]

Kulmhof had been constructed for one purpose. It was not a concentration camp in the usual sense, with a miniscule possibility of survival as a tortured slave. Kulmhof was a center for extermination, a place where living beings became nonexistent.

Silence

There are no more dishes to wash. Nothing still to buy. No further tinkering with the text of this book I am attempting to write. It is time to go with my parents through the double doors.

A former gas van driver, Gustav Laab, describes the scene. The van shakes as the bare feet enter.[29] When the van is full, the double doors are closed and locked. The exhaust pipe is connected to the flexible metal hose leading inside the van. The driver starts the engine. Screams, groans, hammering on the sides. After ten minutes, silence. The driver leaves the engine running for ten more minutes. The pipe and hose are disconnected. The vans are difficult to drive because they do not turn easily.[30] The driver carefully negotiates the three kilometers to the fenced area inside the forest, backing up to one of the four large holes. The double doors are unlocked and opened. The Jewish work details throw the corpses out of the van into the holes. In the process they search the bodies for hidden valuables, pull out any gold teeth, and take off wedding rings.[31]

Adolf Eichmann

Known as the "Architect of the Holocaust," Adolf Eichmann had been charged with the task of facilitating and managing the logistics of the mass deportation of Jews to eastern Europe because of his organizational talents and ideological reliability.[32,33] In 1960, Eichmann was snatched from his hiding place, a suburb of Buenos Aires, Argentina, and secretly brought to Israel. At his lengthy trial in Jerusalem, he was questioned about his visit to Kulmhof for the observation of a gassing. When he described being invited to look through a peephole into a van, he said:

> *I couldn't bring myself to look closely. . . . I couldn't take anymore. The screaming . . . I was too upset. . . . The van drove up to a long trench, the doors were opened, and bodies thrown out. . . . I can still remember a civilian pulling out teeth with some pliers, and then I got the hell out of there. . . . Terrible . . . I am telling you . . . the inferno.[34,35]*

SS *Obersturmbannführer* (Lieutenant Colonel) Adolf Eichmann was tried, convicted, and hanged for war crimes in Ramleh, Israel, on May 31, 1962.[36]

The Jewish Work Detail

The empty van is then driven back to the "castle." The Jewish work detail cleans the inside with water and disinfectant, ready for the return trip to the forest with the next group of thirty-five or forty souls.

The Jewish work detail was selected from incoming victims as they stepped out of the trucks into the "castle" courtyard. They were the young and robust. They wore leg irons. They lasted about a week. At the end of a day in the forest, their numbers were constantly culled by shooting in the neck.[37] A few miraculously escaped and reached the Warsaw ghetto. Their handwritten report of events in Kulmhof, covering the period January 7-19, 1942, was found in 1946 among papers buried in the earth, under the rubble of the ghetto.[38,39]

Eventually, the holes in the forest filled up and, fearing the spread of typhus, the Nazis constructed camouflaged incinerators. Those victims unfortunate enough to be put on the Jewish work detail were now assigned to digging up bodies and the efficient servicing of the ongoing burning.

The Stones Cry Out

A visitor to the village of Chelmno today would be hard-pressed to imagine the violent depravity that took place there seventy or so years earlier. Can it be true that this tranquil village, set in a lush river valley, had such an infamous history? As the Soviet army approached Chelmno in early 1945, the Nazis destroyed and burned most of the evidence before their retreat.

Since the 1980s, a Polish archeologist, with the approval of the Jewish community in Lodz, has led a series of excavations that have uncovered traces of Chelmno's haunted past. Extensive digging at the castle site revealed the remains of the basement rooms and the passageway that led my parents to the grey van. Vast amounts of meticulously sorted plundered property have been unearthed, such as a thick layer of glass medicine bottles, thousands of dental bridges, and false teeth that had been picked over in the search for precious metals.[40]

Why?

How do I bear my burden, the emptiness left by the merciless slaughter of my dearest? How do I face the fiery dragon that destroyed not just my two parents but also six million others?

Still, the fire is not quenched. The survivors and their children are maimed. Even the descendants of the perpetrators and the onlookers are scarred. But, I also ask questions about contemporary evil. How do I live in the presence of darkness? How do I cope with the restraint of God?

Around 640-615 BC, a Hebrew prophet, Habakkuk, cries out to God, "How long, O Lord, shall I cry and Thou wilt not hear? I cry out unto Thee of violence, and Thou wilt not save."[41] Bent under the weight of the truth—the circumstances of my parents' death—I join the Hebrew prophet in his questioning, wailing, listening, and trembling before the Holy One. I look up and take hold of his words—words of hope.

For though the fig tree shall not blossom,
neither shall fruit be in the vines;
the labour of the olive shall fail,
and the fields shall yield no food;
the flock shall be cut off from the fold,
and there shall be no herd in the stalls;

Yet I will rejoice in the LORD,
I will exult in the God of my salvation.
God, the Lord, is my strength.[42]

PART II

"Lucky Girl"

❧ ❧

Events converge
A moment in time
A quota of children
A mystery

❧ ❧

In 2007, George and I attended an interactive performance at the Freilichtmuseum, Kommern, Germany. There were only seven of us in the audience watching young actors from Köln telling the story of their city under Nazi rule. The script, drawn from authenticated letters and documents written during those dark years, was skillfully interpreted in a thoughtful, passionate production. A searing insight came to me during one scene. The seven of us were led outside. We circled the theater and re-entered through a side door, finding ourselves in a small, dark room, standing around a table bearing hundreds of burning candles. Two children, softly, slowly, and solemnly, read the names of all the Jewish children from Köln who had been murdered in the Holocaust. Even today I stop and become still as I remember listening to the names and looking at the flickering flames.

They did not read the name of Hannelore Zack.

8

Auf Wiedersehen & How Do You Do?

ondon is our destination. On the evening of July 24, 1939, the whistle blows, the flag waves, the wheels of the train gather momentum, and we leave the confusing darkness, the bright lights of Köln Hauptbahnhof, and all that is familiar. Oblivious to the costly gift my parents have entrusted to me, I allow myself to be carried away to the unknown. My body occupies a small space among all the other Jewish children. My mind and emotions go into hibernation.

I have no memory now of our crossing the oppressive German border or the communal expressions of relief as we entered a free Holland. The detailed memories of the Kindertransport recorded by older children are like brush strokes on my empty canvas.

A Box of Toys and Two Suitcases

I do remember one incident along the journey of my displacement— only one. I feel the ground steady under my feet after a night of swaying clatter. I am dazzled by the bright daylight; I breathe the bracing sea air. We must have reached the Hook of Holland prior to embarking on the ship that would cross the Channel and take us to Harwich, England. I hear the instructions. Fear and panic permeate the memory of that moment. We have to identify our luggage. We are led into a gigantic shed. I see the floor covered with suitcases and boxes arranged in endless rows. Unaware of my parents' abundant provision for the journey, I do not even know what my baggage looks like. How can I find it?

Hanna Schneider
Koblenz/Rhein
Markenbildchenweg 3o.pt.   2.August 1939.

        Sehr geehrte gnädige Frau,

        Von meiner Schwester, Frau Zack- Köln, erhielt ich den Brief von
        Frau Luise Kohn. Ich kann Ihnen nicht sagen, wie glücklich wir
        über diesen lieben Brief waren, und ich als Hannelores Tante will
        nicht verfehlen, auch herzlichst zu danken, für Ihre grosse Güte
        und Liebe, die Sie Hannelore geben wollen. Sie können sich denken
        welche Sorge wir bei der Abreise des Kindes hatten und wir glück-
        lich wir mit den Eltern waren,als der erste Brief ankam.
        Hoffentlich geht es Hannelore weiter gut,und fühlt sie sich in
        ihrem neuen Heime glücklich,und wir hoffen besonders,dass Hanne-
        lore artig und,lieb ist, und Ihnen nicht gar so viel Arbeit,und
        auch etwas Freude macht. - Wir hatten gerade in der letzten Zeit
        sehr viel Aufregung und die Abreise des Kindes kam so unerwartet
        schnell,dass wir gar nicht wissen,ob wir für Hannelores Gepäck
        alles richtig besorgt haben. Ich denke, dass die 2 Koffer und
        1 Kiste mit Spielsachen gut angekommen sind. Ich habe in den le
        ten Tage vor der Abreise des Kindes das Gepäck besorgt. Falls
        nun irgend etwas an Kleidung, Wäsche etc. fehlt, so bitten wir
        Sie, uns dies nur mitzuteilen, auch, wenn Sie Bettwäsche oder
        sonst irgend etwas wünschen sollten. Wir werden versuchen, diese
        Sachen noch nachsenden zu können.- Ich weiss nicht, ob Hanne-
        lores Mutter dieserhalb schon geschrieben hat, aber vorsorglich
        will ich danach fragen und dafür sorgen,dass die Eltern noch
        alles nachsenden, was gewünscht wird.- Es ging ebense alles so
        schnell, dass möglicherweise einige Sachen fehlen.
        Wir waren auch dadurch noch beunruhigt,dass Hannelore erst kurz
        vor der Abreise eine Blinddarmoperation hatte und wir hoffen,dass
        der Arzt,der sie inzwischen untersuchte, für gesund gehalten hat,
        und dass sie sich weiter wohl fühlt.- Ich habe heute Hannelore
        eine Karte gesandt, ich denke, dass sie antworten wird. Wenn
        Frau Luise Kohn noch bei Ihnen weilt, wird sie vielleicht so
        lieb sein und ihr bei der Antwort helfen,da sie ja deutsch
        schreibt und spricht.- Wir hatten vor einigen Monaten auch mit
        englisch-lernen begonnen, doch seit 2 Monaten gab es so viel
        Ereignisse,dass wir nicht mehr zum lernen kamen. Ich denke aber,

dann wir bald die english-lessons wieder aufnehmen werden,
und ich werde dann versuchen, einmal in englisch an Sie,gnädige
Frau, zu schreiben. Ich wäre Ihnen sehr dankbar, wenn Sie mir
bald einmal schreiben würden. Da Hannelore das einzige Nicht-
chen in der ganzen Familie ist, haben die Tanten natürlich eine
grosse Liebe für sie. Sie können in englisch schreiben,ich denke,
dass ich den Brief übersetzen kann.
Wenn natürlich Frau Luise Kohn noch dort ist, wäre ich ihr aus-
serordentlich dankbar, wenn Sie mir einmal schreiben würde.Denn
ich darf wohl annehmen, dass es ihr leichter fallen wird, hier-
hin zu schreiben. Auch ihr danke ich herzlichst für ihren Brief
und ihre Güte und Liebe zu Hannelore.
Auch meine Schwester Dora, mit der ich zusammen wohne, lässt
herzlichst Grüssen.
          Nehmen Sie für heute nochmals meinen herzlichsten
          Dank für Ihre Liebe und Güte entgegen mit den
          herzlichsten Grüssen Ihre

                    Hanna Schneider

The complete letter that my aunt sent to the gracious English lady.

Today, as if for the first time, I stop and re-read a section of my Aunt Johanna's letter dated August 2, 1939, and addressed to the "*Sehr geehrte gnädige Frau*" ("Dear honored and gracious lady"). She is responding to a letter my mother had received from a certain Luise Kohn, written in German with the news of my safe arrival. Was Luise Kohn helping in the arrangements for the refugees in England? I don't know.

In her letter, my aunt is concerned that my luggage is inadequate. She writes:

> *We have had in these last days so much disturbance, and the departure of the child came so unexpectedly fast, that we have little idea if we have included everything needed in Hannelore's luggage. I think that the two suitcases and box of toys have arrived safely. In the last days before the departure of the child I was responsible for assembling her luggage. In case any clothing, underwear, etc. is lacking, we ask you to please let us know. And if you would like to have bed linens or anything else, we will try to send these on to you.[1]*

The survival of my aunt's worn and faded letter amazes me. I hold in my hands a rare connection to my past. I strain to feel something of my family's anguish and their boundless love for me.

I was indeed travelling with two huge cases, one brown and one black, a large wooden box filled with all my dolls and their clothes, plus my hand luggage—a small black patent leather case with tan trimmings. It has taken years for me to release the anxiety I associate with baggage when travelling.

Back in 1939, at the Hook of Holland, inside the big shed, my loud cries and tears attract the attention of a Dutch railway official, who with patient kindness helps me to find my "stuff." He must have linked my name and number printed on the card hung around my neck with the labels on all that baggage.

England

I have no recollection of the Channel crossing. Perhaps the sea was calm that night. The arrival in Harwich and the train to Liverpool Street Station, London, are a blank. In my next moment of awareness following the experience with the luggage, we have arrived at Liverpool Street Station. I am standing among a small group of eight or so children on another railway station platform, surrounded by noise and flurry. Most of the other children have been claimed by relatives or sponsors, or perhaps collected to live in group homes. Today, I can hardly conceive of how my parents made the costly decision to send me off, trusting I would find someone to receive me but without any certainty. Probably, the same desperation had driven the other seven sets of parents. I feel a sliver of comfort in our shared apprehension as we stand close together.

As if in a vintage movie that jumps and jerks from one scene to another, now the eight of us are sitting in a moving railway carriage with three or four older men in dark suits. The two groups, children and adults, are isolated from each other. The adults speak no German. We children have not one word of English between us. Susi, age ten or eleven, tells us we must behave. I feel annoyed with her.

One of the men attempts to connect with us and tries a little English teasing. He makes motions to take the blue and white circular label hung around my neck. I become agitated and angry. Most probably my parents had strongly emphasized that the round piece of white cardboard must not be removed at any time. This is my identity; I am number 8814. On the back, the handwritten name Hannelore is crossed out, and replaced by Johanna Flora Zack. Horst is also crossed out, and replaced by Köln. I think this is my mother's handwriting. The corrections show something of her turmoil.

Who were these men, attempting to communicate with eight traumatized children? They were Christadelphian leaders from central England. Christadelphians, members of a small sect,[2] had responded to the Jewish plight. A number of families opened their homes to the refugees and volunteered to become foster parents. The harried Kindertransport organizers gladly accepted such offers in this time of crisis.[3]

Kenilworth

It must have been the next morning. We wake up in a very large house in Kenilworth, a small town in the middle of England. We are to sit on a blanket spread over a slightly damp, lush, grass lawn to have our picture "snapped." I am horrified to see my big doll brought out to sit with us. Someone must have opened my toy box and, finding the big doll, had an idea that this toy would enhance the appeal of the photograph. The sun is shining. We are arranged on the grass in the beautiful, landscaped English garden.

Thinking about the incident now, I try to untangle the strong emotions I felt on that day. I was struggling with anxiety. Someone had rifled through my things, but that was not the prime cause of my distress. Rather, my doll and her precious clothes could be marred, get dirty, and I had no say in the matter. My mother had knitted the clothes for me when I was a baby. Were they all entwined—the doll, my own baby clothes, the loss of my mother, and the invasion of my boundaries? I felt helpless in my indignation.

Today, I can understand. The abnormal events of 1939 challenged British adults who were trying their best to respond to the children in their midst. We were flesh and blood, needy children, who were no longer the distant objects of their humane decision to "do something." I am thankful for their willingness to risk the disruption to their lives.

The next scene in the old English wartime movie now showing in the theater of my imagination depicts our little group squeezed into a small car, with Mr. Crowley,* our host, driving us the few miles to Coventry. We stop outside a house. Faces appear at the windows of the car. This pattern is repeated—drive, stop, faces at the window. Inside the car, we are silent and uncomprehending. When I look back and remember that time driving around Coventry, a jolly tune and the words of a song popular in the 1950s play in my mind: "How much is that doggy in the window, the one with the waggly tail? I do hope that doggy's for sale."

We felt as though we were on display in a pet shop window, sitting close together in that car. And, the faces pressed against the glass? They were looking for the cutest puppy. How could such serious decisions be processed in that emergency, our hurried exodus from Germany to an England tense with fears of war? The Calcott family picked me.

The Calcotts of Coventry

I know that I cried the first night, alone in the room the Calcotts had carefully prepared for their new family member. I wept in dread that I would forget all my German and never learn English, and I would be isolated and alone, unable to communicate with another human being for the rest of my life. I was seven years old, abruptly thrust out of my familiar world into a strange, inhospitable universe, bereft of the last traces of security. There was no place to land, no familiar voice, no teacher to guide my untethered soul. Even if the Calcotts could have helped, there were hardly any words we had in common. The first wounds inflicted as I turned on the top step of the train at Köln Hauptbahnhof and the pain I nursed as the train gathered speed remained unhealed. Now, loneliness beyond my ability to articulate rubbed the raw place in my soul. Lying on the bed in my own room at the Calcotts, I was confronted with existential questions hanging in the empty void, unasked and unanswered.

Daylight introduced me to Roddy, the Calcotts' son. He was about my age, an amiable little boy with whom I loved to play in the tiny garden. So my language learning began almost by osmosis, conversing with Roddy. I felt a peaceable atmosphere in the home, a capacity to enjoy simple pleasures. Looking back now, I see myself sitting on the carpet in

Kath and Jack Calcott, probably
photographed in the autumn
of 1939.

Roddy and I shortly after my
arrival.

the front room. Mrs. Calcott is preparing afternoon tea on the low coffee table. We have English white bread, which to my German taste resembles cake. She mashes bananas with a fork, and spreads the gooey mixture on the slice of bread, takes a teaspoon and skims cream from the top of the milk for the finishing touch. This is comfort food.

We are all going to the "pictures"—Mr. and Mrs. Calcott, Roddy, and I. The star of the featured film is Shirley Temple. It is the first time I have ever been inside a cinema. I relish the excitement of the atmosphere— sitting in the curved, plush, tip-up seat, the tension of the lights dimming before an explosion of sights and sounds, the charming little girl with her curls bobbing as she dances and sings. Her cheerfulness, even joy, feeds my starved, intensive gaze, and I step into another world.

The Princesses

If only Mutti and Vati could have seen this photograph ...

Each of us Kindertransport children had received a large hardcover picture book—an introduction to our new life in Britain. I was most impressed by the English princesses. I would turn to their photographs again and again, absorbing every detail of their posed pictures, at play and with their parents—their ethereal, white, frilly dresses, the idyllic setting, flowers, gardens, and rich velvet curtains. To me, they looked like fairies, graced with beautiful expressions, delicate features, waves, and curls. Princess Margaret was about my age, and Princess Elizabeth a little older. What country was this where the rulers looked gentle and shy? I had come from a nation where leadership meant power, might, loud harsh voices—violence. "Be afraid" was the message ringing in our ears. Could leaders be kind and humane?

Disaster

Days later, unexpected disaster struck. I remember clambering up and down the stairs, squirting water on the ceiling. What a powerful feeling—directing the wet stream high, higher. My parents had tried to cover every contingency in their packing. I found a rubber enema bulb, filled it with water, and followed the path of my curiosity. Today, I wonder, "Was the rage simmering within me bursting out like the water spewing upward?"

The next thing I knew, I was with another family. Probably there had been other incidents beside the water on the ceiling. I don't remember. But the Calcotts telephoned someone and asked that I be taken back. They couldn't cope.

I learned a bitter lesson. Be careful, keep everything locked inside, or something bad will happen; the slippery remnants of security you still hold will be yanked out of your grasp and you will fall into nothingness. I was a child, believing I had been abandoned by my parents, focused on myself and totally blind to their agony. Now, with this second blow, I lacked any awareness of the Calcotts' pain in our parting.[4]

Exhall

As train carriages are uncoupled from the engine when there is a change in the gauge of a track, so my life in the English Midlands abruptly disconnected me from parents, home, family, friends, religion, culture, and language. The old familiar rails were gone, and I had no map for the journey. Now, after only a few weeks, another unexpected turn in the road—I found myself in a different house with a new foster family, Mr. and Mrs. Dodd of Exhall.

The grievous story of a little Czech girl, recounted by the Dodds, makes me think my move from the Calcotts to Exhall took place shortly after September 3, 1939. There had been an exchange of letters between the Dodds and Dr. Stefan Jaroschy, Prague XIX, na Dionysce 9. The Dodds had agreed to receive his little daughter into their home and were awaiting her arrival. I have a blurred copy of Dr. Jaroschy's last letter from Prague dated August 28, 1939. He hopes Erika, called by her pet name "Ini," will leave at midnight on August 30, but adds, "Just now I am told that it is still all in the air whether the transport will start the 30. August." The ninth Kindertransport train, containing 250 children, was due to leave Prague on September 3, 1939, the day Britain declared war. The Germans did not allow the train to leave the station.[5]

What happened to the little girl who was awaited in Exhall? She must have been among the 250 children who had said goodbye to their parents and were sitting and waiting in the train. She never arrived at 167 Coventry Road, Exhall, and so it was that I took the place prepared for her.

Why, Ini. . . . Why?

William Henry and Louisa Dodd, a couple in their early fifties, with their only son already married, lived alone in their detached, three-bedroom house. According to the English custom of naming a house, they called their home "Bethel." Beth-El is Hebrew for "House of God." As Christadelphians, they read through the Bible systematically, according to a reading plan: all of the Old Testament once a year and the New Testament twice. I was expected to join the regular evening readings and attend Sunday gatherings that lasted several hours. (I remember coping with my boredom by devising mind games, like counting the number of times the speaker used "but" or "and.") Some of the stories and names I heard were familiar—Moses, David, Esther—but the name Jesus . . . that was new to my ears. Christadelphians saw themselves as outsiders, a remnant, upholding "the Truth" in contrast to the errors of the "church" in doctrine and practice. I received shelter because of the group's close affinity with the Jewish people.

Across the busy main road from the Dodd's house in Exhall, a good location between Coventry and Bedworth, stood "W. H. Dodd & Son," a garage selling petrol, motor bikes, and bicycles and offering repairs. Exhall is a village without a center, a collection of hamlets strung together in the shadow of the city of Coventry, which is located five miles to the south. Exhall extends to the small town of Bedworth lying about a mile to the north. Records mention that Exhall, a modest place with a long history, was in 1275 considered half of the fee paid to a knight's family, the Butlers.[6]

Traditionally, many local men worked in agriculture, coal mining, or the brickworks. But in 1939, after World War II broke out, Exhall was

Dr. Stefan Jaroschy
Prague XIX   Prague August 28th. 1939
na Dionysce 9

Dear Mrs. Dodd,

thank you very much for your letter /to my wife/ of t.
21. august. We are always looking forward to your letters which are really comforting in our sad situation. The feeling that you fully understand what it s:
nify to separe us from the children and perhaps to separe the children from
each other is already a consolation to us. And the hope that your efforts in fi
ding a home for Stephen would be successfull prevents us to lose courage.

In the meantime we were informed that Erikas transport
will start the 30th. august at midnight. The committee asked for a few document
and promised to settle the rest. Last wednesday we were anew informed that the
German authorities do not agree with this proceeding and that everybody has't
ask personally for the permit and that the children too are to be presented.
I won't to inform you what happened, I remark only that once my wife waited at
the office from 10 to 7 and the next day from 7 to 1. At the same time the lug
gage had to be prepared and delivered to the custom-office, where it rests til
the transports departs. By this reason there was naturally not time enough to
prepare all as we wanted. Besides, we got very strict new orders concerning goo
which are not allowed to export and in this way the possibility of fitting ou
the children is quite limited.

I am also sorry because I had the intention of sending
you with Erika a little present as souvenir from Bohemia. My father was a col-
lectioner of Bohemian curiosities a we have several cabinets containing Bohemian old glassware, china and other works of art. Now it is strictly forbidden
to take such things along.

Just now I am again told, that it is still all in the air
whether the transport will start the 30. august

However, Erika - called "Ini" with her petname, her second christian
name is Winifried - is looking forward to be soon by Auntie and Uncle.
She is a child as happy as the day is long, always in good spirits and I am s
you will be content with her. She is already a little woman, always willing to
help and to work. You must only take into account, that it will be necessary a
certain time, till she comes to an understanding with her new company and the
perhaps in the first time it would be a little confusing for her to be separ
from her family. But I know by your letters that you have so much understand
for a little childs mind that we are quite calmed and have perfect trust. in

I hope there are not too many mistakes in my letter, but I am writing in
a hurry and I dont expect, you would take me for an Englishman. But I had neve
time by my profession to learn languages and now I began in May and attended
for a few months the English Institute in Prague.

Thank you very much for your kindness and thank please Mr. Dodd too fro
as

sincerely Yours

D. Stefan Jergely

We both send our
Erika and Stefan.

Letter from Ini's father to the Dodds.

pulled closer into the orbit of Coventry: a center for the world-renowned vehicle industry. The many workshops manufacturing bicycles, cars, and trucks were hurriedly transformed into huge armament-producing factories. Many women rolled up their sleeves for the war effort, while their husbands, sons, and fathers were mobilized for battle in the British army, navy, and air force.

On the lawn in front of the bird bath, probably photographed during the summer of 1940. From left to right: Laurie's mother; Laurie, who was married to Mr. and Mrs. Dodd's son, Cyril; Susan, their first child; Auntie; and me.

Who Am I?

The official name written on my birth certificate issued by the city of Bonn is Johanna Flora Zack. Everyone in Gemünd called me Hannelore, a valid German name. In my case, it could have been created by combining "Johanna" and "Flora." My parents expressed their delight in me with the diminutive "Hannalorechen." An abundance of affection and names surrounded my little person.

The name Hannelore sounded cumbersome to English ears, and so I became Hanna. While my new foster family called me Hanna, I was to address them as "Auntie" and "Uncle." Recently, I learned that my aunt Johanna was known as Hanna—a comfort in the childhood loss hovering around my name.

Looking back at world events after September 3, 1939, I wonder if there was more to the name change than ease of usage—becoming inconspicuous, perhaps? What was the cost for English families taking refugees from Germany? As I melted into the English culture, unknown to me my parents were wearing yellow stars.[7]

War was declared; Britain was tense, expecting an imminent German invasion. We experienced "blackouts"—hiding all lights to prevent enemy aircraft from receiving guidance to their targets. For a household, that meant sewing curtains of heavy black material for every window. No sliver of light was allowed. If your cover-up was inadequate, you would be warned. All Britain held its breath, and yet, nothing actually happened in those first months.

By May 1940, an epidemic of anti-alien fear broke out in Britain. Germany had quickly overrun much of Europe with a new military strategy—*Blitzkrieg*, a concentration of planes, tanks, and artillery along a narrow front, used successfully against Poland (September 1939), Denmark (April 1940), Norway (April 1940), Belgium (May 1940), the Netherlands (May 1940), Luxembourg (May 1940), and France (May

103

1940).[8] Britain stood alone against the Nazi war machine.

The nation gathered courage to resist a powerful enemy. The Anglicization of German-Jewish children living among a vulnerable people was strongly encouraged, and I became Hanna. I was told, "Forget all that German past; what a lucky little girl you are!" So, a new cultural skin was grafted over the surface of my injury. Underneath, the festering infection rose to the surface at unexpected times. One day, I saw Hitler's picture on the front page of the *Daily Mirror*. I took a pair of scissors and stabbed him. I can still feel the intensity of the motion as I raised my hand, grasping the scissors, and brought the sharp point down again and again.

Raining Death and Destruction

Jerked out of sleep by the shrieking air raid siren assaulting our ears, Auntie, Uncle, and I made our urgent way to the bottom of the long garden and entered the newly built structure under the crabapple tree— our small, brick, square air raid shelter. I rather liked the novelty of a break in the order of our lives, being awakened in the night and, especially, sitting close together with our neighbors, Mr. and Mrs. Gibson* and their three young children, Margaret, John, and David, our coats covering pajamas and nightgowns. Getting to know them in this odd situation, listening for the drone of the airplanes and the distant explosions—it was all so exciting! After a long, unbroken silence we would hear the steady whine of the siren heralding "All clear." The adults would sigh, releasing their anxiety, and we all would return to our beds.

In the bright light of a full moon, on the frosty night of November 14, 1940, summoned by the wail of sirens, we scurried into the garden shelter. The heavy thunder of the bombers above us continued endlessly, mixed with earth-shattering booming. Five miles away, we could see all Coventry aglow. Were my parents cowering in the cellar of 14 Horst-Wessel Platz, Köln? Did the German and British planes pass each other in the sky? Today's questions were far from my sleepy, eight-year-old head that turbulent night.

I don't know if we left voluntarily or were directed, but in the morning, we drove to a farm at the edge of Warwick, twenty miles from Exhall. We were part of an evacuation fleeing the hazardous industrial area for shelter in the countryside. Coventry had burned all night, and only hours after the devastation, we were driving slowly, slowly through the smoking piles of debris edging our path to hoped-for safety. I can never forget the sight of tram lines forming huge metal arcs high above us, strange sculptures created by the power of multiple blasts. Coventry Cathedral had been gutted by incendiary bombs, leaving only the tower, spire, and outer walls.

The cathedral provost walked, shocked and sorrowful in the morning light, among the smoking rubble. Maybe we passed him as we crawled our way out of the city. A cross was constructed from charred, medieval roof beams and placed on an altar of rubble.[9] Carved on a still standing wall were the words, "Father, forgive."[10]

I think we probably stayed at the farm for several days, but then, believing bombs would drop only during the night, we began a new pattern. Each weekday in the dark early hours, we returned to Exhall—Uncle to his shop, Auntie caring for the house, and me to Exhall Council Junior School. Evenings brought us back to the large, jolly, and welcoming farm family who invited us to join them playing Monopoly. Eventually, we settled back full time at 167 Coventry Road with the addition of a new air raid shelter. More sophisticated, this was an underground shelter, dug out of the ground nearer to the house, covered by a mound of grass next to the big weeping willow tree. Furnished with bunks and bedding, this place became our bedroom for many nights. I faintly remember the story of a land mine falling in the field bordering our back garden, just next to the old shelter that our neighbors continued to use. A plane had dropped a land mine that lodged deep in the ground—a bomb with a colossal capacity for destruction. It was discovered unexploded.

Gas masks were issued. We had regular practices in our classes at school when we took the ugly "thing" out of its box. At a word from the teacher, we tried to place the uncomfortable, thick rubber membrane over our faces, attaching it with straps over the back of our heads. We could see through an oval, transparent "window," and we practiced breathing through the metal snout. We looked like a cross between a pig and a space alien. The little square cardboard box with a long string loop for carrying the gas mask across our shoulders accompanied us at all times and in every place.

I was ignorant of the dangers and fascinated by all the unusual activities. I was totally oblivious that people were dying.

Auntie and Uncle

Wartime fear and tension must have jostled the balance of our relationships in those first years behind the front door with leaded windows at 167 Coventry Road, Exhall. What was the flavor of our daily lives?

Probably, my memories of life with Auntie and Uncle are filtered through the lens of my suppressed sense of abandonment and emotional deprivation. In my sudden separation from Mutti and Vati, I was like a tree, felled with a single blow and the bark stripped, cut into thin planks at the sawmill. How did the Dodds view their substitute foster child? I suspect my reputation had preceded my arrival: "a problem child needing firm discipline." Yet, it was not all gloom and doom. There are pleasant memories from those early years in England.

I first met my "best friend," Peter, when the front door of 167 opened, and I stood hesitantly on the black and white tiles at the entrance of a dark hallway. Peter looked up at me, his eyes bright and his tail wagging in total acceptance. By the time our friendship began, his frisky "fox-terrierness" had mellowed to patient empathy, and I poured out all my pent-up emotion on his furry black and white being.

Peter, except for the occasional distraction of a bird or two, was our constant companion when I pushed my three well-dressed children—the large, celluloid infant the size of a one-year-old, the middle doll with lifelike rubber head and hands, and the baby—in a simple old-fashioned carriage. We took long walks. Our route began on the square lawn next to the house and continued down the slope past the birdbath to a long rectangular second lawn. At the bottom by the crabapple tree, we turned left, passing the scratchy bushes, and continued up the third lawn parallel to lawn number two. Our journey took us under the clothesline until we reached the giant pine tree marking our return to the beginning. Repeat and repeat.

I grew bored with the monotony of our route and the unresponsive gaze of my three babies. They stared at me with unchanging, vapid smiles whatever current problem I was confiding. There, beside us, was Peter—vibrant, alive. Could Peter be my baby? Out came the dolls. Their new role? Sitting on a bench, an audience watching our adventures. Quickly and carefully I undid the bonnet, the one knitted by my mother as she waited for my birth, and gently fastened the little white hat to Peter's compliant head, lifting him into the carriage. Wonder of wonders, he stayed in place, my companion. We two wanderers hiked around and around.

Maybe a year later, in 1940, the sunny back garden was the setting for another happy, playful memory. How hard it was to wait for the knock on the door. My friend from Exhall Council Junior School, Raymond, was bringing his younger sister Joy to visit and play. Joy was a softly rounded cheerful little girl with curly black hair, while Raymond was a fair, slightly built amiable boy. He was my friend because he always agreed with my ideas and plans.

On this Saturday, we would play weddings. Auntie brought a big box overflowing with old curtains and well-worn hats and set it down under the clothesline. Nothing, not a scrap, was discarded in wartime. I had never attended a wedding, but I boldly took charge. In my imagination, weddings consisted of elegant clothes, a procession, and speeches by the bride and groom. There was no rabbi, pastor, or priest in the picture.

Of course, I was the bride. Joy became the perfect bridesmaid in her too long, flowery dress and big, floppy straw hat. I can't remember the bridegroom's outfit clearly. I think he wore a battered men's felt hat, sitting low on his head, partially covering his eyes, and a slightly frayed silk tie. I was resplendent in two sets of lace curtains, one over my head, the other wrapped around my body and pinned to my German sunsuit. We marched solemnly the whole length of the lawn. Joy obediently lifted the curtain trailing behind me with only a few reminders, "Hold it up . . . hold it up." Raymond and I proceeded, hand in hand, while I gave instructions, word by word, and Peter excitedly circled the wedding party.

During the first weeks of my life with the Dodds, after his midday meal, Uncle would sit by the coal fire and listen to the news on the radio before returning to his business across the road. I would clamber onto his lap and sit still in a peaceful, relaxed atmosphere. That cozy memory contrasts with a later family ritual. At the end of the day, Auntie and Uncle would sit in their easy chairs on either side of the fire, listening to the radio or reading the newspaper. When my bedtime came, I was expected to go to each in turn and say good night with a kiss on their cheeks. There was no reciprocal kiss, hug, or smile. Auntie would say, "Good night, sweet dreams"—rote words and actions, empty of warmth and emotion. How did we grow apart? Was it my inner withdrawal, or their disappointment in the child I was becoming? I don't know.

Auntie had a supply of old proverbs to apply to daily life. At the table, if I became too chatty, "Children should be seen and not heard." Tuesday was cleaning day, and I joined her on holidays from school. When I skipped dusting the curlicues on the fat legs of the heavy table, I heard, "If a job is worth doing, it is worth doing well." When I wanted to give up, "If at first you don't succeed, try, try again." I resisted silently.

Auntie and Uncle, on holiday at the seaside, probably in 1951 or 1952.

Taste the Difference

A child eating tasty, familiar food feels comfortable and loved.

I have the quirkiest memories of my first encounters with the English diet. Drinking tea was a trial. I remembered tea as a fragrant, delicate drink, diluted with lemon. The words "tea" and "Tee" (the German word for "tea") sounded the same to my ears, straining for understanding. But what I tasted was a strong and bitter brew, made more unpalatable with the addition of milk. In the search for a familiar taste, I persuaded Auntie to let me eat a slice of raw bacon, thus confirming that my mother had shared with me her "un-kosher" enjoyment of smoked ham. I chewed and chewed the salty, raw bacon with only the faintest of echoes from an unreachable home. Mustard cured me of my restless search. Spreading the oh-so-mild German mustard on hearty rye bread must have made a delicious snack. I tried a thin smear of English mustard on a slice of white bread, and my nose and entire head exploded!

Sometimes, mealtimes became battlegrounds. Perhaps the strict application of rules was part of the Dodds' philosophy for rearing a problem child. It could have been that my reputation as a "difficult child" contributed to the stringent control. In those first weeks, I would sit at the table for hours after the meal was over until I ate every bite. I hated boiled cabbage. Gradually, this indulged child learned to chew and swallow her distaste.

Ration Cards

Wartime rationing affected us all. We carefully used the limited supply of clothes, petrol, and food. My parents were just across the English Channel, so near and yet so far—I had no inkling of their discomfort, the hunger, the cold. Our lives at 167 Coventry Road were very ordered. On the same day every week, before I began to attend school, I would go with Auntie to Pattersons.* We turned right out of our gate, walking

Happy Memories

My first school picture, 1941.

with a basket, crossing over the busy road, turning left onto Hayes Lane, passing the council houses. Reaching the end of the lane, we opened the door. The bell rang, and we stepped into the tiny grocery store.

Mr. and Mrs. Patterson were a gentle, elderly, rounded couple. They were both experts in cutting the thin wedge of cheese allowed for three ration cards without waste. They carefully scooped the sugar from a sack into a paper bag. I can still hear Mr. Patterson's chesty, rumbling voice. I don't recall seeing their adult daughter, Kate, but many years later, I would learn that she saw and remembered me.

An Unfortunate Question

One cool morning in 1939, as my first English summer was ending, there was a knock on the front door. Today, I can still see in my mind's eye the place in the road where I looked up at the reassuring presence of Pat, a tall girl who was taking me with her for my first day at Exhall Council Junior School. I sat next to her at the big, wooden desk, swinging my legs that didn't quite reach the floor. The teacher said, "Draw a margin." I whispered, "What is a margin?" Pat thought this so amusing; she raised her hand to share the funny question with the teacher and the class.

The next thing I knew, I was sitting in a smaller desk in another classroom. This exposure of my language inadequacies had a good outcome. I was placed in Mrs. Farrell's* class. The last time I visited Exhall—I think it was in 2007—I happened to meet our old neighbor, David Gibson.* He delighted to recount the stories of the past, and he remembered how Mrs. Farrell cared for each of her pupils and was much loved in return. The affirming environment in her classroom and the stories she read to us at the end of the school day stimulated my imagination, nurturing a delight in words and pictures.

A'Peth o'Suck

Except for that glitch with "margin" on the first day of school, I gathered the necessary English vocabulary as if by osmosis. Oh, but there was the experience in December 1939 when I was standing with my class, singing Christmas carols. They all knew the familiar words; there was no need for books. With some shame I moved my mouth, pretending to join in. Even today, I try to gauge the atmosphere with great intensity when I am interacting with others.

Britain is rich in regional dialects, and each small area has unique pronunciation and singular words. In Exhall, we spoke with a dialect peculiar to the Coventry area. "We speak with an accent exceedingly rare," is a phrase in an old Coventry song. Walking to school, I would stop at the small corner market, entering the door between boxes of cabbages and turnips displayed outside. The bell would clang, and the shopkeeper would look at me across the counter and say, "'Ello, luv," and I would reply, "A'peth o'suck." (Translation: a half penny of candy.) The most delectable "suck" and a great bargain was a three-inch paper roll filled with powder that you could suck through the black licorice tube sticking up from the top. The powder tasted sweet, tingly, and frothy as it touched the moisture of my tongue. A wise investment, the powder lasted a long time with an added bonus—chewing the licorice straw.

A Hole in the Heart

On a special day in 1940, maybe just before the summer holiday began, our class was allowed to bring a favorite toy to school. Of course, my selection was the big doll in her beautiful clothes, the one that had caused so much anxiety on my first day in England. I have a clear memory of walking across the playground, carefully holding the huge, celluloid doll. My path took me a little too near the big boys and their boisterous game. Sudden catastrophe! The doll flew out of my arms. She struck her head on the concrete ground. I picked her up, weeping at the sight of a large hole in her head.

Why do all these painful memories surface when I describe my childhood? Perhaps the many little losses have lodged in my heart because I was not grieving the greater hurt.

9

Stuff It in the Bag

All day I sat in the silent classroom. Only the scratch of pens, punctuated by an occasional shuffle or cough, intruded, until a dislocating voice announced, "Pens down, time is up."

A room full of apprehensive ten to eleven year olds was squeezing out every ounce of limited knowledge, and when the tube was empty, they hazarded the best guesses they could. The rest of our lives would be marked by this day. Isolated in rows, our desks far apart, we were "sitting for a scholarship." In Britain at that time, for most children, an academic education depended on winning a scholarship. This was your only chance if your parents could not pay school fees. Lacking fees or a scholarship, you were directed to a comprehensive school, making a grammar school or high school education unattainable.

Lunchtime was the only pause during that intense day at the big school in Ash Green. I went home with Diana who lived nearby. Since both of her parents worked, she prepared her own lunch, usually a boiled egg. I ate my cold meat sandwich, left over from the Sunday roast. She taught me how to make a hot drink with a spoonful of dark red bramble jam and hot water—so exotic to my mind! It was wartime. We were surrounded by limitations.

The Academic Door Opens

I struggled through endless papers and numbers. Respite came in the afternoon when we were directed to write a "composition." I selected

"The Story of a Journey" from among the choices offered and lost myself in a mystery boat trip along the Rhine River. Probably, that piece of writing tipped the balance. Exhall Council Junior School was allocated one scholarship—only one. A boy and I had equal results; he was probably good at mathematics. His age allowed him to retake the exam the following year, but I was too old. So the privileged door to Nuneaton High School for Girls opened to me.

Many Kindertransport children suffered the loss of educational opportunities, and you would think this rare gift of an academic education would have inspired me to work hard and excel. However, after the initial scary anticipation and excitement with the novelty of it all, I settled into habits of doing as little homework as possible and listening only if the teacher was interesting and confident.

We were required to wear school uniforms. On the first day of school, I realized that everyone else's mother had chosen a beret from the list, while I was wearing a felt hat with a brim and ribbon. The shame of being different! When we travelled, we had to wear a hat every school day. Auntie believed that a hat covering the head prevented sicknesses, such as a cold. So, I had to wear the wretched thing even on Saturdays, when it was my job to go by bus to Bedworth and buy meat for the Sunday roast. The bus stopped by the metal railing surrounding the alms houses at the center of town. I would walk the short distance to the butcher's shop, stuffing the hat into the shopping bag along the way. I was charmed by the butcher's assistant. His name was Melvyn; he was an amateur boxer. I eagerly looked forward to the words we would exchange as I counted out the pounds, shillings, and pence, uneasy with my desire to appear "normal" and the deception of "breaking the rules."

The darkest recollection from those high school years is the time I chased Hilda Boyle* around and around the large grass playing field, a bone out of the natural science display case in my hand. Hilda, a classmate, was a thin, pale girl—nervous and fragile. I bullied her. How could a child who had been subjected to discrimination and contempt do such a thing? I

116

think it is all too easy for the persecuted to become the persecutor; the powerless to mistreat those who are weaker yet. Oh Lord, forgive. Bless and heal Hilda Boyle from the harm I did her.

Sheila Deeming was a bright ray of light in my life at Nuneaton High School for Girls. She was a loyal, caring best friend. Recently, after sixty-five years, we reconnected. She wrote, "As a girl, I never dared to ask you, I had no idea how terrible things were in Europe, and I just didn't want to upset you and perhaps make you cry. Somehow, it was taboo—something nobody spoke about—as were such a lot of things in those days." To my question, "What was I like then?" she answered, "Within you there was a deep sadness."

I asked her if she recalled the time our headmistress, Miss Kerr,* cautioned her about our friendship. She didn't remember. In my memory, a scene took place in which Miss Kerr, a tall, regal, angular woman, with an aquiline nose and grey hair knotted at the nape of her neck, took Sheila aside, bent down, and quietly suggested it would be better for her to find another friend. I wonder—did this warning come because of my troubled behavior or from a sense of class distinctions? Sheila's grandfather was a respected member of the local government in Nuneaton and owned a large, well-known butcher shop. Or could it have been because of my German-Jewish background? I was the only "foreign" child attending Nuneaton High School. Sheila responded to the story by saying, "Well, that didn't stop us, did it?" She added that Miss Kerr, ready for retirement at that time, was probably carrying a lot of wartime burdens. The advice Miss Kerr gave to Sheila could have been a combination of all those influences.

Classes taught by Miss Jacobs* were fun, and I wanted to please her. She was a small, plump woman and scraped her frizzy hair into a little bun on the top of her head. Her tight, black suit looked shiny and grey from constant wear. She taught English literature enthusiastically by allowing us to experience the power of creative words. We would study Shakespeare by throwing ourselves into the drama as we acted scenes in the classroom.

My favorite was *The Taming of the Shrew*. I would hold my breath as the parts were assigned, unconsciously seeking the release of my hostility in the words of Katherina the Shrew.

The War Was Over

The war was over. Britain erupted in relieved and joyous celebration. It was 1945, and I was in my thirteenth year when the letter regarding my parents' fate arrived from the Red Cross. I read the words but would not allow my emotions to respond. I could not swallow the bitterness. My parents were dead. I closed my heart and turned away. I withdrew behind the internal barricade I had erected as a protection from the unbearable pain of my loss.

Today, I can still remember a song I heard for the first time in my early teens. I see myself again, under the table kneeling and dusting. I stop and listen. Paul Robeson's deep rich voice flows out of the radio. He is expressing my own inarticulate cry—

Ah, gits weary
An' sick of tryin'
Ah'm tired of livin'
An' skeered of dyin'
But ol' man river
He jes' keeps rollin' along![1]

Counseling, grief therapy, or even the encouragement to express sadness were little known in those days of sorrow. I must have been deeply depressed if I identified so intensely with words like "tired of living" and "scared of dying." I connected with the indifference surrounding the singer, the Mississippi River just rolling along. I was passive and fatalistic, but I intended to stoically go on. I told myself not to anticipate anything pleasant or good because I would be disappointed.

How did I cope?

Another Flashback

I remember being alone in the front room amid the dark wood furniture and heavy navy blue velvet chairs with gold dots. My eyes fell on an old hymn book. Aimlessly turning the pages, I selected Horatius Bonar's composition because the notes were uncomplicated.

Perched on the piano stool, firmly and loudly picking out the tune with the fingers of my right hand and drowning my off-key rendering, I sang along.

> *I heard the voice of Jesus say, "Come unto Me and rest;*
> *Lay down, thou weary one, lay down thy head upon My breast."*
> *I came to Jesus as I was, weary, worn and sad;*
> *I found in Him a resting place, and He has made me glad.*
>
> *I heard the voice of Jesus say, "Behold, I freely give*
> *The living water, thirsty one, stoop down, and drink and live."*
> *I came to Jesus, and I drank of that life-giving stream;*
> *My thirst was quenched, my soul revived, and now I live in Him.*
>
> *I heard the voice of Jesus say, "I am this dark world's Light;*
> *Look unto Me, thy morn shall rise, and all thy day be bright."*
> *I looked to Jesus, and I found in Him my Star, my Sun;*
> *And in that light of life I'll walk, 'til travelling days are done.*[2]

As a teenager, I was touched by the melancholy tune and the words "weary . . . worn . . . sad . . . this dark world . . . travelling days." As the music reached my suppressed emotions, I had the rare experience of actually feeling my feelings.

I never remember hearing the word "Jesus" in Gemünd. In the synagogue, when I accompanied my father on a Sabbath (Saturday), or in our home celebrations of Jewish feast days such as the Passover Seder, we would use the word "Messiah," but the name "Jesus" was not uttered.

After six or so years in England, "Jesus" sounded familiar. At school, I had heard all those Christmas carols. And, His name must have echoed in my ears when I sat through those long Christadelphian Sunday meetings. Yet, although I had grown accustomed to the word, the person of Jesus remained hazy and unreal, a distant figure hovering at the edge of my awareness. As I sang, repeating the verses over and over, His invitation to come evoked profound yearning for the tenderness and love He offered. Yet, I didn't know how to respond beyond my fleeting deep desire.

The School Door Closes

The novel idea that to pursue learning could be enjoyable and satisfying dawned on me in my fifteenth year, and I began to delight in the experience of reading more than the required amount and crafting good papers. At this time, however, Auntie and Uncle let me know that this would be my last year of school and that I needed to find a job. What did I want to do beyond study and learn? I had no idea. Prospective employers came to our class and gave their presentations to us school-leavers. I decided to join the Civil Service. Why? Because it offered job security and a pension. Imagine a sixteen year old choosing a career because of the pension! Such was my fear and insecurity.

My coworkers would sometimes stand together smoking, a convivial group, and I was at the edge, the newcomer, a clerical officer at the National Assistance Board. Winston Churchill had failed in his postwar bid to remain prime minister. The Labour Party had replaced the Conservatives, and social welfare received fresh attention. I followed the easy banter among familiar acquaintances. On one particular day, there was a joke. I can't remember the words or images, but the content had an anti-Semitic tinge. I winced and remained ill at ease, silent like a spy hiding behind a false alibi.

My assignment at the National Assistance Board was to interview applicants who were requesting legal aid. Most of the clients were seeking financial aid from the government toward the legal costs of a divorce, and to assess their eligibility, I had to ask intrusive questions.

Eventually, I woke up and realized why I felt uncomfortable as a civil servant—I was a "square peg in a round hole!"

10

Fear of Flying

Waking as if from a long, deep sleep, with my blinking eyes adjusting to the daylight, I could see the obvious: I was out of place working among administrators who were clearly at ease, enjoying job satisfaction and fulfillment in the Civil Service. The scary question, "What do I really want to do?" hung in the air. The desires of my heart had long been covered by a thick layer of scar tissue. I continued filling in the forms, calculating income versus valid expenses, and asking hurting people probing questions, while in my own life a strange interplay of flickering signals penetrated my defense system, and I was prodded inch by inch to break free from my constricted life patterns. In one seven-day period, several notable events interrupted my everyday boring life.

Alone

I was alone at 167 Coventry Road. Auntie and Uncle were taking a seaside holiday in Morecambe on the northeast English coast. One morning, on the way out of the house to catch the Coventry bus for another workday, I picked up a rectangular envelope lying on the doormat. It looked foreign and official. With nervous hands, I tore open the envelope, pulled out the folded paper, and read it. The German government had awarded me a sum of money in restitution for the death of my parents. The amount seemed large to me in my inexperience. In reality, it was quite small.

As I experienced fresh stabs of grief over the deaths of my parents, I had yet another blow to absorb—a "break-up." Bill Pritchard* and I had met at a Christadelphian gathering in Coventry. Our first date was afternoon tea at the Tea Room in Leamington Spa. Bill drove a white convertible, an unusual luxury in the postwar England of the early 1950s. He was my first boyfriend. The Pritchards enjoyed an affluent lifestyle funded by the family scrap metal business. Bill was the youngest. His siblings, two brothers and a sister Eileen, were married. Sitting across the damask-covered table, looking at the tall, fair-haired, bold-featured, confident young man in the posh Tea Room, I was catapulted out of my dull and frugal existence.

In those days, such a friendship meant you were considering marriage, and Bill and I had been "going out" for several months by the time the German letter dropped into my life. That same week Bill let me know that "it's over . . . finished." He said, "You are emotionally unreachable." The breakup felt unbearable. I wallowed in the tragedy. Food was nauseating; the world drained of color; and the future seemed bleak.

At night, alone in the house, I lay awake and pondered life. I could not place my hope for lasting love and security in family. What about money? Money would not feed the hunger of my heart.

The constant rumble of traffic flowing along the main road outside my bedroom window gradually ceased. Silence slowly filled the night. In the quiet stillness, a simple thought entered my mind: "I need God." "But how can I reach Him?" It seemed as though I was engaged in a dialogue. I heard a clear answer to my question—"Jesus is the Bridge." "Yes," I replied.

The next day I followed the routine, familiar patterns: breakfast, bus ride, desk, interviews, reports, lunch, calculations, bus ride, supper—but my misery had been replaced by a genuine, tangible comfort.

Sadly, the vitality brought by my new understanding gradually drained away, and I was left arid . . . dry. The religious environment in which I remained contributed to the leakage. I had been warned so often about the errors of those outside Christadelphian beliefs that there was no room in my fearful mind to consider searching beyond my constricted environment for an enduring relationship with God.

Waiting

Weeks later, I was standing alone outside the Flint railway station in North Wales, waiting for a ride to join a group of young Christadelphians. No one came, and I had no idea how to reach the gathering place. I didn't even know the address. Carefully I re-read the instructions. An hour or more passed while I anxiously waited. Perhaps my past experiences with railway stations increased my disquiet. Standing there, I had the opportunity for reflection. Normally, I would seek the diversions that crowd out time to ponder. Instead, waiting in the same spot without other distractions, I began to look within: "I am dead inside. I am involved in religious activity, but I am not alive." I thought back to the night I had seen the Bridge to God, and I wondered, "Was that a genuine encounter?" There on the street, I gave God an ultimatum: "Unless something happens this week to show you are real, I am bailing out."

Eventually someone came, and I joined the small group. A young man told me about his friends at university—friends who were fully alive and talked to him about being born again by the Holy Spirit. His words reverberated for me. At the same time, I could see that if I chose to explore this path, I would end up leaving familiar beliefs and heading into the unknown. Fearing the loss of security, my agitated thoughts brought inner turmoil, and I said to God, "If this is true, then give me peace." Far beyond my expectations, the confusion and turbulence melted away and a settled quietness inhabited my soul.

Leaving

As a result of my impertinent demand at the Flint railway station, I somehow discovered the courage to step out into the unknown and leave the drudgery of security. I left the Civil Service and began to train as a teacher. Why did I choose teaching? I wanted to study, and I had the necessary qualifications to enter Teacher Training College. At that time, the Labour Party enacted many laws benefitting people in the lower social classes. As I began further education, giving up any regular income, I was the recipient of this largesse. My education, food, and housing were fully covered, plus I received a small stipend.

I had continued to live with Auntie and Uncle. As I launched out on the adventure of a college education, Uncle communicated that I would be welcome to visit, but this was no longer to be "home." Inside, I was distraught—another experience of being cast away. Today, I have a different understanding. By pushing me out of an uncomfortable nest, they gave me a gift. It was time to fly! Drawn onward in the journey to become an authentic person, I left my assumed name of Hanna Dodd, a wartime cover, and returned to my original family name—Hanna Zack. Now, after all these years, I can honor William Henry and Louisa Dodd for their courageous step in receiving a German-Jewish child at a risky time and providing what they could.

College

In vivid contrast to the apathy of my high school years, I plunged into college studies with boundless enthusiasm. Midway through my final teaching practice, my education professor called me into her study for an interview. I had been assigned to an underperforming school and a difficult class. I complained. She responded, "Miss Zack, you are very ambitious." She looked at me with kindly eyes, but did the firm tone of her voice contain a note of warning? I walked out of my professor's study pondering the unexpected gift she had given me: self-awareness.

Under the surface, tension, anxiety, and doubt flowed like a subterranean stream. Did I have the capacity to complete this program? The lectures and readings in the psychology of education led me to question my encounters with God. I had understood those exchanges to be authentic and had experienced their beneficial effects. Had I been grasping at an emotional crutch? Were the times I had met the Unseen Real ephemeral? Merely a product of my dire need?

My questions about God were soon smothered. The satisfaction of graduation was eclipsed by the daily challenge of facing live children in a village classroom and finding a way to teach so they would learn to read, write, add, subtract, and divide.

A Village School

With eyes focused on the task at hand, I don't think I realized the liberation and enjoyment I was experiencing in my daily life as a teacher. Located in the center of Slinfold, a tiny West Sussex village, the Slinfold Church of England Primary School comprised only three classes.

I had applied for the position of teacher for the second class, children aged 6½ to 8½ years, and received the appointment. My Coventry friend, Shirley Webb, who had initiated our Sussex venture, became the teacher of the first class. The headmaster, Mr. Knight,* taught the "top" class. He had requested the board to appoint young teachers with modern ideas. Up to that time, the children had been taught in a circumscribed Victorian manner. So, in 1960, we moved into an apartment above the newsagent's shop in Horsham, a small town four miles from Slinfold.

Shirley and I were stimulated by the freedom and opportunity to try out all the innovations we had learned in college. The school was built in 1849, and despite the limitations of our physical surroundings, we were encouraged to nurture the children's creativity. Even the self-conscious boys joined the eager girls in the dining hall for my version of "modern dance." We were guided by classical music, played on the school turntable and selected for vivid drama. As we listened, we created a story in movement. Such fun, except when two reluctant and tardy boys, unnoticed, stayed back in our classroom across the school yard. They got into a fight. One boy hit his head on the heavy metal legs of the desk . . .

blood everywhere,
a scared first-year teacher,
an upset mother,
and a calming and supportive headmaster.

I was often stretched beyond my ability and training, but I caught the joy of the children in the release of their pent-up desire for learning and discovery, as together we explored the edges of a vast world of knowledge. Close beside the confining old school buildings, the expansive West Sussex countryside called us to come and see the rhythms of seasonal change. My class, familiar with plant names and insect habits, would take the lead in our nature walks. We would come back to the classroom and write and draw and press our discoveries.

In retrospect, I wonder if my own stunted school days were being redeemed. I was 6½ when I was put out of my first school in Gemünd; among the children who looked at me every morning with eager eyes in our narrow, old classroom, the youngest were 6½ years old.

PART III

"You Touched Me"

ॐॐ

Late have I loved you, O Beauty ever ancient, ever new, late have I loved you!

You were within me, but I was outside, and it was there that I searched for you.

In my unloveliness I plunged into the lovely things which you created. You were with me, but I was not with you. Created things kept me from you; yet if they had not been in you they would have not been at all.

You called, you shouted, and you broke through my deafness. You flashed, you shone, and you dispelled my blindness. You breathed your fragrance on me; I drew in breath and now I pant for you. I have tasted you, now I hunger and thirst for more.

You touched me, and I burned for your peace.

Confessions, St. Augustine
354-430 AD[1]

ॐॐ

11

What's a Nice Jewish Girl Like You Doing at St. Mark's?

In my first year of teaching, I wobbled between competing drives. My push to succeed and my longing to fit in were constrained by buried vulnerabilities and a fear of failure. Gradually, I became aware of the hardness binding my heart. At times I disliked myself. I was not a "nice" person. I labored to produce acceptable behavior, but occasionally a harsh word would pop out, inconveniently and uncontrollably. The hidden bitterness and nurtured resentments could not always be contained. Now, as I turn over the old memories, I think my lack of love troubled me most of all. My ex-boyfriend had been right. I was emotionally unavailable. Most days, though, I avoided such thoughts and followed the daily pattern of life in the calm of the lovely West Sussex countryside.

An Ordinary Day

On a fresh spring morning in 1961, Shirley and I emerged from "The Flat," 13 Queen Street, Horsham, Sussex, our upstairs apartment. We climbed down the steep exterior wooden stairs to the miniscule, scrubby back garden behind the newsagent's shop, carrying our load of school materials. We were oblivious to the pivotal moment we were approaching in our life journey. We walked the now familiar route, passing the Horsham shops. I remember looking for changes in the window displays as we made our way to the bus stop for the daily ride between Horsham and Slinfold. It was an ordinary day like any other.

We did notice numerous posters announcing that Billy Graham would be in Manchester, May 29 to June 17. Britain was still recovering from the depletion of World War II, and Graham had captured the national imagination. And, he was coming to St. Mark's Church, Horsham! Not exactly—on two or three evenings there would be a landline relay from Manchester to Horsham. These were the days before the advent of video links. As Graham described it in his autobiography: "During World War II the General Post Office had constructed telephone-type message lines throughout the country."[1] These landlines, originally created to broadcast news of the war to the watchful British people, would now carry the words of a forty-three-year-old American evangelist, reaching even scattered small towns such as Horsham. Our curiosity was awakened, and we wanted to be part of the current attraction.

"The Soul's Sap Quivers"[2]

I don't remember the exact date when Shirley and I—two short, young women in long skirts, with traces of Coventry in our speech, and all our inner defenses firmly in place—cautiously followed the crowd to the center of Horsham, continuing on through open doors into St. Mark's. Sitting in the old wooden pew felt strange and unfamiliar. Why? The warnings I had absorbed in all those long Christadelphian Sunday meetings began to bubble up: "The church is in error . . . be careful . . . keep away."

The rich sound of many voices singing lively choruses filled the staid church that evening. I remember my smug English thoughts: "This is so American—so enthusiastic and showy!" When Billy Graham began to speak, my preoccupation with externals faded, and I listened. It was as though the words were addressed directly to me. Inexplicably, God was gently opening up my tightly closed, dried-up heart.

As I retrace the events of that evening, I can still remember hearing a quotation from a speech made in Athens around AD 50 by Paul, a Jewish follower of Jesus Christ: "And the times of this ignorance God overlooked, but now He commandeth all men everywhere to repent, because He hath appointed a day, in which He will judge the world in righteousness by that man whom He hath ordained; concerning which He hath given assurance to all men, in that He hath raised Him from the dead."[3]

I no longer noticed the stained glass windows, the soaring ceiling, or my Horsham neighbors. It was as though my inner being was wide open before God. I saw Jesus, hanging dead on a cross, and then in one luminous moment I knew He was gloriously alive. I felt His love for me, and I could look with candor at the chaos within my soul—the despair, bitterness, selfishness, narcissism, anger, hatred, and hardness of heart— and my inadequate attempts to break free and effect lasting change. Gently, but unequivocally, God spoke to me: "Repent."

I remember Graham recounting a family tale describing a father with his little son in a boat on a lake. The father plied the oars as they moved across the large body of water. The little boy wanted to row; he asked persistently for the oars. The father refused his son's request. Why? Although the water appeared calm and smooth, he knew the dangers lurking under the surface. "Is this a picture of your life?" Billy Graham asked. "Are you in charge of your life and oblivious to all the hidden hazards?" The question reverberated within me. My own past experiences had convinced me that danger lurked in this world. And, what about the inner scars left by the rage and hatred—my own responses to the evil done against me? "Yes," I said, "I am tired of trying to run my own life."

We were asked to stand up and go to the front of the church. I sat, stuck in my seat, appearing calm and still on the outside, while the battle raged within. How could I reveal my inadequacy to the curious eyes all around me? I was the school teacher! Aware of my need and knowing God was waiting to receive me, I struggled. Could I hand over the oars of my life to God, my Father, and release my tight control? My thoughts skittered back and forth. In spite of my fear of exposure, I was inexorably drawn to respond to a loving God. I stood up and walked tentatively to the front of the church. So did Shirley.

The Rubicon

There we all stood—packed together, apprehensive, yet aware of the strange sequence of events that had brought us, poised, before the Rubicon.[4]

I can't remember her name, but in my mind I can see her—a winsome, gracious, tall, middle-aged woman. She talked and prayed with me. Hearing I was a Christadelphian, she looked a little flummoxed. She didn't know what to do, so she excused herself to consult the Anglican in charge. She came back and without comment, we continued our conversation. I think if she had expressed her actual thoughts—"You need to get out of that sect"—I would have run for the door. I stayed, and this lady became a wise friend.

In turning the faded pages of my book of memories, a haziness surrounds the timing of events following that evening in St. Mark's. But, I remember certain experiences with clarity, as if they were deeply chiseled letters carved into a rock.

Some days later, kneeling on the faded carpet in the front room of our apartment above the newsagent's shop, I felt my head and arms pressed into the soft, old, armchair. I had come to the quietness of that mundane setting with a heart strangely warmed. Several nights earlier, lying awake on my narrow bed in the tiniest of bedrooms, I had received the unmistakable impression: "God loves me." Thus comforted as I knelt, I could accept the light shining on my soul, further penetrating the hidden places where darkness lurked. I saw the suppressed rage and bitterness like shoots growing from the robust weed of unforgiveness deeply rooted in my being. I knew my life was marred by the poisonous plant I was tending in the soil of my heart. I hated Germany. I hated Germans for what they had done to me, to my parents, to my family. Forgive? Never! I wrestled, repelled by the ugliness of my own diseased responses but feeling justified in my refusal to unclench my grip on unforgiveness. I wanted to forgive, yet I could not.

Healing the Wounds

Viewing my life journey from today's perspective, I can detect a progression of heavenly nudges drawing me to become a whole person. In those spring days of 1961, my grave wound of unforgiveness began to be healed. What transpired? I saw Jesus Christ—His arms stretched on the cross. From my soul's depth, I gave Him my shame, my wrongness, my sin, my responses to the evil done to me. I saw Him take that unbearably heavy load from me, and I began to understand the meaning and purpose of His death. I experienced a lightness of being.

After I tasted forgiveness for my own sinful responses to the evil done to me, I experienced the lifting of an unmanageable burden, and I began to think a new thought: to forgive was far beyond even my most strenuous effort, but Jesus could give me the ability to forgive those who had wronged me so grievously. The barbarous atrocities hatched in the nest of anti-Semitism remind me of the stealthy rats in the Middle Ages that transmitted the plague during the Black Death epidemic. Healing of my own infection came as I released my desire for revenge and retribution and deliberately turned the crushing problem over to God. He is just. At the end, His judgment will be righteous.

My personal encounter with Jesus, His death on the cross, and the reality of His resurrection have assured me that history is leading to the day "when God will wipe away every tear from our eyes."[5]

"My Song Is Love Unknown"[6]

Could there be more to the story than the voice of Billy Graham carried strong and clear over landlines, my voluntary response after intense inner debate, the sensitive woman who talked with me, followed by days alone when I experienced vivid interaction with God who was speaking to me?

In those days, Shirley and I met a group of twelve or so people. We felt warmly welcomed and accepted among them. We tasted a quality of friendship we had not known before. They came from different local churches and were diverse in education, work, and life experience. What was the secret of their connection?

My eyes opened wide in wonder when I heard how the group had prayed earnestly during the last weeks for their town, their neighbors, and especially for young people. Here we sat all together, awed by the physicality of answered prayer.

More details of the dynamics of my slow steps toward God were yet to be disclosed.

Kate Patterson[*]

Maybe five years later, Shirley, now married and living back in Coventry, was invited to share her story with a group of ladies in the suburb of Allesley. She concluded her talk with a detailed account of the fateful evening in St. Mark's, mentioning our mutual encounter with Jesus. She sat down. To open her life in such a public way was a new and scary experience. What would happen now?

A tiny middle-aged woman approached. Shirley saw her sensible shoes, her thick ankles, and looked into an unforgettable face, with soft skin and a gentle inner beauty revealed through tear-filled eyes. The woman said, "I know the girl who responded with you at the Billy Graham meeting. I'm Kate Patterson, and my parents owned the small grocery store on Hays Lane. In the autumn of 1939 when I saw the little foreign refugee Mrs. Dodd brought with her to buy the weekly rations, I felt compassion for the sober, sad child, and I began to pray for her."[7]

Weeks later, Kate and I sat together in her home, enjoying the tiny sandwiches and buttery cake she had carefully prepared for afternoon tea.

She recounted the amazing way her life and my life had interconnected through the years, and we both reflected on the meaning of all this new information we were hearing about God and ourselves—far beyond the smallness of our usual thinking.

Kate had worked in the office of J & J Cash Ltd., a large, well known, old Coventry silk weaving company. Next to her worked Eileen Pritchard.˙ Yes, that Eileen Pritchard, the sister of Bill Pritchard, my old boyfriend. As they chatted in one of their tea breaks, Kate learned that Bill had just broken up with his girlfriend, Hanna Dodd. Hanna Dodd . . . Kate's memory carried her back to the day, thirteen years earlier, when she caught her first glimpse of the forlorn little girl from Germany. Hearing the news of the broken relationship, she was moved by the pain of my rejection and renewed her prayers. Unknown to me, Kate was praying the very week that, depressed and alone in the house, the thought "I need God" had popped into my consciousness.

We continued sitting, still and silent before empty tea cups and the last cake crumbs, amazed by the unveiling of God's hand on our lives.

12

"On the Road Again"

"Goin' places that I've never been
Seein' things that I may never see again" [1]

Back in West Sussex after Billy Graham's visit, life was comfortingly predictable. The children at Slinfold Church of England Primary School were enthusiastic learners and added spice to our days. I wonder if time has added a golden glow to these memories?

Yet, even our first days in Horsham were tinged with hints of the changes to come. While we were eating our first meal at the kitchen table, having unpacked our suitcases, we looked around. Everything we might need had been provided. But the walls were bare and the furniture worn and faded. We decided to liven up our bland setting with posters. We searched a directory and found addresses for embassy travel departments. We selected countries randomly from the "I" page and politely requested a poster from each. How we enjoyed returning home, opening the door, and catching a glimpse of the decorated walls inviting us to imagine the unfamiliar world beyond. Three countries had responded: Italy, Israel, and India.

In a Field at the Edge of Town

On a day free of commitments, I found myself in a field. I wanted to consider the future, and had walked to the edge of town to be alone.

The presence of God pervaded the unhurried stillness, and I became aware that I was to make myself available to do anything and go anywhere, and He would show the way. This was unfamiliar territory for me—scary. What would He ask me to do? I knelt down on the turf and put my future in His hands. Nothing dramatic appeared to happen.

Now, as I mull over the past, fresh insights come to me. That internal conversation in a field decades ago ushered me into the most surprising adventures—hard, bitter, boring, joyous, satisfying, and altogether wonderful—with Italy, Israel, and India featuring prominently in the unfolding story.

I had already begun to experience relief from the paralysis caused by my childhood uprootings. I had left 167 Coventry Road, Exhall, the Civil Service, and life in the Midlands. I had a satisfying, new career, a measure of maturity—running a household with Shirley—and I was adapting to the cultural differences between the Midlands and southern England.

I don't remember the date, but some months after my response at St. Mark's, I was among a group of Christadelphians in Crawley, West Sussex. The fetters attaching me to this belief system had been gradually eroding, and on that Sunday morning, I had the unmistakable impression that I was to make a clean break. Leaving brought freedom. Changes beyond my wildest imagination awaited me.

Hoist the Anchor!

Among our new Horsham friends, we met Audrey, who shared stories from her experiences living and teaching in France. Shirley was already in a process that would eventually lead her to the Pestalozzi Children's Village in Switzerland and marriage to John from Holland. Audrey invited me to join her on her next adventure—teaching in Italy!

As Shirley and I left all that had become familiar, our feelings were a mixture of eager anticipation and poignant sadness. Saying goodbye to the Slinfold children and to a significant period in our lives was painful, but the time had come to go.

Italy

Audrey and I landed in Torino, northern Italy, teaching English in a local school. The children knew no English; I knew almost no Italian; and I lacked creativity to bridge the gap. Audrey enlivened her assigned lesson plans by singing English songs with the children. My inability to carry a tune prevented me from copying her great idea. So the daily struggle with classes of thirty to forty *vivace* (lively) Italian city children aged seven to eleven contrasted sharply with the glow of success I had experienced in an English village school.

Further reflection on those Torino days brings more pleasant memories to the surface. I enjoyed relating to a new culture, the delicate taste of profiterole and panettone, attempting to learn the musical language, and adapting to the expressive Italian ways of interaction. This time, I was in another country as an adult and by my own choice.

In the summer of 1963, I joined an international group of young people called "Operation Mobilisation." I was attracted by their high ideals and vision for sharing the message of new life in Jesus—the gospel. Was I also influenced by the desire for a family, somewhere to belong, when I made that decision?

We travelled in teams, visiting European villages, using old reconditioned trucks and vans. Recalling my adventures in Italy, I am amazed by our childlike trust in God's provision for our most basic needs: food, water, and shelter. As I look back, decades later, the cautions that come with age cause me to question some of our exploits. Nevertheless, I am deeply grateful for such opportunities to depend on God alone. My life has been marked by those months, living in community and encountering tangible expressions of God's care for us every day.

Toward the end of that summer, about eight of us young women were travelling together with an old van and car in northern Italy. We would knock on doors, engage people in conversation with our rudimentary Italian, give tracts, and sell books to those who expressed interest. We found the village people warm, friendly, and hospitable. Many lived in homes built by their ancestors.

We had no income other than the books we sold and a limited supply of cash. In northern Italy, the nights began to be cold, and we could no longer sleep in our tents. We decided we would trust the Lord for a free place to sleep each night—having four walls and a roof. Up to now, we had experienced the provision of a field with the permission of the farmer. Now our faith would be further stretched.

At the end of one particular day, we drove into a small town. Our hearts sank. This place was larger than a village, and our map revealed that we had arrived at a tourist attraction. Our bold confidence in finding free accommodation evaporated. At this late hour, what could we do? Should we drive on? Our questions hung in the air. In the silence, we turned to God for help, and a venturesome idea surfaced. We approached a large historic hotel and told our story. The hotel was so old that the extensive grounds included empty stables where horses and carriages had been housed. Amazed, we accepted the offer of a roof and four walls. We drove our old Volkswagen van and little car inside a stable. We still had room to spread our sleeping bags on the floor and close the large wooden doors against the cold wind.

In the early morning we stood together on the cold flagstones of the ancient stable and asked the Lord out loud for gloves and coats. Within the next day or so, we received a message—the teams were reorganizing. We were directed south—into the sunshine of southern Italy.

Land of My Fathers

My first visit to Israel took place in 1964, as an enthusiastic member of Operation Mobilisation. I had lived in a Gentile environment since the age of seven. In the war years, the hiding of my Jewish identity was influenced by the prevailing atmosphere of suspicion toward anyone who was German or "foreign." The British population was admonished to look out for spies in their midst. In the following years, I continued the pattern of being closed off to my true identity, ignoring my Jewishness.

We stood at the railing of our Turkish ship as we slowly entered the Haifa harbor. I heard the cacophony of sounds coming from the busy port; my skin felt the balmy Mediterranean air—a contrast to the winter chill of England. Nestled among my small group of Gentile friends, I looked out with curious eyes at the people—Jewish people, my people.

Reflecting back to that time, I try to remember my feelings climbing down the steep gangway as we entered the port of Haifa—swept along in the crowd, surrounded by the strange new sound of Hebrew. What was going on in my soul? Perhaps, I was transported back to the parting with my parents. Our separation was like a carefully sewn garment being torn into two parts. I heard again the sound of the ripping. I saw each piece left with raw, uneven edges and broken threads floating in the air. This assault on my carefully constructed persona must have been unwelcome.

The daily round of life in Israel also brought cultural challenges. Waiting for the green light at a street crossing, if I put a foot beyond the pavement my fellow pedestrians would admonish me. On the one hand, I liked their concern. But, I resented the intrusion. More to the point, I recognized my own tendency to police those around me. When standing at the bus stop or waiting for an official in a bank or government office, my emotions would engage with the push toward the front bubbling up in the crowd around me. My English sense of orderly queuing was in conflict with my inner anxiety, the fear of being left behind, and I felt a strong urge to use my elbows to secure a place. I did not enjoy my emotions in the midst of a crowd.

My emerging sense of being Jewish also clashed with the feeling that I was an outsider. In 1964, unlike today, the number of Jews who followed Jesus as their Messiah was small and cautious. What did I do with my ambivalence? I swallowed painful things whole, without chewing, and medicated the indigestion with activity and daydreaming, a pattern that had begun when I was sitting in the train that took me away from my parents. So, scattered among the novelty and adventure in Israel, I experienced days of doubt and depression.

One hot summer day, I was in Arad with Dorothy, another English friend. It was lunchtime, and in the midday heat, the practice of siesta was widely practiced. Knowing we would not be welcome to visit anyone for a couple of hours, we decided to hitchhike to the Dead Sea. On the map, the twenty-five kilometers from Arad to the Dead Sea and back seemed feasible. At this time in Israel's history, hitchhiking was an acceptable means of transport. Buses ran infrequently, and a car would have been considered a luxury.

One of the massive trucks that carried chemicals up from the salty sea stopped. We climbed the huge wheels and settled into seats with the driver in the front cab, joining him on his way back down to pick up a fresh load. There was no air conditioning. The engine noise and hot air pulsing through the open windows precluded conversation. We felt as if we were enduring a foretaste of hell as we descended lower and lower to 420 meters (1,385 feet) below sea level. The scenery on the way down reinforced our discomfort. We passed the location where judgment had fallen on Sodom and Gomorrah at the time of Abraham, and to our eyes, it could have happened yesterday. The wild and barren rock formations spoke to us of the turbulence of Israel's history.

We did reach our destination safely. I can't remember how we returned to Arad. But in March 1997, celebrating our twenty-fifth wedding anniversary, George and I retraced my route of thirty-three years earlier down to the Dead Sea, this time in the luxury of a little rented car.

Which brings me to India . . .

13

India

We were a group of around sixteen "OMers" (Operation Mobilisation members) travelling in two large, reconditioned trucks. We left Zaventem, Belgium, toward the end of October 1968, making haste to cross the eastern Turkish mountains before the winter snows would hinder our safe arrival in New Delhi. In those days, we would hold our breath until we crossed the Yugoslavian and Bulgarian borders; the Iron Curtain was firmly in place. Iran was a pleasant interlude; the shah welcomed Western visitors. We rested in Teheran, preparing for the last push through Afghanistan, Pakistan, and finally India.

Christmas day dawned sunny and cold. Walking in *chappals* (flip-flops) had caused the skin on my bare heels to crack. Without familiar lotions and potions, or even socks, my experiment with a local folk medicine—dripping melted candle wax into the split—proved painful and ineffective.

I was in Chandigarh, a modern city in northwest India, commissioned by the first prime minister Jawaharlal Nehru. Chandigarh served as the capital of two Indian states: Punjab and Haryana. It was a planned city, built to reflect the nation's modern progressive outlook after gaining independence from the British in 1947. I was intrigued by the angular, concrete buildings; the streets laid out in an orderly grid; and the huge, imposing government offices. Eeva, from Finland, and I were guests of a small group of young women, from India and Europe, who lived together in a small apartment on the ground floor in one of those gray, cement buildings.

An Unconventional Celebration

We came from a mixture of Indian and European cultural traditions—Kerala, Karnataka, Sweden, Finland, and England. Together on this significant day, we were feeling a little sad, missing our own unique family customs. And, our common purse was almost empty. How would we celebrate Christmas Day together?

Eeva, Kerstin, and Karen—the three Scandinavians—closed the door to the room used for eating, conversation, and sleeping, while the rest of us, four young women—three from India and one from England—waited outside. At last the door opened, and to our surprise, the barren room had been magically transformed. Delicate snowflake sculptures cut from white paper filled every ledge. We stood surrounded by these expressions of joy and beauty. As we contemplated the wonder of Christmas, gradually an idea emerged for our own unique celebration.

On the southeastern boundary of Chandigarh, a seasonal stream had been dammed in 1948 to form a lake. Sukhana Lake was three kilometers long and provided tranquility and relaxation for the inhabitants of a bustling, crowded city. We counted our money. We had slightly more than the bus fare for eight of us to reach the lake, but what about the return journey? What would be the menu for a Christmas Day picnic?

In the silence that followed our questions, there was a knock. A friend stood on the doorstep, a young neighbor in her Punjabi clothes—a long patterned dress, full pants, and an elegant casually draped scarf. Our eyes focused on the covered basket on her arm. A few days earlier, she had promised to teach us how to make *paratha*, and December 25 was her chosen day for a cooking lesson. She lifted the cloth from the basket and took out *ghee* (butter), flour, potatoes, onions, and spices. We scurried around looking for a frying pan and a rolling pin. Soon our senses engaged with exotic smells, and the flat, round shapes piled up around the kitchen. We invited our generous neighbor to join us on our Christmas picnic. She carefully layered the hot delicacies into

146

the basket, and the next thing I remember, we were stepping out of the bus.

I think we were expecting to see an expanse of water and green vegetation where we would enjoy a solitary picnic. Bemused, we looked around. To our eyes, half of Chandigarh was walking, talking, sitting in family groups like bright, animated, colorful flowers all around the lake. We found our own little spot and ate an unforgettable Christmas dinner together.

The sober reality of our situation intruded on this pastoral scene. How would we return to Chandigarh? We had spent our last *rupees* and *paisa* on the bus fare to reach Sukhana Lake.

Usually, the team obtained money for rent, food, and toothpaste by selling books, knocking on doors, and engaging interested housewives in conversation. There were few bookshops beyond the largest cities. But, our little group had run out of books and had sent a letter days before to the Bombay office requesting a fresh supply. In those days, cell phones did not exist and, like the majority of homes in Chandigarh, the apartment had no telephone.

Late in the afternoon of December 24, a large truck had braked noisily in front of the apartment. We looked out of the window and watched two young men unload a pile of boxes—the books from Bombay! Over cups of *chai* (Indian tea), we eagerly listened to all the latest OM news. Our visitors carried a message for Eeva and me: "Take a train to Bombay as soon as possible in order to fly back to Europe for the annual January conference in Belgium." On their Christmas Eve visit, the young men had brought books and the urgent message, but no money.

That Christmas morning, as we left the apartment for the outing on the lake, each of us had picked up ten or so books, just in case we met someone who might want to buy a copy. We decided to lay out our book selection on a wall near where we were sitting. At that time, the lake did not offer much entertainment other than walking, sitting, and talking, and our casual display was a magnet for the crowds. One curious onlooker purchased a book, breaking an unseen barrier, and before we knew it, we had sold every book we had brought. We were not stranded at the lake, and we had the money for those two train tickets. Within a couple of days, Eeva and I were sitting in a train. On the platform, our friends waved goodbye as we began the twenty-eight-hour journey to Bombay.

Back in Europe

In January 1971, after several more trips to India, I was back in Europe recovering from a visit to the dentist. As the effects of Novocaine receded and I began to feel a dull throbbing in the hole left by my pulled wisdom tooth, a small package was handed to me. Curious, I quickly tore off the brown wrapping paper and discovered a cassette recording sent from India. I grabbed my cassette player, clicked the tape into place, and lay back down to listen. I heard a number of introductory sentences, and then the voice asked me to marry him! This was not quite how I had pictured a proposal in my romantic daydreams. It was George Errett Miley, sitting on a Bombay harbor wall, looking out to sea, and speaking into a microphone.

How did we meet, George and I? We first noticed each other at a campsite in Belgium at the end of the summer of 1966. We were seated in a group around a large table grading test papers at the conclusion of a short conference based on a leadership manual compiled by Operation Mobilisation. We took note of each other, but there was no exchange of greetings or conversation.

Over the next five years, we would "happen" to meet, always as colleagues in team settings. I remember our fleeting encounters in scattered places. There was the small town of Beziers in southern France, close enough to the Mediterranean to catch the smell of the sea. Another time, we crossed paths in Mantova, Italy. I was in town to visit a women's team, and George arrived driving a truck full of people on the last lap of their long overland journey back from India to Europe. Gradually, we became friends.

December 10, 1971

Late in the afternoon of December 10, 1971, I was standing in the middle of a sparsely furnished room in Hebron, Hyderabad, Andhra Pradesh, India. Two close friends, Annamma and Aleyamma, were helping to arrange my *sari*. The length of ivory material they were skillfully folding into pleats was slippery; it was not real silk. With the help of strategically placed safety pins, I stood at last, elegant in my wedding dress. Sister Daisy, part of the Hebron community, caught a glimpse of my high-heeled silver sandals, peeking out from the hem of the sari. As I twirled around for a final check, she blurted out, "Oh, Brother Bakht Singh won't allow that!" The marriage ceremony would take place in a *pandal*, an open Indian structure: mats on the floor,

The way we were.

posts supporting the roof. This was a holy place, and all who entered left their sandals or shoes in orderly rows at the entrance. Bakht Singh, the founder of the community, would conduct the ceremony. I pleaded with Sister Daisy to request special permission for me to wear the heels.

How dissimilar we were. George was six feet two inches tall; I was four feet eleven and a half inches. He was a white Anglo-Saxon Protestant from Virginia, in the United States of America. I was . . . what was I? The added height of the heels on my wedding day seemed important to me, but back came the answer: "No." Now we were in a quandary. There was insufficient time to redo the sari. It had been constructed "just so"—no ankle showing and the hem an inch above the ground. As I walked down the middle of the pandal where everyone was waiting seated on the mats, women on the left and men on the right, I was anxious not to trip and with each step kicked the too long sari forward.

A Hidden Treasure

Hidden within our chosen setting and a ceremony devoid of Western custom was a jewel of great worth. Bakht Singh gave us an enduring wedding gift. The lengthy vows he required from any couple who asked him to marry them included a promise that we would pray and read the Bible together every day. Although there have been days we have missed the target of praying and reading the Bible together, this promise has been an anchor in the ups and downs of married life for more than forty years.

Our wedding reception took place in the extensive courtyard of the walled compound—a peaceful place in the middle of Hyderabad, a large city throbbing with noise and movement, buses, cars, bicycle rickshaws, cattle, and people filling the air with dust, exhaust, and clamor. Orderly rows of mats were laid on the ground in this island of tranquility. The ground was freshly swept, not a scrap of litter in sight. We took our places on the mats and noticed the bright colors and variety of exotic scripts decorating the pure, white walls—scripture texts written in some of the many Indian languages, and here and there an English verse.

Friends from Europe, America, and a wide variety of Indian states joined the local Christians. All were welcomed to the wedding feast, which was hosted by the Hebron community. We observed and attempted to copy the Indian way of quietly and gracefully easing the body to sit on the ground before our "plates," large freshly washed banana leaves. Assigned members of the community carrying steel buckets came quietly up and down the rows, spooning out a pile of steaming, fragrant rice, followed by spicy vegetable curry, gently laying accurate portions on each leaf.

We all sat still until everyone had been served, followed by the communal prayer. Only then, we extended our right hand, squeezed a small portion of rice and curry together, and placed the ball of food into our mouths. So different from all the wedding day fantasies of my Coventry childhood! Yes, there was loss in the absence of Western cultural traditions. But, we were enriched as we embraced an Indian Christian wedding, stripped to the bare bones and focused on the magnanimity of a community celebration and the solemnity of a covenant before God.

A Bombay Home

In December 1971, George and I made our first home in a city dating from antiquity. By the third century BC, the emperor Ashoka ruled Bombay. In 1536, the territory was surrendered to the Portuguese Empire. On May 11, 1661, the city was part of the marriage dowry of the king of Portugal's daughter when she married Charles II of England. Bombay (now "Mumbai") was leased to the British East India Company in 1668 for £10 per year. In 1857, commercial interests reverted to the crown. India achieved independence in 1947.[1,2] Yet, I hardly thought about Bombay's past beyond noticing the imposing Victorian buildings rooted in the city center.

We lived in a large room, sharing the house with two families and their little children, and a team of young men. On hot nights, without air conditioning, we would take our foam mat and sleep on the balcony. In the early morning, we awakened to murmurs, smoke, and spices wafting up around us. The street dwellers directly under us, in their tents of cardboard and old cloth, were enacting the rituals of a new day. Our balcony jutted out above the intersection of three main thoroughfares, and the relentless sound of traffic continued late and began early. Often we awoke to the gritty taste of dust on our tongues.

Our home was a short walk to Bombay Central, now called Mumbai Central Station. The British had inaugurated the first Indian railway line in 1853. Many Sunday mornings we would escape to the luxury of being on our own for breakfast at the Bombay Central Railway Station restaurant. We climbed the stairs and entered the cavernous, almost empty restaurant, taking our seats at a table covered with a white, linen cloth. Everything was ancient. The cloth had endured many washings; the waiter surely had served under the British.

I suppose we could have gone to a modern, fancy restaurant. In 1971, Bombay was a thriving city and the commercial capital of India. But, Bombay Central had a romantic air for us; we felt as though we were touching history. We liked the quaintness, even though the dark shadows of the colonial past hovered like the pigeons in the rafters above. We relished the omelet, cooked just right, with little pieces of onion and chili, the crackly toast, the chai for George and milk coffee for me, served in old porcelain stamped with the Indian Railways crest.

Why were we escaping to an illusion of the past? I think we were seeking privacy—identity as a couple. It was our first year of marriage, and we were submerged in an abundance of people. Our community welcomed the constant flow of visitors, and extra chairs would often be pulled up to the large, oval dining table. Squeezed together, we would share our rice and *dahl* with anyone who happened to join us. And, the population of India in 1971 was more than 500 million,[3] with about 8 million living in

Time to relax outside the city.

Bombay.[4] Every time we stepped into the street, we were inundated by taxis, trucks, buses, and rickshaws, ringing bells and blowing horns and exhaust. We learned to maneuver through the press of humanity—men, women, and children crowding the sidewalks—and to find opportunities to be alone with one another.

Fully absorbed by the challenges and possibilities of daily life in India, we never stopped to consider the healing journey still ahead.

PART IV

Steep Steps

ↄ❧ ❧ↄ

Our five-day visit to the Ancient City of Aleppo, Syria, in January 2010
leaves a bundle of vivid, unforgettable images in my mind.

Many times each day we negotiate stone steps
connecting the restored old houses that now form one hotel.
The staff skip up and down, speedily and with great ease,
while we huff and puff and lift our legs slowly, with painful effort,
encouraging ourselves by saying to each other,
"This is good exercise in the rarest of settings."

The rigor of those steep old Syrian steps
ushers us into joyful exhilaration
once we reach the architectural grandeur
of the vast and lofty Ottoman courtyard.

Not unlike my soul's exertion as I journey
toward wholeness and freedom …

ↄ❧ ❧ↄ

14

Risky Adventures in the Land of Forgiveness: Summer 2000

George and I approach the front desk. Our eyes are focused on the congenial face of the receptionist. It is the morning after a disturbed night.

The previous afternoon, while driving along ul. Sadowa in the small Polish town of Brodnica, we noticed an exotic display of flowers in the garden surrounding the Magnat Hotel. We stopped, climbed the steps of the attractive new building, and entered the lobby.

To allow for unhurried exploration of the area, we planned to stay for several days and so were relieved when we opened the door to our clean, bright, and comfortable room. Tired and happy, we lay down to sleep, only to find a fly in the ointment. The hotel restaurant stayed open twenty-four hours a day. We were sleeping over the kitchen, and the energetic cook banged and rattled the saucepans at irregular intervals all through the night.

The friendly receptionist gives us her full attention, but we fail to find even a few simple words in common, and we feel helpless in our foreignness. How can we bridge the gap? Motivated by our need for rest and sleep, we set aside any reticence and begin to mime our nighttime experiences. Head laid on hands, eyes closed, pleasant dreams, smiling face, a sudden shake, eyes open, startled expression, repeat. . . . The young woman understands. She hands us a new key, smiling apologetically.

How did George and I end up performing amateur theatricals in a hotel lobby in the middle of Poland?

An Unexpected Question

The adventure begins with an unexpected question. It is 1999. George and I are in Phoenix, seated across from each other at our dining table.

"If you could fly anywhere in all the wide world, what place would you choose?"—an unusual question from George.

His words hang in the air. I look at his eyes, focused on the computer screen between us. He counts the frequent flyer miles accumulated in our account. His question is not casual or "make-believe." There are enough miles for an unlimited adventure, and we both need a break.

"I would like to visit the places where my mother and father were born." I surprise myself by this quick response. My answer bypasses all the other tantalizing options. The words have come up and out from deep inside and express my real longing. Often in the past I was out of touch with my genuine desires. Now, after so many years, I want to connect with my parents.

Becoming Willing to Face the Past

In 1991, Ruth Holden—the fellow Jewish survivor from Gemünd who had walked with me to the Kino, intending to see *Snow White and the Seven Dwarfs*—mentioned a newly published book written by Hans-Dieter Arntz, *Judenverfolgung und Fluchthilfe im deutsch-belgischen Grenzgebiet* (Persecution and flight of Jews in the German-Belgian border region). Our German friends, the Gottliebs,* purchased the 784-page hardcover book and mailed it to us in Phoenix.

I unwrapped the package and searched the index, turning the pages. I wanted to find my family's story but feared what I might discover. On page 352, I read: "*Der jüdische Kaufmann* (the Jewish businessman) Markus Zack, born 1878 in Strasburg, West Preussen. . . . His wife Amalie Zack, born Schneider 1891, in Heddesheim, Kreis Kreuznach."

I stared at the names, dates, and places. I shut the book and pushed it firmly between the other books on a distant shelf. There the printed words stayed undisturbed between its covers for more than seven years.

Now, the book is on my desk, its cover black with a bright yellow title spread above a large grey and white drawing, titled *Inferno*. The artist, Mathias Barz, was a Gentile born in 1895. His wife, Hilde Stein, born in 1896, was a Jew. He disobeyed the 1935 race laws by refusing to divorce her, and together, they endured years of danger. They were smuggled by friends from one hiding place to another, always on the run.

In December 1944, the couple was hiding under the roof of a *Pfarrhaus* (rectory) in Kirchheim, Eifel. The region was in turmoil as German soldiers assembled in towns and villages along the Belgian border for Hitler's last offensive, the Ardennes Campaign (or the Battle of the Bulge). A small SS group had taken possession of the ground floor of the rectory. After the war, *Dechant* (Dean) Edmonds recounted how the persecuted ate the food of the persecutors.[1]

Both Mathias and Hilde survived. In 1946, he created *The Inferno*.

ᘏᘏ ᕙᕗ

In 1999, I once again pick up *Judenverfolgung und Fluchthilfe im deutsch-belgischen Grenzgebiet*, deeply moved by its cover. I pull it toward me and examine the white spaces, the grey and black strokes drawn by a man who has narrowly escaped the inferno. Mounds of skulls lie in the

159

background; hundreds of sorrowing Jews stream toward me. They look at me and ask, "Will you engage with the sorrow?"

A large, realistic Christ hangs high in their midst—naked, arms raised, eyes downcast. All share the same expression and features: Christ, the men, women, children, young, middle-aged, and elderly. In my mind's eye, I see His hands nailed to the wood beyond the frame of the drawing.

Mathias Barz inspires me to attempt my own little journey out of illusion into reality. I know so little about my parents' beginnings. Why do I lack even basic information about the Zacks? In the worry and hurry of the sudden parting with my Mutti and Vati in 1939, I carried no documents, no photographs, nor any factual information. My luggage contained only dolls, their varied outfits, and clothes suitable for a seven-, eight- or even nine-year-old well-dressed German *Mädchen* (little girl). I remember a sleeveless sunsuit, with tiny red, blue, and green flowers scattered over a cream-colored background. All these years later, I feel again the warm sun on my skin as I lounged in a deck chair on a rare sunny day in Exhall, wearing the pretty outfit. I must have been about nine years old.

In 1941, clothes were rationed. There would have been no coupons or money for such an extravagant item. My recollection of this luxury once again calls to mind the merciless disintegration of our little family's way of life. As harsh as the change from my comfortable German existence was for me, how much more cruel it was for my parents.

Surrender to the Search

In the summer of 2000, driving out of Gemünd in our rented car, we pass the church, look toward Dreibornerstrasse, my childhood home, and ask ourselves, "Will this Polish adventure turn into a wild goose chase?"

The unlimited, detailed information continually bubbling up from our computers today was unavailable eleven years ago, at least to us. The names "Strasburg" and "Heddesheim," where my father and mother were born, have vanished. How did we begin to uncover something of their lives?

An Old Map

On a short stopover, travelling between Kazakhstan and Phoenix in 1999, we explore London. A trestle table, loaded with cardboard boxes, stands outside a map shop on a small street off Trafalgar Square. Browsing, not really searching, I pull out an old map at random from one of the boxes. The map has been torn from an atlas, and I read the title: "Preussen." Holding my breath, I run my finger across the clear plastic envelope protecting the fragile sepia paper. I scrutinize the tiny printed place names set on the jumbled black threads of road, rail, and river. The tip of my finger seems to tingle. The letters form the word "Strasburg," my father's home, far to the east, south of Danzig, next to the border with Russia.

A Polish Travel Agency in Phoenix

Now, we know the location of the old Prussian town, Strasburg. But what is the Polish name today? Back in Phoenix, we visit Stefania Travel, a Polish travel agency. Stefania herself searches the huge map of Poland covering half the wall and writes "Brodnica" near the larger city of Torun. She goes on to add the address and telephone number of the consulate general of the Republic of Poland, 12400 Wilshire Boulevard, Los Angeles, CA. "Write there," she says, "and ask where you can find your family records."

Start in Torun

The consulate general's prompt reply in English, on official paper headed with a crest and title in Polish, advises us to visit the district office in

Torun. With a population of approximately 207,000, Torun is the chief town of the area, and documents for citizens of Brodnica would be stored there. Little did we know that this piece of paper would be the key to opening local government doors despite the language barrier.

On August 21, 2000, we enter the walled city of Torun, founded in 1233 when Teutonic Knights built a castle by the River Vistula. The city appears serene despite a tumultuous history. After World War I, the Versailles Treaty assigned the Prussian city to Poland, as part of the Polish corridor. The local people had to acquire Polish citizenship or leave.[2] I wonder if my father's decision to uproot and go from the eastern edge of the former Prussian Empire far to the west, almost to the Belgian border, was influenced by the Versailles Treaty? The railroad between Torun and Berlin was opened in 1861. Would he have looked out of a carriage window and waved goodbye to his parents standing on the platform of the Torun station as he began a journey that would end in Gemünd? We have covered the same ground driving in the opposite direction from Gemünd to Torun.

Early the next day, we begin our search. We walk to the district office and hand the letter from the Polish consulate in Los Angeles, together with our handwritten note, "Markus Zack, born Strasburg, West Preussen, 24.9.1878," to the porter sitting in his cubicle just inside the door. We are politely ushered from office to office, our letter and note carefully examined, smiles and nods our only communication. Finally, we are handed a slip of paper with the words "Archiwum Panstwowe ul. Idzikowskiego 6." We recognize the word "archive" and realize that my father's records, if any still exist, are no longer filed in the district office among regular family records. How do we find a street whose name we cannot pronounce? We show the paper to anyone we happen to meet in the street. We watch closely and try to remember their hand signals. Finally, we reach the door of Archiwum Panstwowe, a modest entrance on a quiet street.

Anna

The door opens and we step into a peaceful place. The senior archivist is expecting us. The district office has telephoned, introducing the foreigners and their search. Anna, a middle-aged woman wearing a silky, black and white, flowered dress, pearls, her hair dyed the fashionable European shade of auburn, introduces us to Lukas, her young assistant. His long, fair, wavy hair is tied back in a ponytail. I look into Anna's eyes and see gentleness, intelligence, and sorrow. She speaks English! Our request for the Zack family record falls on a sympathetic ear.

She explains the process. Research in Poland's archives is welcomed, and the rules are clear and reasonable. You can spend as much time as you wish looking through the volumes of records, or you can pay the staff to search for you.

We are overwhelmed by the impossibility of the task. We have come so close, yet any concrete evidence of my father's family story still seems out of reach. So many huge books, each holding innumerable documents! How will we read the spidery, 122-year-old German script? The office is about to close, and Anna suggests we return the next morning.

Are We Too Early?

Will the archive office be open? We arrive with fresh energy to scale the mountain of papers and examine the unfathomable script. Anna is waiting for us. Barely hiding her excitement, she leads us to a wooden table in the middle of the room. "I took several books home with me last night," she says, pointing to one of the heavy old books lying open.

We peer at the old German script. Document Nr. 161, dated September 30, 1878, Strasburg, signed by the *Standesbeamte* (registrar). We find "Markus" and discover my grandmother's name, "Caroline Zack born Salomon." My grandfather, Joseph Zack, signed his name with an "X."

A surreal moment. I have roots; I no longer float, unattached, in empty space.

There is more. Among the books Anna had taken with her to study at home were volumes dating from 1840, filled with Jewish marriage certificates. She opens to Nr. 36, and we look at the same sloping pointy script. My grandmother, Caroline Salomon, was born on May 8, 1856. She married Joseph Zack in Strasburg on November 24, 1877. She must have been twenty-one years old. Joseph was born in Rypin on August 29, 1852; he was twenty-five years old when they wed. Rypin lies just across the border, only twenty-three kilometers from Strasburg. In my grandfather's day, Rypin belonged to Russia. He was a *Händler* (merchant). Was he unable to write his name due to lack of education, or could he write only in Cyrillic?

Anna hands me her carefully copied English translation of my grandparents' marriage certificate. She declines any payment and confides that she enjoys Klezmer music and loves helping Jewish people. She lost her husband three years ago to cancer, and she herself wrote a book about Brodnica, trying to keep her mind active while recovering from cancer surgery. "Chernobyl," she says.

I still have the official handwritten receipt, Nr. 118/2000, signed by Lukas, dated August 22, 2000, for our payment of 2 *zloty*, the cost of several photocopies.

As we leave Torun, we make a last stop at the Archive Office, carrying the biggest bunch of flowers we can find.

Strasburg/Brodnica

On the way to Brodnica, a sixty-five-kilometer drive from Torun, we talk about the last two days. We came to Poland seeking a treasure. Now, holding two photocopies in our hands, we mull over the twists and turns of the journey along the way to our discovery.

The Magnat Hotel, just outside the city center, is our base. We set out to explore the town my father called home all those years ago.

Brodnica, like Torun, had been ruled by the Teutonic Knights in medieval times. Today, a lone, restored castle tower and a gateway, part of the city wall, are the only remnants of their 1320 fortifications. The elegant German architecture in the town center and vestiges in two churches point to the years of Prussian rule. Rows of bulky grey concrete boxes climb the hill and overlook the center, built after 1945 when the Red Army "liberated" Brodnica.[3]

Are there any Jewish traces to be found?

The Jews of Strasburg

The earliest known settlement of Jews in Strasburg dates from the 1770s; a Jewish cemetery was established at around the same time. A synagogue and Jewish school were founded in 1839. My father was born in 1878. The Jewish population of Strasburg peaked at 626 in 1871. During the next fifty years, the Gentile population increased from 5,854 to 6,923, but the Jewish population steadily declined. By the 1920s, only a few Jewish families remained.[4,5]

What was going on in Strasburg at the beginning of the twentieth century as Markus Zack reached manhood? At the end of World War I, the area became Polish. Strasburg ceased to be Prussian. Jews were beaten; documents record four cases in 1923. The 1922 presidential election generated a stream of anti-Semitic propaganda. The Jewish community felt increasingly isolated. Many emigrated to Germany.

Germany invaded Poland on September 1, 1939. On September 29, the few Jews left in Strasburg were arrested and shot, together with a group of Polish citizens. That evening the synagogue was burned; the cemetery closed; the gravestones destroyed. Later, the stones were used to pave the streets.[6] Since the time of the Communists, a factory producing furniture has stood on the site of the cemetery.[7]

What about the ground where Jews had worshipped and studied Torah for 100 years?

In 2000, we walk around Brodnica looking for clues; our only certainty is the knowledge that my family lived somewhere in this small spot on the surface of the earth. We see a plaque on the wall of a medieval brick building, beautiful, tall, and spare. We read the word "*Muzeum*," and just then, a young man opens the door. He is in charge. A university student, he speaks some English. We buy tickets, look around the few exhibits, and begin a conversation about the Jews of Strasburg. He remembers hearing about the destruction of the synagogue from his mother. "The local market stands in the place where the synagogue used to be," he tells us, slowly and carefully. He is embarrassed that there is no plaque of remembrance.

We find the market bustling with people, filled with produce and merchandise, sheltered by faded awnings and colorful umbrellas. I walk between the stalls, oblivious to the noise and activity, my eyes glued to the ground. I see the worn cobblestones and cracked concrete and say to myself: "Joseph Zack, Caroline Salomon Zack, my father Markus Zack and all their friends and relatives walked here." This is sacred ground. Probably it is as near as I will ever be to their embodied lives.

We explore the narrow streets radiating from the marketplace and find tiny, old houses built close together. We listen to the sounds of the children playing in the street. Through the open windows, we smell the food being cooked by their mothers. Could this have been the Jewish quarter?

My father was religious. Did the Zack family live near the synagogue in order to stay within the distance permitted for a pious Jew to walk on the Sabbath?[8] I don't know.

I stand awhile on the little bridge and look around. The small Drwęca River flows gently beneath me. I see the cloudy blue sky and dark, lush, green trees reflected in the water. I wonder if my father ever stood on the little bridge over the narrow Urft River near our home in Gemünd. When he looked at the shapes of the trees in the water, did he remember the Drwęca River and his home in Strasburg?

15

"It's a Pity That the Village of Heddesheim Doesn't Exist Anymore"

W e enter the Nahe Valley, and our eyes take in vineyards hanging from the peaks of surrounding hills like the warp of some vast green tapestry.

According to local lore, Romans planted the first vineyards above this tributary of the Rhine, the Nahe River. Indigenous Celtic tribes may have dug the rich earth, lifted the stones, and crafted the terraces for their new rulers around 2000 years ago.[1] Is this the land my mother called home, her *Heimat*? Her *Zuhause*? Did she run up and down these hills with her younger sister Johanna? Did they hitch up their long skirts and chase each other among the vines, laden with grapes, on the very same paths we are seeing today?

No trace of Heddesheim can be found on a modern German map of the Nahe region. The name of my father's home town, Strasburg, West Prussia, was changed to Brodnica, Poland, but Heddesheim was absorbed. On June 7, 1969, three villages—Breitenfelser Hof, Heddesheim, and Waldhilbersheim—became Guldental.

Preparing for our journey of discovery, trying to locate Heddesheim, asking where records for the Schneider family could be found, I wrote letters to every likely address. A prompt reply came from the *Arbeitsgemeinschaft Pfälzisch-Rheinische Familienkund eV* (a regional working group for information on local families). Oskar Pawlak* wrote back in English on June 27, 2000: "It's a pity that the village of Heddesheim doesn't exist anymore. It is incorporated to [*sic*] Guldental D-55452."

Now, it is August 14, 2000, and we stroll through Guldental in the afternoon heat and stillness. Our senses are captivated by flowers growing in every nook and cranny, their perfume, the bright colors. Arched vines span the small streets. Such peace . . . beauty. . . .

"The Little Foxes That Spoil the Vineyards"[2]

I become aware of a dissonance between the idyllic scene before me and the uneasiness I have felt with the name "Heddesheim" ever since 1992, when I first read the entry on page 352 of the book *Judenverfolgung und Fluchthilfe*: "Amalia Zack, born Schneider (1891-Holocaust) from Heddesheim, Kreis Kreuznach" (Kreuznach district).[3]

Pink geraniums spill over a wooden wheel at the corner of a street. Part of the corner has been cut off, and embedded in the flat wall, we notice two oval decorated wine cask lids. Under a hot sun, we shade our eyes with our hands and read the small street sign "*Judengasse*" (Jews' lane). Are we in Guldental or are we in the old Heddesheim?

We walk slowly along Judengasse. I wonder: "Did my mother play in this narrow street? Did she hear her mother's voice calling from the window of one of these little houses, 'Amalie, Amalie, come home; dinner's ready'?"

At the end of Judengasse, a tablet on the wall, plain as the nose on your face, spells out "Heddesheim."

We wander along the *Hauptstrasse* (main street) and reach a pale, brick, double-story building. Two open wine casks, rims painted red, lie on their sides flanking stone steps leading to old carved wooden doors. I climb the steps and read the painted letters on yet another wine cask lid attached to the wall above a trailing vine: "*Heimat und Weinbaumuseum*" (Museum of Local Heritage and Wine Production). I try the handle. The doors are shut. Then, I notice a handwritten paper note with directions to Grabenstrasse 17, signed Günther Lukas.

"Are You Looking for Günther Lukas?"

Two workmen stand in a shaded alley next to the museum. Maybe they can direct us to Grabenstrasse. I wait for a pause in their conversation with a white-haired man holding a bundle of pictures. He turns to me and asks, "Are you looking for Günther Lukas? I am he." He unlocks the doors and ushers us inside. Upon hearing of my family connection to Heddesheim, he seems as excited as we are. He leads us through rooms brimming with maps, pictures, documents, posters, antique wooden implements hanging and standing on the creaky floorboards and on tables—Heddesheim history entwined with viniculture.

Günther Lukas is a retired banker, well-known wine-taster, local historian, and the father of the museum. In the last room, a wall and table are dedicated to Jews who once lived in Heddesheim. He steps out of his role as curator, his practiced presentation, and whispers, "My closest boyhood friend, a Jew, died in a concentration camp. Even today I feel pain in my heart for my friend, and I want to keep Jewish memories alive."

We have lunch together at the elegant *"Der Kaiserhof"* (imperial court) restaurant. We all drink glass after glass of cold water as we recover from walking in the hot sun. We stroll through Judengasse again, this time with Günther. He tells us that in the Nazi times the street was blocked off and turned into a ghetto.

With Günther as our generous and enthusiastic guide, we explore his home village. We meet his cousin on a neighboring street, and he invites us for a tour of the family's cavernous, cool, dark wine cellar. Surrounded by rows of casks, we smell the wine and appreciate the patience of transformation. This family is just one of the forty-one wine producers among 2,900 Guldental inhabitants.

Outside in the bright light, Günther points to the old school at 14 Hauptstrasse, built 1895-1896, hardly changed externally from the time my mother attended the "new school." Lutheran and Jewish children studied on the top floor, and Roman Catholic pupils had their own teachers on the ground floor. As my mother watched the impressive brick building take form, was she eager to go to school?

Behind St. Jakobus Church

Behind St. Jakobus Church, 8 Hauptstrasse, the three of us approach a small, single-story house with a wavy, overhanging tile roof. Günther tells us that this was the Schneider family home!

The noise of saws and hammers, the loud voices of workmen, the music of the organ pipes and sounds of the processions must have penetrated the windows and walls of my mother's home during those first years of her life. The church building was completed in 1894. My mother would have been three years old and Johanna two.

The man who recently purchased our old family home, according to the story making the rounds in the village, is a Russian. We knock on the door tentatively. Stefan, the new owner, opens the door. He wears an earring, and his arms sport several tattoos. He is from northern Germany. He welcomes us despite our unannounced visit. We shake hands, and he invites us inside. "I noticed the name 'Schneider' on the deed listing previous owners," he says as he takes us on a tour.

In the kitchen, I look at a black, decorated iron tablet attached to the wall. A sudden, vivid memory surfaces. Maybe I was three years old. I am standing on the kitchen table, surrounded by people, perhaps my mother's family, and my father spanks my legs, only a light touch. An aberration; I don't remember my father ever disciplining me. He indulged my every wish and comforted my tantrums. I must have done something very naughty. Was it climbing up and standing on the table? Did my behavior trigger feelings of shame in my proud Vati, squeezed into the tiny kitchen with his wife's family? I clearly remember the group around us rebuking him—one more step in the development of a spoiled little princess.

Before we leave my old family home, Stefan takes us to the cellar, and I climb down steep, narrow steps to see the entrance to a tunnel. Günther confirms Stefan's story. Between 1630 and 1635, when Sweden invaded Germany during the Thirty Years War, local citizens dug the long tunnel, an escape route leading to the vineyards.

Were my grandparents the first Jews to own the old house?

I lay out the scraps of my mother's story, turn them over, and hold them up to the light, thankful for each little detail made known to me and mourning the loss of all the missing pieces.

The Synagogue

In 1910, the Jewish community living in Heddesheim and Waldhilbersheim, the neighboring village, was small. Records show ninety persons in 1858. Emigration reduced the numbers to twenty-nine by 1925.

The *Allgemeine Zeitung des Judentums* (General Jewish Newspaper) reported the dedication of the new synagogue on September 16, 1910, in Heddesheim/Waldhilbersheim. Political and religious leaders from the region attended the celebration, which ended with prayer for the *Kaiser und Reich* (king and country). Herr Augustus Schneider, president of the synagogue, then invited everyone present to a *gemütlichen Beisammensein* (a joyful reception).[4] Herr Augustus Schneider was my grandfather. He had four daughters. In 1910, Amalie was nineteen years old, Johanna eighteen, Dorothea fifteen, and Elisabeth thirteen.

Mutti, did you sew beautiful new dresses for yourself and your sisters? Everyone would notice the Schneider girls. Did you dream about meeting a handsome Jewish boy among all the visitors?

Today, you can still see the synagogue building at 83 Naheweinstrasse, standing at the edge of town like a simple barn, the windows covered with brick and board.

Günther leads us to the house next door. The neighbor, working in the garden, delights to show us his flowers, the different varieties, the vivid colors. He hands Günther the key to the barren brick building.

Near the locked door of the former synagogue is a small, blue, enamel plaque, decorated with a white painted border, indented to give place for four nails, one at each corner. The nails still secure the metal plate close to the wall. In the center of the rectangle is a hole. As I look, the crack of a gunshot echoes from the past. Rusting metal is exposed around the hole, and only the white letter "f" on the blue background can be read.

In the dark winter night of November 9-10, 1938, two Torah rolls; seventy-five prayer books; silver lamps, cups, and plates; curtains; table covers; and an oven were stolen or destroyed. In January 1939, the structure was sold.[5]

Günther struggles to turn the key. Finally the door opens—partially. Something is blocking access. We poke our heads inside. A stream of light shining through the narrow opening reveals old carriages, the kind drawn by horses, packed tightly together in a jumble of wheels and carriage frames.

I scrutinize the ceiling and walls and note the architectural remnants left from the joyous, inclusive celebration of 1910. I take in the intricate design of the plaster circle on the ceiling. One of the missing lamps must have hung from the empty hole in the middle of the circle. The peeling walls still show the original white and tan paint and pale blue molding. I imagine my grandfather and his friends, their heads covered with prayer shawls, bowing low and reciting Hebrew words on ordinary Sabbaths between the High Holidays of the Jewish year, delighting in the bright newness of their holy place.

The synagogue existed for only twenty-nine short years.

The Cemetery

Without a guide, it would be difficult to find the Jewish cemetery, even though there is an official address: *Auf dem Engelroth*, Waldhilbersheim.[6] Led by Günther, we drive into the forest along overhung, narrow lanes just wide enough for a tractor or a car, turn after turn, until we come to a small enclosure. Forty-two gravestones and some fragments stand upright inside low, wooden, crisscross fencing. The trees give us shade, respite from the hot sun.

We open the gate and see the large black marble stone that reads:

Hier ruhen in Gott
Unsere lieben unvergeßlichen Eltern
(Here rest in God our beloved unforgettable parents)

. . . and inscribed under Hebrew letters:

August Schneider	Flora Schneider, geb Mayer
geb. 20.1.58	geb. 18.1.64
gest. 19.5.35	gest. 3.4.30

(August Schneider, born January 20, 1858, died May 19, 1935, and Flora Schneider, maiden name Mayer, born January 18, 1864, died April 3, 1930)

I am filled with a strange joy: they both died natural deaths. And there in the quiet graveyard, I feel my heart expand to accept my middle name, "Flora." I never liked Flora. "What an odd choice," I used to think, unaware that I had been named after my maternal grandmother. Under the trees, in a forgotten place, I embrace my grandmother, Flora Schneider.

The kitchen table incident in the family home must have happened when my mother and father and I came from Gemünd to Heddesheim for my grandfather's funeral. Have I been here before, in this cemetery, among the mourners accompanying the coffin into the woods?

Did my grandfather order the stone in 1930 when his wife died, leaving a blank space for his own name?

Below my grandparents' names, spreading across the base of the stone in a single line, carved letters spell out a quotation without referring to the source:

Die Liebe höret nimmer auf
(Love has no end)

Why was this text—from the New Testament, the 1545 Luther Bible, 1 Corinthians 13:8—chosen? Did my relatives make their selection from a list offered by a Gentile stone mason? Was this saying popular among Jews without an awareness of its origin? Or are these the words that best describe my family's longings?

I take a cursory look at the other stones and stop before Amalie Schneider, geb. Schosser, 1821-1890. Have I been led to the grave of my great-grandmother?[7] My mother was born in 1891 and must have been named after her paternal grandmother according to the Jewish custom, which gives the first child born after the death of a grandparent the same name, in this case, Amalie Flora.

You Are a Mist

What is your life? . . .
you are a mist that appears for a little while,
and then vanishes.[8]

My grandparents named my three aunts Johanna, Dorothea, and Elisabeth. In daily life, they were called Hanna, Dora, and Lisbet. They never married. Who were the Schneider girls? Their identity, character, and essence have vanished. They left no photographs behind, only a few words written on several pieces of paper—a postcard from *Tante* (Aunt) Lisbet, an envelope and a letter from Tante Hanna, and a page torn out of an autograph book written by my Mutti. Tante Dora is silent.

I try to bring their hazy memory to life—I only knew them as a self-absorbed young child. Tante Hanna I picture as a dark, well-built, strong, smart businesswoman. Tante Dora has mousy hair. She is slight in build, tentative, and occupied with housework. Tante Lisbet is more mysterious, entering my life only at brief, exciting intervals. Her hair is curly and dark. She is attractive, sophisticated, and she is laughing.

I remember staying with Hanna and Dora in their Koblenz apartment on the ground floor of Markenbildchen Weg 30 pt. An elaborate chandelier hangs over a large, shiny, dark, wooden table where a typewriter sits, the keys waiting for Hanna's fingers. Did she learn her business skills from her father? She is dressed in a dark, well-cut outfit, the cloth fine, the style somewhat severe.

Dora is wearing an apron. I follow her down the narrow, dim corridor to the small kitchen and sit at the table. I can smell gas. She is preparing a boiled egg for my breakfast. She butters the rye bread and cuts narrow strips ready for me to dip, one by one, into the perfectly textured runny yolk. With one swipe of the knife, she expertly cuts off the top of the egg. As I write my memories of this time, I can taste the toast and egg, and then I wonder, "Is this a true-to-life memory?"

Lisbet spent time in southwestern Berlin, Ernst-Ring Strasse 2, Schlachtensee 14129. I examine the postcard she sent from there on July 18, 1939, to Room 154 of the Köln Jewish Hospital where I was recovering from the appendix operation. Lisbet's exuberant words fill the back of the postcard to the edges. The lines are even and precise, but the letters are hurriedly formed. The "a's" and "o's" are left open. She concludes, "Greet all, and for you many, many tender kisses from your Aunt Lisbet."

I pick up the envelope and letter Tante Hanna wrote on August 2, 1939, from Koblenz. In her own handwriting, she addressed the envelope *"An die Dame in England, die das Kind in Empfang nimmt."* (To the lady in England who takes in the child.) The two-page letter inside the envelope is typed and begins, "To the honored, gracious lady." Tante Hanna continues, "Hannelore is the only niece in the whole family and naturally the aunts have a great love for her." She expresses that love in practical concern, asking if anything is missing from my baggage, clothes, or bedding.

I Google the Berlin and Koblenz addresses. Both still exist. Are these the original buildings or were they bombed and restored?

Kith and Kin

My parents named me Johanna Flora Zack. The measure of my disconnection with the past is revealed by a recent gut-level awareness that my aunt Johanna and I have the same name. Oh, I knew that vaguely, but it is only by living with the memory of the Schneiders in these days of writing that I have grown in love for my family, reaching my hands out to their shadows.

Why was Johanna selected for my first name? Did my mother admire her sister? At home, I was called Hannelore, but in England and even today, I am known as Hanna, just like Tante Hanna.

As far as I know, I am the last living member of the August Schneider family. George and I are childless.

Silhouettes

How did they vanish, the Schneider sisters? How can I find their faint trail and give a trace of dignity to their lives?

After our visit to Guldental, Günther Lukas mailed to us a copy of a Guldental high school student's term paper dated 1994/1995, titled *"Die ehemalige jüdische Gemeinde in Guldental"* (The former Jewish community of Guldenthal). Encouraged by Günther to study and record the history of the local Jews, the student mentions the forced sale of the Schneider home at a price far below the true value. Johanna dealt with the sale, and Dorothea was admitted to a Jewish clinic with a nervous breakdown.

On August 31, 2007, I receive a thin file folder, hand-delivered by the Phoenix office of the Red Cross, containing the response of the International Tracing Service to my request for information about my parents and aunts. Since 1946, the International Red Cross has administered this research and tracing facility containing a vast cache of Holocaust documents and some personal effects in Bad Arolsen, a small town in northern Hesse, Germany. The general public gained access to the store of information only in 2007.

I open the plain, yellow file. What will be revealed about my family? The dates and places of birth for my parents and their last address in Köln are confirmed. These records take them only as far as Lodz on their last journey.

I turn to the covering letter introducing the information about my aunts:

SCHNEIDER, Johanna, born in Heddesheim on 23.8.1892
SCHNEIDER, Dorothe, born in Heddesheim on 10.8.1895
SCHNEIDER, Elisabeth, born in Heddesheim on 22.1.1897

Underneath lies a blackened copy of a card addressed to Elisabeth Schneider dated June 9, 1937, from the *Staatspolizei* (federal police), refusing her request for a passport in order to travel to Luxembourg. It was 1937. Was she attempting to flee?

The remaining papers in the file from Bad Arolsen are copies of a printed list issued by the *Geheime Staatspolizei* (Secret State Police, abbreviated to "Gestapo") in Koblenz. The heading is *"der am 22.März.1942 aus dem Stadt und Landkreis Koblenz evakuierten Juden"* (Jews evacuated from the city and surrounding area of Koblenz on March 22, 1942). All is correct: their names, dates of birth, place of birth. Schneider, Dorothe is number 250; Schneider, Elisabeth 251; and Schneider, Johanna 252. In the column titled "Last address," all three are listed as living at Adolf-Hitler-Strasse 15, Kobern. Dora must have left the hospital, and at some point, Lisbet returned from Berlin and joined her sisters.

There surely were more pages listing the names of deported Jews, but I have only the two relevant pages with ninety-six names. I notice that a number of families lived together at the same address in a handful of "Jew houses." Perhaps, like my parents, they were forced to move into a building with other Jews. My aunts were the only ones listed as living in Kobern at Adolf-Hitler-Strasse 15. The distance between Koblenz and Kobern is seventeen kilometers.

When they entered the train that would carry them on their final journey, did they, like the others, try to believe they were being sent to work in the East? Was there any comfort in their companionship, the three of them together?

Their place of death is recorded as Izbica, Krasnystaw, Lublin, Poland. Beside the category "Victim's status end WW2" is printed the word "missing."

I am unsettled by the voiceless past.

Izbica

Izbica, a small Jewish town, a *shtetl*, in the Lublin province, was chosen by the Nazis as the main transitory ghetto for Jews from Poland, Germany, Austria, and Czechoslovakia because of its convenient location on the main railway line to the Belzec and Sobibor death camps.[9,10]

My aunts left Koblenz from *Güterbahnhof Koblenz Lutzei* (freight train station Koblenz Lutzei) on March 22, 1942. They were packed into the first train carrying Jews to the East.[11] Between March and June 1942, 11,000 to 15,000 European Jews were brought to Izbica. To make room for these incoming transports in the small shtetl, brutal deportations to the death camps Belzec and Sobibor began on March 24, 1942.

Conditions in Izbica were unendurable—overcrowding, famine, typhoid. Historians estimate that four thousand Jews were buried in the Jewish cemetery, two thousand of whom had been rounded up and shot.[12] How did you die, Hanna, Dora, Elisabeth? From starvation, disease, a bullet? Or did you run naked up the ramp to the bathhouse in Belzec or Sobibor?

You were concerned for my every whim and need. I couldn't even give you a cup of cold water.

Three of the Schneider sisters died in Izbica or Belzec or Sobibor, Poland, as spring turned into summer in the year 1942. That same year on May 3, their older sister died with her husband in Chelmno, Poland. I was ten years old.

Langenlonsheim

In 2000, I found the birth certificates of the four sisters in the *Rathaus* (town hall) in Langenlonsheim, where records for the seven surrounding villages are stored.

As I attempted to read the obscure script filling the spaces on the copies of the old printed documents, I connected with my grandparents' joy the four times they made the journey from Heddesheim to Langenlonsheim to register the births of their daughters. Maybe by number three they swallowed a measure of disappointment—another girl.

What was that word in front of my grandfather's name? The letters, more than one hundred years old, spell out "*Weinhändler*" (wine merchant). My grandfather was a Weinhändler!

There, right in the middle of the page of my mother's birth certificate, written in copperplate, the upstroke thin and the downstroke bold and black, leaning to the right, was the word "Amalia."

Amalia, Amalie, Milla, Mally

A locked glass case stands just inside St. Nicholas Church, Gemünd. A large book lies open under the glass, supported by a carved wooden ledge. A memorial book for the citizens of Gemünd, its pages are turned daily to display the names of the dead on the dates of their death. Years ago, Willi Kruff carefully formed each letter, each word, influenced by the formal Blackletter script so popular in the Germany of his youth.

Every November 9 and 10, the book is turned to the left-hand page with the heading "9-10.November.1938" and on the right-hand page, under the heading "Reichskristallnacht," Willi's memorial words appear:

> *In the early morning of November 10, orders were given for the synagogue on Mühlenstrasse to be set on fire. The fire department was standing by to protect the neighboring houses. On these days we especially think of the Jewish citizens, who were killed in concentration and internment camps.*[13]

Twenty-three names, arranged in alphabetical order, fill the rest of the two pages. The last three names on the list are Zack Marcus, Zack Milla, and Zack Georg.

I cannot recall hearing my father or anyone else call my mother "Milla." The name on her birth certificate is "Amalia," whereas her name is written as "Amalie" on the official list of Jews leaving Köln for Litzmannstadt (Lodz) on October 30, 1941.[14] Perhaps an "a" at the end of a hasty, handwritten "Amalia" was misread and printed as an "e," or maybe in daily usage, four syllables actually were shortened to three and she was called "Amalie." Was my mother's nickname "Milla?" Or did Willi write from a confused childhood memory?

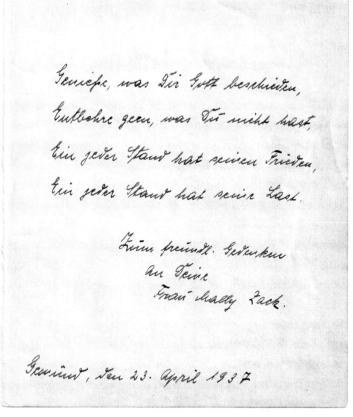

A page that my friend Ruth tore out of her autograph
book, signed by my mother.

I can no longer sit with Willi and ask my questions. On a bleak, cold Sunday in November 2010, he drove his car into a wall on the way to church. He died instantly. Willi was a careful driver; he may have had a heart attack.

A year later, as I write my story, I linger with the loss of my friend. Then, I remember the page Ruth tore out of her autograph book and gave to me. I dig it out. There, in my mother's fluid handwriting, dated April 23, 1937, Gemünd, she has written her contribution, a well-known quotation:

> "Enjoy what God has given you,
> Accept graciously what you don't have.
> Every condition has its blessing.
> Every condition has its trials.
>
> With friendly thoughts, yours, Frau Mally Zack"[15]

I repeat the name to myself: "Mally" . . . "Mally". . . .

Mutti, Wer Bist Du?[16]

Even though my mother's life has faded into obscurity, I am grateful for the slivers of light revealed in our visits to Heddesheim. I wonder if the legacy my mother has left for me is not the glorious setting of her childhood years—peace, simplicity, order, wholesomeness, fruitfulness, gladness, celebration?

When she came to Gemünd, did she bring a dowry of warmth and joy? Did she balance my father's sadness? He had lost his family, his home in Strasburg, and then his first wife. Light, peace, order, and love bathe my own childhood memories of our home, 174 Dreibornerstrasse, Gemünd.

PART V

Sacred Adventure

꩜

Notes Scribbled along the Way: Spring 2010

You have called us to walk with the forsaken,
to understand those who were suffering
as You did.

Hans-Peter Lang
in a prayer on our first evening in Lodz

I am a traveler on the way to a sacred place,
where God holds me in the palm of His hand.

Henry J. Nouwen (1932-1996)[1]

꩜

16

Drawn to Follow Their Steps to the Bitter End

As I wrote Chapter 6, "What Happened to My Parents?" in the cocoon of my Phoenix home, surrounded by piles of books and Internet printouts, I was shaken by the description of their experiences as they were caught up in the disaster after we separated in July 1939. I wanted to know the truth, the details. At the same time, I was repelled by my discoveries. Do I have to dig deeper? Haven't I already forgiven?

Emerging from the protection of time and distance, I am drawn to follow their steps to the bitter end.

Wednesday, March 24, 2010. We land in Frankfurt and take the intercity express train to the Köln main train station. Arriving here and looking up at the 4711 sign has become so commonplace that I no longer have to suppress the thought, "This is the place where we parted, my parents and I." After years of denial, I am beginning to accept the role Köln played in my past.

The Romans built an aqueduct in AD 80 to bring drinking water from the Eifel to Köln, beginning in Nettersheim, eighteen kilometers from Gemünd. Except for a few bridges, the water was carried almost entirely underground. Nearly two millennia later, at the end of 1939, one little Jewish family left a faint trail between Gemünd and Köln. Deep in the hidden chambers of my heart, the neglected memory of our move had almost evaporated.

Our longtime friend Detlef Wurst is waiting on the railway station platform to take us to our home in the Eifel. We embrace.

Fourteen days later George and I drive back to Köln. Our previous excursions from the Eifel to Köln are now converging to launch us on a longer journey; a pilgrimage further into forgiveness and deeper healing.

With Walter in Köln

Wednesday, April 7, 2010. Promptly at 10 a.m., George and I stand on the doorstep of a small brick house on Offenbachstrasse, Köln. The door opens, and a smiling Walter Volmer stands with arms outstretched in welcome. A tall, slim man with fair, thinning hair, he leads us to a sunny sitting room where our eyes are pulled toward the riot of spring flowers blooming in the tidy garden. Walter invites us to the table, carefully and generously prepared for a hearty, German breakfast. We smell the coffee. We relax together, enjoying the tranquility and good food after the challenges of an hour-long drive through roadwork and city traffic.

We are meeting for the first time after an exchange of emails, yet all three of us instantly feel at ease with each other. Walter is now retired. He was the criminal police commissioner for the city of Köln. These days, among his many activities, he guides tours focused on Köln's past. In our correspondence, I have shared the meager pieces of information I have gleaned about my parents' time in Köln, beginning just after the events of Kristallnacht in November 1938, until their deportation on October 30, 1941. Walter took my few facts and thoroughly researched and planned our day together. I feel as though I am living in a dream, awed by the timing of such a gift.

Slowly, slowly, ever since I first read the printout handed to me by Barbara Becker-Jakli at the EL-DE-Haus in March 2009—saying that my parents lived in the Lodz ghetto before their gassing in Chelmno in May 1942—

the impression has grown that I should do something to remember and honor my parents. Now, thirteen months after I was handed those cold, bitter facts—where they died and how they died—I have absorbed that nauseous medicine and am preparing a journey, following their steps from Gemünd to Köln to Lodz to Chelmno.

In three weeks, on April 28, the journey to Poland will begin, and I am discouraged by the failure of all my efforts to find the actual route taken by their train from Köln to Lodz. Yet, I have a conviction that we should follow them as closely as we can. I share with Walter my desire to find the route taking Köln Jews to Lodz.

We have been walking the streets of Köln for several hours, and I need to find a bathroom. There are no public facilities around, but we find ourselves near the EL-DE-Haus, the very place I received the news of my parents' deportation to Lodz and gassing in Chelmno. Walter suggests we stop there. Behind the desk, in the miniscule reception area, the genial, elderly, literary gentleman in his black beret tells George he is puzzled by the rancor expressed in the American political scene and asks for help in understanding the latest TV soundbites.

Meanwhile, Walter and I scan the small number of scholarly books offered for sale. Haphazardly, Walter reaches for and pulls down the book by Dieter Corbach—*6.00 Uhr ab Messe Köln-Deutz Deportationen 1938-1945* (Departure: 6.00 a.m. Messe Köln-Deutz deportations 1938-1945)—which I left behind in Phoenix. He opens the book, and there, printed inside the cover, is a map clearly showing the various routes of the deportation trains from Köln to Riga, Minsk, Lublin, Theresienstadt, and Lodz! Shocked, we read the carefully researched and precise information. I had opened this book many times without even glancing at the maps. I sense the gentle, strong hand of my Heavenly Father leading me, and I am strengthened to face the darkness ahead.

A Pile of Shoes

Sunday, April 11, 2010. We are back in Köln four days after our tour with Walter, this time with our friend Thomas Cogdell from Austin, Texas, who has been closely following our journey. He is on a European business trip and squeezes in a quick weekend visit to the Eifel.

The three of us are unaware that it is Holocaust Remembrance Day, yet how fitting a day to retrace the unstable ground on which my parents had walked. We follow the same route that George and I took with Walter. Around the corner from the EL-DE-Haus, we approach a sprawling sculpture, growing out of the pavement, revealing the story of Edith Stein's life—a silent testimony to the Jewish Carmelite nun martyred at Auschwitz in 1942, calling out to passing cars and pedestrians. We circle and gaze and absorb the narrative.

More visceral than words, the sculpture symbolizes the agony of entering the abyss. I look at the heavy tablets of the Law, rising from the ground, askew, staggering under the weight of an overflowing mound of worn shoes. I grieve the cruel injustice done to Edith Stein and the six million, including Markus and Amalie Zack. My eyes return to the silent cry rising from the concrete, and I take in the deeply carved footprints of bare feet driven forward. I look closely. Among the feet, two are turned to face in the opposite direction. They are pierced. Jesus was there when Edith Stein, her sister Rosa, and all the others took their final steps into the Auschwitz gas chambers.

Like a soft breeze, I feel the comfort of God—not an explanation, but a tenderness that beckons me toward the bitter reality of following my parents' final footprints, ending in the agony of the gas truck in Chelmno.

With the Chevra Kadisha in Gemünd

Wednesday, April 28, 2010. Will we find the way that my parents took on the final part of their journey from Lodz to Chelmno? Can I go through with this? The activity of preparation had assuaged my anxious thoughts. Today, our journey begins; preparations are over. We drive from Dahlem through soothing, undulating fields—fresh green trees and yellow dandelions. We check into the Kurpark Hotel, our Gemünd gathering place, hosted by Detlef, the burly, tender-hearted innkeeper. For years, he has been a dear and faithful friend.

Gradually, we come together—Ryan and Megan, Americans from Phoenix; Verena and Hans-Peter, Austrians from Wieselburg; Julia, British from Berlin; and Jutta, German from the Westerwald across the Rhine. We will meet David, British, and Greetje, Dutch, in Berlin along the way. There will be ten of us—a *minyan*.[1] A small, diverse group, we are Roman Catholic, Lutheran, Anglican, free church, and Messianic Jews. Our ages span generations, from the mid-twenties to seventy-eight.

I hardly dare receive the showers of love and care pouring over me from George and these dear friends who will be my travelling companions, and those others who are closely accompanying us from a physical distance. I think of them as my helpers—*Chevra Kadisha*, who in Jewish tradition volunteer to assist in the mourning process, honoring the dead and caring for the grieving.[2]

We welcome our fellow travellers, and after everyone is settled into their comfortable rooms, we make our way to the top of Dreibornerstrasse, a pedestrian zone and shopping area in the heart of Gemünd. On this sunny day, we sit at tables in the street, eating *doner kebab* at the Turkish restaurant. Across the road, in clear view, stands the yellow apartment building erected on the foundation of my former home. Wide steps lead up to the glass entrance, placed between two large, street-level windows. Women's clothing and accessories, expensive and stylish, are elegantly displayed. As I read through my journal notes, the two windows where my father displayed china dishes, and everything else a housewife might have desired and needed eighty years ago, appear like a mirage before my eyes.

I have no real memory of my father's actual shop, which surely played a

Eifel friends welcome the minyan. Photograph by Ryan Thurman.

central role in my family's daily life. However, I vividly remember Willi's tale of the broken milk jug. He was seven or eight years old, and he had broken the little jug, an important part of his mother's coffee set. Taking his own few *pfennig,* he came across the road, searching with anxious eyes for a little jug among the treasures packed behind the glass. My father, as usual, was standing on the steps, and he led Willi inside. He found a matching jug that just happened to cost exactly the number of pfennig Willi was holding in his hand.

We walk further down the street and introduce everyone to the delight of *italienisches Eis* (Italian ice) and collect the twelve white roses we had ordered from the flower shop. At 4 p.m., we stand outside the Kurpark Hotel with six of the roses. Several of our Eifel friends join us. We cross the Marienplatz and reach the top of Dreibornerstrasse again. Our diverse group begins to flow together. We are a little cautious, yet certain we are supposed to do this. Though following a planned route, we are aware of entering the unknown. What are our thoughts as we place our feet on the ground? Me, I am questioning my ability to cope with the emotional fallout that surely lies ahead.

In the introduction to an eyewitness account of daily life in the Lodz ghetto, Allen Adelson observed that "insidious stages of individual diminishment . . . preceded mass death for a great many Jews of Europe."[3] Diminishment began for our family in Gemünd, and so it is fitting that our journey toward forgiveness and reconciliation starts in this very place.

We want to lay two white roses, one for each of my parents, at locations connected to their lives. Where should we begin? We are a conspicuous group in a small European town. If we assemble in front of our former home and shop, will we bring blessing or apprehension to the families who call this yellow building home today? An idea surfaces: Maria Schmitz-Schumacher is waiting to join us next door at their home on Dreibornerstrasse. Her parents were our neighbors when I was born, and her mother, Frau Schmitz, led me to the only remnant of my childhood— the apple tree—when we visited her in 1992.

On this warm, spring day, branches and leaves pour over the wall of the Schmitz garden into the former Zack courtyard. Maria and her husband, Dieter, are *Zuhause* in the family home. This is their place, where they belong, and they gladly invite us into the garden. We lay our two roses on the earth between the base of the tree and the fence. Standing in a semicircle around the old tree, we remember Amalie and Markus Zack and the former Jews of Gemünd, and pray for the healing of the past.

Maria enthusiastically joins us as we walk over the bridge, crossing the street at the traffic light. We enter tiny, narrow Mühlengasse, where the synagogue, the center of the Jewish community, had stood from February 27, 1874, until November 9-10, 1938.[4] A small, dingy, grey repair shop with startling blue window frames and door now sits on the synagogue's foundation. Wheels and vehicle parts spill into the street through the open doorway. A visitor today would be hard-pressed to picture the former scene, a beloved house of worship marking the rhythm of the Jewish year.

At the rear, behind the busy façade, under a canopy of brambles and weeds, the original foundation stones laid in 1874 are supporting the post-war structure. The modest building sits snugly at the foot of a sloping hill. Holding two roses, George and I approach the back by a small, open, paved side area between the workshop and the neighboring house. We begin to climb the ancient, crumbly stone steps, carefully stepping over the encroaching undergrowth. Did the men who burned the synagogue carry the gasoline up these same steps? I want to leave the roses as near as possible to the only remnant left of the place where I sat close by my father, swinging my legs, watching the reading of the Torah.

The group waits across the narrow street. Maria follows us to the paved area. On our right, the sun is bright, and I dimly see the outline of a neighbor whom I do not know leaning over her balcony. I feel her disapproval penetrating my skin as we gingerly climb the steps. Are we trespassing? Maria engages her in conversation, and George and I cast our roses in an arc to fall among the weeds at the base of the building.

As we all continue down Mühlengasse, Maria tells the story of her grandmother who had lived on the hill behind the synagogue. As a child and a Gentile, she had been asked to put out the lights in the synagogue. Her finger on the switch helped sustain the Jewish sabbath when no work was allowed. Maria's talk with the neighbor revealed new information: after World War II, nearby houses had been rebuilt with the rubble from the synagogue.

Our path to the Jewish cemetery, our last stop, passes behind the railway station from where we must have left Gemünd after Kristallnacht. No longer used as a train station, it is a melancholy, backwater place. The low, metal gate clicks open. We are soothed by the peaceful atmosphere we find inside the *jüdische Friedhof* (Jewish cemetery), trimmed and tidy under the care of the municipality.

George and I pull two *tallit* (prayer shawls) and one *kippa* (skull cap) out of a large, yellow plastic bag. The tallit, one for a man and the other for a woman—new, white with the prescribed corner threads hanging—have been sent to us from Baltimore. Chris and Lisa, a couple closely following our journey from afar, were prompted to buy the shawls at their local orthodox Judaica store. The shopkeeper, who had helped in the selection of a man's tallit, looked nonplussed when Lisa requested another tallit, one suitable for a woman. Finally, a smaller version emerged from a box on a high shelf, a stole that a girl would wear for her *bat mitzvah*.[5] The two tallit arrived with the request that we wear them as we pray in places associated with my parents. George had received the kippa, a small blue satin circle, at the solemn service closing the seventieth reunion of Kindertransport in London. As I was packing in Dahlem, I came upon the kippa at the bottom of a basket and, on the spur of the moment, threw the little, blue disc into our suitcase.

Praying hands. Photograph by Ryan Thurman.

It is Jewish custom for a man to wear a prayer shawl over his shoulders and to cover his head with a kippa when praying before the holy God. The two of us stand close together, clad in our prayer shawls, George with a kippa, facing the memorial stone for my parents. If they had died a normal death, this would have been their actual place of burial. Our time in the cemetery ends as we choose small stones to take with us to the forest near Chelmno.

Back at the Kurpark Hotel, our invited guests, Willi Kruff and Helmut Scheler, an elderly, kindly, retired Lutheran pastor, and his wife, are already waiting for us. We sit, one big group together, and enjoy a simple meal of soup and salad. Willi is eighty-nine years old, walking with a cane, lonely after the death of Annemarie, his wife, but still able to tell a story with grace and humor. We egg him on and once more, he recounts the time he set the curtains on fire when he was four and a half years old, and how my father came to the rescue. Could there be a better way to end such a day?

With the Chevra Kadisha in Köln

Thursday, April 29, 2010. After breakfast, we pick up generous lunch packets, take the last six white roses out of the water, wrap their stems, and head out to catch the early train to Köln. Today, we will honor my parents' lives during the twenty-three months or so they lived there. We stand together on the platform in Kall, a ten-minute drive from Gemünd. Detlef has joined us. Walter is waiting for us at the *Hauptbahnhof* (main train station). He will be our guide.

Our first stop is Rathenauplatz 14, the home I dimly remember when it was known as Horst-Wessel Platz 14. We gather on the green island facing the building. Behind us looms a massive Victorian structure, the Roon Street Synagogue, restored and functioning once again. Where should we leave the two roses? A woman has been observing us from her open window on the second floor and abruptly turns away. We decide to stand the roses upright on the doorstep, propped against the wall, as an act of remembrance for the Jews who once lived in this particular *Juden Haus* (Jewish house) and an expression of blessing for those who live there today.

Under Walter's careful direction, we then travel by streetcar to Müngersdorf, 6.5 kilometers to the west. My parents were forced to leave Horst-Wessel Platz 14 in the autumn of 1941 and enter the internment camp prepared there for the Jewish citizens of Köln. As we enter Müngersdorf, I pause for a moment to contrast my journey with that of my Mutti and Vati. Their living conditions were harsh, their travel inflicted upon them. Yet, here we are on a warm April day in 2010, guided by Walter, walking in sunshine along paths winding through grass and trees dressed in their variegated shades of spring greenery. Müngersdorf is part of the "green ring" (a system of parks) circling the city, a refuge for sports and relaxation. We enter a growth of trees and stop before a large rock. Walter points to a small metal plate, the only visible evidence of the time when my parents had been held here before their deportation. We read the inscription:

A Memorial to the Dead and a Reminder to the Living

During WWII the former Fort V and the area around it became known as the Müngersdorf camp for Jews. Jews who had been forcibly driven from their homes and apartments were interned here and subsequently transported to the Nazi death camps in the East.

The City of Cologne 1981[6]

❧ ☙

It is hard to connect a history of war and cruelty with this peaceful, refreshing place. However, on this site in 1874, the Prussians built Fort V as a defense against the French, one of twelve forts circling the old city of Köln like beads on a necklace. In 1941, the area of the old *Kasematten* (protective vaults of Fort V)[7] was selected for the hurried construction of barracks.[8]

How to comprehend the fearful misery endured by my parents, packed close together with all the other Jews, behind barbed wire in the wet, dark, cold barracks?

⋘ ⋙

Walter came to Müngersdorf two days earlier, searching for solid evidence of the past. He met a lady walking her dog and asked if she knew of any fort ruins. "There, inside the wood, right next to us," she pointed. At the end of our visit to the site of the internment camp in the old fort, Walter presents me with a box. I open it, and there lies a lump of rusty red rock, a piece of the old fort. He hands me a signed certificate of authenticity. How did he understand that some little material fragment of the past would mean so much to me? My parents had really existed; this actually happened to them.

Five Germans—Walter, Detlef, Jutta, Maria Jonas, and I—stand together by the rock with the plaque of remembrance and pray for God's mercy on victim and perpetrator.

We take the streetcar and travel the 7.3 kilometers toward the Köln-Deutz Tief railway station, following the route that the Köln Jews took in October 1941. Walter reminds us that this mass of men, women and children, each wearing the yellow star and carrying their luggage, walked for hours in full view of the citizens of Köln.

We sit on the steps facing the Rhine. It is sunny and hot. Quietly, we drink our bottled water and eat our fruit and sandwiches—for us a welcome respite before going on to face the dark scene played out on Platform 5 of Köln-Deutz Tief sixty-nine years ago.

Five Germans after prayer at the plaque of remembrance.
Photograph by Ryan Thurman.

Walter leads us over the Rhine, and we look down on the river as we cross the bridge. Did Amalie and Markus Zack, driven forward among the crowd of frightened Jews, take in the water below, or were they focused on their exhaustion? As our group walks together, I carry on an inward conversation with my parents.

"Mutti und Vati, my heart was closed to you while you were walking this same path all those years ago. But today I come with friends to think of you."

I feel the cobblestones pressing on the soles of my feet.

"Were your shoes worn? Did your feet hurt? Were your cases heavy? Were you weeping? Or had you already wept all your tears? Did your dread increase as you entered the darkness of the underground platform? Vati, did you hold Mutti's hand?"

We follow the original, short, cobbled path skirting the side of the railway station.

"Mutti, did you think of me?"

Across the street stands the *Messe* (exhibition halls). The old interior is hidden under the refurbished façade. It was often used as an assembly point during the deportations. Were my parents processed in these buildings? It is hard to be certain.

Without question they were in the crowd on the dark, hidden, lower-level platform on October 30, 1941—hurried, pushed, cursed, beaten, and packed into the ancient railway carriages. Finally, they heard the doors slammed shut and locks turned on the outside.

"I have come to remember you today, with my friends."

Our little group is here by choice. We sit or stand alone in the shadows—in the silence. Then, George and I cast two white roses on the tracks.

17

The Wheels Roll East

*F*riday, April 30, 2010. 7:42 a.m. and we leave Kall on our way to Berlin via Köln. I try to capture the thoughts tumbling over one another as I sit in the train, scribbling fast in my new, pocket-size, orange notebook. It is April 30th, a sunny, green, and glistening day. We have been sent off with kindness, our lunches packed, luggage loaded, and driven to Kall *Bahnhof* (train station) by Detlef and his crew. As we glide toward Köln, the soft murmurings of German voices surround us. My parents and I left Gemünd stripped of dignity and possessions, objects of contempt. Yet, here I am, seventy-two years later, hugged and loved by my Gemünd friends, surrounded by the tenderness of my travelling companions and the strong protection of my husband. Could there be a greater contrast?

Probably, I was travelling on this train line after Kristallnacht toward the end of 1938 with my Vati and Mutti when we left Gemünd to settle precariously in Köln. Did they speak to each other or to me? Or, were they silent in their grief, despair, and depression? Did any of our things come with us? What about our fine furniture, dishes, pots and pans, and clothing? I have no memory of that journey. We were leaving everything my father had built, the outer expression of his labor and creativity. Since 1933, his identity had been systematically and diabolically dismantled and stripped, while old neighbors looked away—some sorrowful, some fearful, some indifferent, others complicit.

Herr Arntz described to us his experiences in Gemünd, while doing research for his book *Judenverfolgung und Fluchthilfe im deutsch-belgischen Grenzgebiet*. He would visit older people in their homes, and after an hour or two of conversation, sharing a glass or two or three of good German wine, he would hear tongues loosened by alcohol, opening hidden doors to the past. "See this? It came from such and such Jewish family." O Lord, forgive! Help me to forgive!

Rolling through the Eifel, seeing blossoming trees, gently curving hills, orderly houses, freshly dug gardens, and the yellow expanse of rape fields (seed used to make canola oil), you can start to question, "Did all that stuff really happen?" It all seems so normal. How could such depravity overflow and submerge an entire people?

Was it the "frog in the kettle" syndrome? The water heats ever so gradually, from cold to warm and then boiling, while the frog stays, oblivious to the change in temperature. Souls were marinated for years in contempt, hatred, lust for power, and the desire to belong to the "in group." Even Martin Luther added his sticks to the wood pile, begun by some of the early church fathers.[1] Hitler only had to throw a lighted taper, and the bonfire burst into flame, the sparks ascending to heaven. The fire, he prophesied, would burn for 1,000 years. Just ten years later, Germany, land and people, sprawled in smoldering ruins.

We negotiate a very tight connection in Köln to catch the intercity express train to Berlin and slide into our reserved seats, two sets of four, around two tables across from one another. We hear a soft, recorded voice welcoming us in German and English and wishing us an enjoyable journey.

We look down on the Rhine through the arch of the Hohenzollern Bridge as the train leaves Köln, the same bridge we crossed yesterday following my parents' path. I see the hundreds of locks, the kind of small padlocks used to protect personal property, clamped shut, affixed to the mesh railing—a local custom with no apparent practical purpose. Yesterday, Walter spoke about the official concern that their weight might eventually break the railing. I settle back in my seat and think of the contrast between the constrictions of life in Köln during the 1930s and 1940s and today's freedom to publicly express an offbeat fad.

The train stops for nine minutes in Hamm. What would my parents have seen? Theirs was an autumn journey. I see a profusion of lilac trees in full bloom. For an instant, the lovely scent tickles my memory, an aroma faintly reminiscent of my mother. Were the lilac trees perfuming our intimate world when the two of us had our picture snapped close together in our garden?

Berlin

Now, there are ten of us: Megan, Ryan, Verena, Hans-Peter, Julia, David, Greetje, Jutta, George, and I standing with all our luggage on the platform of the Berlin *Hauptbahnhof* (main railway station). David and Greetje have joined us here, and from this point our trains will pick up the actual route of the deportation of Jews from Köln—Berlin, Frankfurt (Oder), Poznań, and Lodz. Kirstin, a Berliner, has come for the brief moments we need to change trains and platforms, to hug us and help carry our luggage down and up the steps. What a strange day to be in Berlin. In this city on April 30, 1945, around 3:30 p.m., Hitler committed suicide.

❧ ☙

He sat on a couch next to his "just married" wife. They were in his private suite inside the bunker, fifty feet under the Reich Chancellery. He knew that the Soviet ground forces were only one block away. His teeth crushed the glass coating of the cyanide capsule; simultaneously, he shot a hole in his head.

His last will and testament, written and signed on April 29, 1945, at 4 a.m., ends with these words: "Above all I charge the leaders of the nation and those under them to scrupulous observance of the laws of race and to merciless opposition to the universal poisoner of all peoples, International Jewry."[2]

⁂

We wave goodbye to Kirstin standing alone on the platform of the Berlin Hauptbahnhof. From now on we will be travelling with slower, regional trains. The computer printout lists the stations where we will stop before we arrive in Poznań later this evening. I count them; there are thirty-three!

Did the train carrying my parents stop at all those places? Or, were they sped through as anonymously as possible? Were they halted at sidings away from population centers? Maybe sitting cramped together for hours without information, food, or water?

On the Way to Poznań

Just outside Berlin, work on the line disrupts the normal flow of traffic, and so we must change trains again at Erkner. We walk the length of the platform and climb steep stairs carrying our luggage, following the sign for Poznań in the midst of a small crowd of German and Polish travellers. We think we have reached the place where our ongoing train will stop. A number of the other travellers warn us that we are on the wrong platform. We must retrace our steps to the platform across the tracks. There is no official in sight. Confused, we join the majority, leaving a remnant behind. The two groups look at each other separated by the railway lines. David walks to the signal box and looks up. He shouts his question to the official high up there. The reply is inconclusive. Will we miss the train? I wonder: Do our feelings of helplessness connect us with the Jewish journey, marked by confusion and a search for facts in the midst of innuendo and rumor?

At last we are on the way again. Thirty minutes later, we reach Frankfurt on the Oder, still in Germany but close to the border with Poland. Another change. We go in search of a hot drink while Hans-Peter and Verena decide to remain on our departure platform and keep an eye on all the luggage. They lean back on a bench, enjoying the respite from constant motion. A tall, graceful, young woman quietly comes and sits beside them. After several minutes of silence, they begin a conversation. Joanna is Polish, and she is leaving Frankfurt on the Oder after a short visit for a job interview. She is a scientist, near graduation from Dublin University. She confides that she has been crying out to God for help in deciding her future. Should she take the job offered? Hans-Peter and Verena listen and share the story of our journey with her.

As the rest of us return to the bench, we become aware that our meeting with Joanna is "out of the ordinary." With luminous eyes, she tells us that God answered her prayer as she sat down beside Hans-Peter and Verena, and they talked together. We exchange email addresses just as our train arrives. We separate as though we are family.

We find seats, and as the train moves away, all of us are mulling over what just happened. We feel as though we had been swept into an encounter, and we are to hold those transient moments with Joanna like a delicate piece of hand-blown glass—to treasure and turn so we can see the many colors shining in the light.

By the time our train reaches Poznań three hours later, we are all tired. We scatter in disarray, looking for transport to the Royal Hotel in the city center. At last, George and I lay our heads on the pillow and think of the good things that happened through the day. But, we also feel a little uneasy about the tension in our group when we discussed the arrangements for paying the hotel bill, just before we separated to sleep in our rooms. We have reached Poznań, and the menace of Lodz and Chelmno awaits us. How can we enter the valley of the shadow of death without mutuality, without harmony? . . .

Saturday, May 1, 2010. Our train will leave early, and after breakfast in the hotel, we meet to pray and read one of the Psalms of Ascent. Ancient Israelites sang Psalms 120-134 on their pilgrimage to Jerusalem, and we know deep down that our journey is also a sacred adventure. First, though, we have a robust discussion about last night, with apologies and the exchange of forgiveness.

Twenty-Eight Stops and Four Hours to Lodz

We are in Poland in the midst of forty days of mourning. On April 10, 2010, the president, Lech Kaczyński, his wife, and more than ninety of the country's leaders were in flight to mark the seventieth anniversary of a massacre. In 1940, 20,000 members of Poland's elite officer corps and leadership had been shot in the Katyn Woods by the Russian Secret Police. The plane carrying Kaczyński and the other leaders crashed near the infamous woods. We encounter a nation wounded afresh at the site of an old scar, a loss poignantly repeated in place and time. Like a very young American child born on July 4, who confuses the fireworks with the celebration of his birthday, I find myself moved by the surrounding national grief that touches my own loss. I am also back in a dark place for the anniversary of two deaths among six million, cut off before their time.

May 1 is Labor Day in Poland. May 3 is National Day, with Sunday sandwiched between. People are on the move. As we lift up our luggage and climb onto the train, we discover that it is packed. We leave all the bags and cases stacked high near our entry point and join the other passengers, standing close together. Lodz is three hours away.

Through all the stops and starts, David stands relaxed beside our luggage. I become aware of repeated references to "the luggage" as I read through my journal notes. Why am I so concerned about suitcases? I think about July 1939 when I was in the cavernous shed trying to identify my baggage, and I remember my fear and anxiety. A deep chasm opened at that moment in time. On one side of the split, everything had been lovingly done for me. I had no memory of the cases being packed. I didn't know what was inside or even what they looked like. Suddenly I was responsible, on my own, unprepared, and incapable. Like the unexpected blow of a weighted hammer falling on my unprepared child's soul, the loss of parents and their love and protection was made known to me in the form of lost luggage.

Next to me, a lady lifts her toddler from the opposite seat, places the child on her lap, and motions for me to sit. I realize the advantages of white hair. Trying not to stare, I observe the little girl, about three years old, holding her rag doll, enveloped in her mother's arms, accepting as her due all the loving attention so tenderly poured upon her. Out of the mother's large, pink, plastic handbag comes a picture book, and they read together. A juice box appears, and then a sweet roll, the crumbs gently brushed away. She leads her little daughter's attention to the sights flashing by the window. I am reminded of a Jewish mother. Her kisses, whispers, and gentle strokes are like a piano, accompanying the singer of a love song.

Why am I sitting in this seat on the train? Why did this Polish lady make room for me? Why am I given a place on the front row to observe a mother's love? Despite the lack of a common language, I learn the little girl's name is Patricia. The mother points to the pendant I am wearing, a stylized silver fish entwined with a menorah, and indicates her understanding of the symbol. I sense a sadness lying deep within her. What is her story? I turn to my own story. Is Patricia's mother allowing me to see how Amalie Zack, my mother, interacted with her small daughter, Hannelore? This Polish mother bends down and with a paper tissue gathers all the crumbs from the floor, and they leave without a trace.

As the wheels turn east, we all find a place to sit. While I have been absorbed with the mother and child, I think that the young couple sitting next to the window, who are continuing on to Pabianice—only one stop before Lodz—have been wondering about me! We begin a conversation in English. They are Marzena and Chris. She is a political science graduate, working as a receptionist, and he is a fencing coach. He writes his name in my little book with three crossed rapiers. They ask why our group is visiting Lodz; why not Krakow, which is so beautiful? There isn't anything to see in Lodz.

When we stop at the tiny station of Zduńska Wola, they point with excitement to a large banner. They translate, "Maximilian Kolbe was born here in 1894." A year earlier, George and I had visited the starvation bunker in Auschwitz, the place where Kolbe had died in 1941. Maximilian Kolbe was a Franciscan and prisoner number 16670. When the vicious commander selected ten men to enter the starvation bunker in reprisal for the disappearance of a prisoner, one of the ten cried out, "My wife, my children." Kolbe volunteered to take his place.

There in the dark, deep underground, the others slowly died. Kolbe was the last survivor. When they came with carbolic acid, he calmly raised his left arm to receive the injection. The missing prisoner was found, dead in the latrine. The family man survived. And the name of Maximilian Kolbe and the Lord he followed is lifted high.[3]

18

Endlich Litzmannstadt[1]

The train stops. We climb down the train steps to the platform and make our way to the taxi stand. The Ibis Hotel, near the top of the main street, ulica Piotrkowska, has been booked. We can take three taxis; maybe with all our luggage we will be a little squeezed together. . . .

My parents left Köln for Lodz on October 30, 1941.[2] What was it like for them when their feet touched the hard, grey stone, and their eyes first saw Radegast, the freight railway station?

A few weeks after our journey is over, I discover *The Diary of Dawid Sierakowiak—Five Notebooks from the Lodz Ghetto*, written between June 28, 1939, and April 15, 1943, and published in 1996—a description of his daily life in the ghetto as a Polish-Jewish teenager.[3] In January 1940, when the ghetto was created in Baluty, the poorest and most neglected northern part of the city, any Gentile living there was forced to relocate. Almost five years later, the Russians liberated the city, and the original owner of the Sierakowiak family apartment returned. He found a pile of notebooks lying on the stove. The diaries bring the darkest realities of life in the ghetto to my reluctant attention.

My parents reached Lodz in weather described in Dawid's diary entries for October 1941. He wrote on October 14, "Although Sunday's snow has almost disappeared, it's terribly wet, cold, and nasty." The arrival of Austrian, Czech, German, and Luxembourg Jews placed great pressure on the overcrowded ghetto.

There is a gap in the diaries from October 24, 1941, to March 17, 1942, four months of testimony gone up in flames for a few moments of warmth. The notebook for March 18 to May 31, 1942, when my parents would have lived in the ghetto, has the title, "We Live in Constant Fear." I lose count of the number of times he uses the word "hunger." I am reading the words written by an eyewitness to the hell my parents were about to enter in November 1941.

Lodz Beckons

As we are about to enter Lodz on May 1, 2010, approaching the doors that will lead us to the taxi stand, we notice the word "Information" on our left. The office looks closed. We peer in and try the door. A small, dark-haired man with an open, friendly face welcomes us, almost as though he is expecting our arrival. It could be that he is happy to see any tourist visiting his city. The office is too small for ten of us, so Verena shares our plans while the rest of us wait outside. She is able to talk by telephone with Monika, an official English-speaking guide, and we agree to meet the next morning, Sunday, for a tour of "Jewish Lodz." We are encouraged as we step out into the city, holding bundles of ghetto literature and maps.

At the close of the day we pray together. Will there be a meaningful connection with my parents? We feel like archeologists excavating a general area. Will we find authentic locations along the way to Chelmno from Lodz? Information beyond the Lodz ghetto is sparse. Hans-Peter prays, "You have called us to walk with the forsaken—to understand those who were suffering—as You did."

Sunday, May 2, 2010. Gradually I awake and become aware of my surroundings. I am lying in a comfortable bed next to George, snuggled under feather duvets. I look around the large, simple, modern room. I step into the sparkling shower, close the curved glass doors, and turn on the shiny faucet. I luxuriate under warm, abundant water. I allow the refreshing experience to continue, disregarding the reminder printed in Polish and English, "Consider saving water."

I am confronted with the extreme contrast between the physical comfort I am relishing here in Lodz and the privation my parents experienced day after day for six months in this city. In 1942, each square kilometer (one kilometer is six-tenths of a mile) of the ghetto was inhabited by 42,587 people. They would have lived in the section of the ghetto assigned to Jews from Germany, in a crowded apartment building with six to seven souls in a room—primitive sanitation, difficult access to water, often cold, without comfort.[4] How can I enjoy the abundance around me?

Hungry, we enter the hotel restaurant and stand before the buffet. How to choose without becoming a glutton? I press the button for my second cup of coffee. Should I have a cappuccino this time or another caffe latte?

I am stricken by the recognition of my parents' sufferings in this place. My little mother, who delighted in creating beauty and perhaps remembered playing in the vineyards surrounding flower-drenched Heddesheim with her sisters, and my multifaceted father, who was energized by his entrepreneurial ventures and freely tramped the Eifel hills breathing the pure healing air—how could they bear the ugly, fetid oppression of Litzmannstadt?

Monika, Our Guide to the Past

Monika is waiting for us in the hotel lobby. She stands ready with her umbrella. Small, maybe in her thirties, a sensitive soul, she will open the past for us in fluent English. She asks, "Would you like to begin our tour with the biggest Jewish cemetery in Europe?" I am thinking, "I would rather focus on places connected with my parents; they were not buried in this cemetery." But then I surrender to the flow of her suggestion.

We follow a narrow path beside the wall enclosing the cemetery, and as we enter the small gate, we notice an older, heavy-set man sitting on a bench to our left. We greet him and our attention is drawn to an imposing brick building on our right. Monika explains, "No one is allowed inside. This is the original funeral house where bodies are still prepared for burial."

We move toward the nearby *Memorial for the Victims of the Lodz Ghetto*—a large, solid sculpture standing on a stone platform. We absorb the symbolism in silence: a tall obelisk resembling a chimney, a broken oak tree, and a menorah—the Jewish nation cut off by burning. The only sound is the crunch of our feet on the gravel. Halfway there we hear a loud yell: "Hey!" We turn and see that the man has left the bench and is standing on the top step by the door of the *Bait ha Tahara* (funeral house). Holding a key in one hand, he motions with his other hand for us to come. We approach, and he opens the door.

Bait ha Tahara

The Bait ha Tahara (funeral house). Photograph by Ryan Thurman.

We slowly file into the first of two huge rooms as if moving in a dreamscape. I wonder if the ancient funeral hearse standing at an angle would have been pulled by horses to bring the ghetto dead to this hallowed place? Or, would the hearse have been pulled by starving men? Eventually, my question will be answered by three eyewitness accounts contained in books that come into my possession after I return home to Phoenix, and I will learn more than I want to know.

ⵣⴻ ⴻⵣ

With a Camera in the Ghetto, published by Schocken Books, contains seventy surviving pictures secretly photographed by Mendel Grossman during the first years of the Lodz ghetto.[5] A blurry photograph on page 56, dated August, 4, 1941, shows a cart loaded with bread and the flank of a horse. On page 61, another cart loaded with bread is being pulled by two men, harnessed between the shafts, matchstick thin, leaning, straining forward.

The five surviving notebooks containing *The Diary of Dawid Sierakowiak* contain such an honest, matter-of-fact record that it is too gut-wrenching to read more than a page or so at a time. On March 6, 1943, Dawid describes his father's death by starvation and disease after four years of utter deprivation in the ghetto amid great inequalities and painful family tensions. On page 243, under his entry for December 28, 1942, a black-and-white picture of a hearse appears. Is it the one that stands in the funeral house today? I think snow is on the ground. A woman looks on as two men carry a stiff body, wrapped in white, feet pointing toward the hearse. A horse stands between the shafts. Below the picture are the words "The black hearse is becoming extremely popular again."[6]

Sara Zyskind is the third eyewitness. She is the lone survivor of the three voices from the past, speaking to me as I search for my parents. In her memoir, *Stolen Years*, she writes about transportation within the confines of the ghetto.[7] Sara remembers that by 1942 only five horses remained.

One was used by Chaim Rumkowski, the Elder of the Jews. Another was available to a Jewish veterinarian, Doctor Leider, who treated German animals. The remaining three pulled vehicles for public use: a bread van, an ambulance, and the hearse. She writes: "The inmates of the ghetto were therefore compelled to supply their own horsepower, by harnessing human beings to wagons. . . . People pulling wagons also disposed of our garbage and waste, since the sewage system of the ghetto had ceased to function long ago."

How did my parents cope? I think a strange thought. Their brutal death on May 3, 1942—could there be an element of severe mercy in their exit from a living hell before the bitter winter of 1942? Between 1940 and 1944, 43,000 died within the ghetto from starvation and disease and were buried in the cemetery.

⚜

Moving to the spacious, clean, bare, inner room of the funeral home, I feel uneasy in the empty stillness. We could be in a primitive operating theater. We are in the room where the bodies are prepared for burial. Dominating the space is a solid, grey, marble chaise lounge. Above is a hose for the flow of purifying water, and at the foot a grating to receive the water. I am gripped by the reality of death and, at the same time, with the care and honor given to the body in Jewish burial practice.

Flickering images scroll through my mind—figures holding plastic bags, scouring broken streets, looking for body parts—Israel on the evening news after an explosion. Even the tiniest fragment is worthy of respect. I become aware of the desecration of my parents' bodies; they were not buried honorably. Until this moment, here in the funeral house, I have pictured coming to the end of our journey in Rzuchowski Forest with a *Yahrzeit*, a memorial service on the anniversary of my parents' deaths at the place where their bodies were thrown into a prepared pit and later dug up and burned. An unformed thought edges into my awareness as I stand before the chair of cleansing water. Tomorrow, should our planned memorial service be combined with a ceremony honoring their bodies and the bodies of their companions—a symbolic burial? But first, more experiences are waiting for us today in Lodz.

Umschlagplatz in Lodz
(A Place for Goods and Humans to be Shipped in and out)

Walking from the Jewish cemetery to Radogoszcz (in German Radegast) Station, we are on the northeastern outskirts of the former ghetto, an area then known as Marysin. We see few vehicles or people. I become aware of the lack of sound and feel an atmosphere of depletion. Is that my charged imagination?

Today, Radegast Station is a silent memorial. Barbed wire surrounded the modest freight railway station when barracks for goods and people were hastily erected in 1940.[8] Food, fuel, and raw materials for the production of clothes, shoes, and uniforms for the German military arrived here. Ready-made goods were shipped out. The enclosed ghetto of Lodz Jews became a productive slave labor camp. Between 1941 and 1942, approximately 20,000 Jews arrived here from western Europe, another 20,000 Polish Jews from the surrounding region, and more than 5,000 Gypsies from Austria.[9]

Umschlagplatz (transfer place) is the term used by the official website www.lodz-ghetto.com to describe Radegast Station, "the site where people were assembled just prior to being shipped out, in most cases to die." The shipping out of Jews from Radegast began on January 16, 1942. Their destination? Chelmno-nad-Nerem (Kulmhof in German) to the northwest. The last train left from here on August 29, 1944, taking its human cargo to Auschwitz/Birkenau to the southwest.[10,11]

As I write "Umschlagplatz," I repeat the word to myself. I dismantle the word "umschlag" and look for the exact meaning of "schlag" in the

German dictionary—blow, punch, whack, lash, shock, thud. When my mother and father received their notification to report for deportation, did they say the word "umschlagplatz," or did they use another common term: "the loading platform in Marysin"? Either name would have been laden with foreboding.

Sixty-eight years later, on Sunday, May 2, 2010, I am looking at three empty freight cars from the 1940s standing open on the original track. Our feet tread on the original stones of the loading platform, and we follow my parents' fearful steps into a cattle car. The ten of us and Monika, confined in the dehumanizing box, stand in a circle and pray. As we begin to leave, Monika, with genuine sadness, softly adds some of the horrible details she has learned in her training as a city guide. She describes bodies pressed so tightly together that the dead were discovered only on arrival, still standing upright.

I feel claustrophobia. I could have been standing, squeezed between my parents. I would have been ten years old. I step out and away from the suffocating air. I want to shut out the image, push it far from me. Knowing we are on the original platform adds to my distress. Next to our cattle car, we notice the old, dark, heavy steam engine, like the ones that pulled human souls without mercy, standing on the original track, stamped with the name "Krupp."

To our right is a simple wooden building displaying a new white sign and the word "Radegast" in the old, black German script. The original shed had lain in ruins until the restoration in 2002. We have reached the actual place where my parents were processed. As I enter, I am aware of open doors and the freedom to come in and go out of a structure that had been formerly closed and with only one exit. There, inside the restored one-room building, stand rows of long, rectangular tables bearing reading lamps at regular intervals. Weighty files are arranged on the tables. Some are open, revealing pages of lists protected by plastic sleeves—the names of passengers.

Inside the cattle car. Photograph by Ryan Thurman.

All of us dive in and start a frantic search. I feel overwhelmed. We are looking for two needles in a haystack. I am desperate to find Amalie and Markus Zack, yet at the same time, I want to hide behind the old, familiar door, blocking out the fearful past.

My Fingers Touch the Plastic

The atmosphere crackles with our intensity. Julia's eyes run down a page. She pulls me forward. My fingers touch the plastic. Written in old German script, I see "Amalie Zack" and on the line below "Markus Zack." Flurries of thoughts jostle my mind. They really existed! Could there have been a measure of doubt? I am startled to realize the absurdity of my thinking. For years, I had blocked the memories of my parents, seeing them as figments of my imagination. Now, I am overwhelmed by this evidence of their being. The first glimpse of their names ignites love in my shrunken heart.

The search. Photograph by Ryan
Thurman.

My finger on their names.
Photograph by Ryan
Thurman.

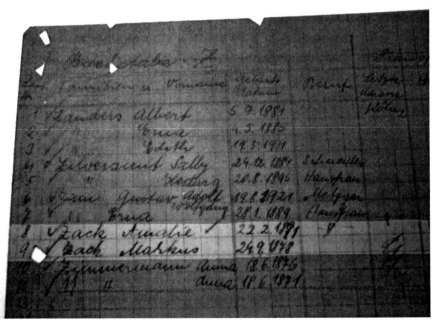

Zack Amalie and Zack Markus on the list.
Photograph by Ryan Thurman.

Ryan photographs the moment of discovery, my hand on one page among the tiniest details. The squared paper helped the German official divide the page into neat, hand-drawn headings. The title is *"Buchstabe* (letter) Z" with a bar across the slope of the "Z," and I remember learning to write the letter "Z" just this way in German school.

The heading of the first column is *"Lauf* (sequence) *Nr."* and my parents are numbered 8 and 9. Their names are followed by their correct dates of birth. Were they standing in abject misery before the official seated at a table, carefully and clearly registering their presence? Under *"Beruf"* (occupation) for numbers 8 and 9 there are two blanks, not even *"Hausfrau"* (housewife) as in the previous entry, number 7. Under *"letze Addresse Köln"* (last address in Cologne), there is no entry for any of the eleven listed on this page. This must be the record of their arrival in Lodz. We could find no list showing their deportation to Chelmno in May 1942.

Behind us as we leave Radegast Station, a tall brick chimney pierces the sky. We take a last look, and even at a distance we can still read the words on the chimney plaque, written in Hebrew, Polish, and English: THOU SHALT NOT KILL.

Ulica Piotrkowska

We part from Monika and walk along ulica Piotrkowska, lined with grand, neo-Renaissance and Art Nouveau buildings, some restored to their former grandeur. We are looking for a place to have lunch among the many shops and restaurants. In her book *Stolen Years,* Sara Zyskind recalls sitting on the curb in September 1939, when she was eleven years old, watching German soldiers marching down ulica Piotrkowska: "The forest of swastika banners accompanying the goose-stepping soldiers deepened the impression of military might and made me tremble with fear."[12] Days later, Jews were prohibited from walking along ulica Piotrkowska, although many of its shops were owned by Jews. But on this day, May 2,

2010, as we enjoy the holiday atmosphere and recover from the drama at Radegast Station, we are unaware of the violations enacted against Poles and Jews along this main artery of Lodz.

Preparing for Tomorrow

Over lunch at a "traditional" rustic Polish restaurant, we begin to think about the next day.

Located almost next door to our hotel is the glittering *Galeria Lodska*. Jutta, Julia, Megan, and I are searching for a glass, a wooden board, and a bunch of white roses—a shopping list far too basic for such a sophisticated place. After searching among the dazzling distractions and buying a T-shirt or two at a Swedish store, we finally find a drinking glass and a bread board at Tesco, a British grocery store in the basement. But the florist offers no white roses—only pink. Should we continue the pattern begun in Gemünd and Köln or give up the idea of white roses? What symbol could we use as we pray along the trail left by my parents?

Verena had given me a plump, ruby rosebud at the memorial stone in the Gemünd Jewish cemetery on the first day of our journey. We both felt a "rightness" about her act, but we did not understand why. When we left Gemünd, I wrapped the bud in damp tissue inside a plastic bag. That morning in Lodz, the much travelled rose was still pliable, and I plucked several petals and scattered them on the floor of the Bait ha Tahara and inside the cattle car. Now, on the evening before the anniversary of my parents' deaths, as we wonder how we can honor them, Hans-Peter asks the question: "Should we use apple blossoms?" In my mind's eye, I see the old apple tree next door to my parents' home, the only remaining tangible connection to our life in Gemünd.

19

Light Glimmers in the Darkest Night

Monday, May 3, 2010. It is 9 a.m., and nine of us are sitting in a small bus parked outside the Ibis Hotel on Al. Pilsudskiego 11. We appear calm and quiet, but internally we feel like astronauts listening to the countdown before blastoff. Today, we will accompany my parents on the anniversary of their death. We are launching into the unknown. The journey will be beyond our control. We are fearful and excited.

Hans-Peter and the driver are at the front desk inside the hotel. Between the ten of us, we speak German, Dutch, Mandarin, and English, but not one word of Polish. Our driver speaks only Polish, his mother tongue. We solve our communication problem with the help of a detailed map of the Warthegau region[1] and the hotel staff, who translate our route for the day to the driver.

Hans-Peter takes his seat beside the driver, who turns the key, and we merge into the morning traffic. Our van is comfortable, the highway is well maintained, and our ride is smooth. The driver turns off the jarring music that had filled the van. In quietness, we can connect with our thoughts. We look out on tranquil villages in all their spring finery, rich with flowers and blossoming fruit trees. Do any of the old people remember the time they were children, when their neighbors disappeared and the Warthegau was declared *Juden rein* (cleansed of Jews)?

Kolo

We have reached Kolo. Hans-Peter points to the railway line on the map. Our driver speaks with a passerby, and we think he is asking directions to the railway station. Kolo is a town, not the village I had imagined. After several turns and past the incongruous sight of a McDonalds, we are relieved to see a small railway station. We park and walk around to the back of the building. We want to physically connect with a patch of ground where sixty-eight years earlier, on or near this day, my parents had been driven out of the packed cattle car. Yesterday, at Radegast Station, Monika told us that Jews deported from Lodz to Chelmno could have been travelling for two or three days without water, food, or toilets, and yet the two places are only 70.5 kilometers apart.

In 1942, the normal rail line from Lodz ended at Kolo. Here, at this station, human cargo was transferred to smaller, open cattle cars, designed for the narrow-gauge tracks that would carry full loads ever closer to their final destination. I imagine my parents emerging from the cattle car, among a great crowd of degraded, dazed, hungry, thirsty souls stumbling across the platform.[2]

Today, we are searching for any remnants of the old, abandoned, narrow-gauge rails, somewhere near the tracks in current use. I am surprised by my first glimpse of the main track. I climb down from the deserted platform for a closer look. Are my eyes deceiving me?

Flowers Appear on the Earth

For lo, the winter is past; the rain is over and gone.
The flowers appear on the earth,
the time of singing has come,
… the voice of the turtle (dove) is heard in our land.
The fig tree puts forth her green figs,
and the vines in blossom give forth their fragrance.

Shir Hashirim[3]

Standing here on the main track, I am surrounded by wildflowers in full bloom. I bend down and pick a bunch of forget-me-nots. I become aware of the birds, their songs blending in harmony. I feel the warmth of the sun. I am overwhelmed by the discovery of beauty in a place where my people were herded with savage injustice.

The group has reached a green patch farther on, and they are signaling for me to come. They have discovered the narrow rails, hiding in shame under a wild garden of plants and trees. We walk together beside the old track, and there before our incredulous gaze, growing between the rails, clothed in a gown of exquisite petals, appears an apple tree, six feet tall!

Hans-Peter asks, "How many branches should we cut?" I ask, "Is it permitted?" He explains, "These fruit trees have been planted by the birds on public land." I pluck a few red petals from the rose given to me in Gemünd at the memorial stone in the jüdische Friedhof, and scatter them on the railway track. We are silent as we return to the van, carrying five apple blossom branches and a bunch of forget-me-nots. Our Polish driver is patiently waiting. Is he wondering how he will describe his unusual assignment when he returns home tonight?

The Mill

My mother and father spent their last night locked inside a mill in the village of Zawadka. Could they sleep lying on the dusty floor? The narrow rails had brought them to Powiercie Station. From there, they had walked 1.5 kilometers through a forest to Zawadka.[4,5]

We park among a cluster of houses. Zawadka is very small. Can we find the mill? Does it still exist? I feel a desperate urgency to connect with my parents in this haunting place. I stand in the middle of the road. Should I knock on a door, even though I don't know the word for "mill" in Polish? Just then my questioning presence disturbs a dog. The dog barks loudly without pause. I feel scared.

A woman comes out of her front door. Her face is friendly and, spurred by my longing, I start to wave my arms in circles like the turning of a mill wheel. I say to her in English, "We are looking for the mill." Her face registers understanding. Immediately and with certainty she leads me to a green mound and points to a pile of old bricks clearly visible under all the weeds. At the same moment, Hans-Peter, knowing that the mill must have been at the water's edge, has worked his way along the bank of the river. He reaches the remnants of the foundation, still jutting out into the river, just beyond the pile of rubble.

We all gather close together. One of us points to an old tree stump, rooted near the foundation of the mill. The stump is split. Out of the gaping slit in the dry, dead tree, a virile, young sapling grows, with branches lifted high, bearing bright, green leaves. David takes a small Bible out of his pocket. He spontaneously reads aloud the words of Job:

> For there is hope for a tree,
> if it be cut down, that it will sprout again,
> and that its shoots will not cease.
> Though its root grow old in the earth,
> and its stump die in the soil,
> yet at the scent of water it will bud
> and put out branches like a young plant.[6]

Without deliberation or discussion, George and I break off two twigs from the apple blossom branches, gently lay them in the river and watch as they swirl in circles before floating away.

A lone fisherman on the opposite bank stands up, stretches, and continues to focus on his line.

Chelmno

On December 7, 1941, as the first seven hundred Jews were being

The river, a new shoot, and me. Photograph by Julia Stone.

deported to the death camp at Chelmno, Japanese aircraft attacked
the United States Fleet at Pearl Harbor. Unknown at the time either
to the Allies or to the Jews of Europe, Roosevelt's day that would "live
in infamy" was also the first day of the "final solution." [7]

Back in the van on the short drive from the ruins of the mill to Chelmno,
I feel a tightness in my throat. Can I go on?

I first heard the name Chelmno (or Kulmhof in Nazi times) in April 2009,
from the lips of Dr. Barbara Becker-Jakli, the historian in Köln, as she
handed me the printed record from her computer. Amalie and Markus
Zack died in Chelmno, May 3, 1942. The name Kulmhof/Chelmno is
repulsive to me. It is forever tainted with vile moral evil. My parents were
asphyxiated, murdered, here on this day sixty-eight years ago. I want to
shut out the malevolent echoes.

⋙ ⋘

As I write this chapter, four months after the journey to Poland, I reread
my journal and relive the events of May 3, 2010. I feel angst (fear) again.
I take a break and chop tomatoes for lunch. An unbidden thought
surfaces: "Being with my parents in the place where they were murdered
is such a small gift to offer them." Then I ask myself, "How would I have
endured being there with them in 1942?"

At the Gate

On this calm, sunny day in May 2010, a festive crowd is coming out
of the church next door to the former Manor House. We stop near a
wrought-iron entrance gate. We are the only visitors. We can easily see
the grounds through the metal bars of the gate, and we recognize the
layout from the Internet photographs we have studied. All that remains
of the baleful Manor House is a large concrete slab, swept clean, between

two huts, surrounded by an expanse of dirt and small stones. On April 7, 1943, the Germans blew up the building where their victims had given up the last of their possessions—watches, wedding rings, clothing—and were quickly herded with shouts and blows up a ramp into the gas vans waiting in the enclosed courtyard.[8,9]

We push down on the handle. The gate is locked. There is no one inside the compound. We linger, perplexed, in the hollow emptiness. A small, elderly man approaches us from a house on our right next to the gate. Our driver talks with him, but, of course, we don't understand their conversation. Is the driver enquiring on our behalf for a way to get in? Whatever he has said, the Polish neighbor of the museum of death is eager to communicate with me. We begin to talk together using our fingers to count and write in the dust! I learn that he is eighty-four years old. He must have been about sixteen on May 3, 1942, when my parents entered the courtyard. He indicates that he has lived in the same house all his life. I write "1942" with my finger in the dirt, and say, "Mama, Papa." I think he understands.

Suddenly, a large tour bus drives up and parks at the gate. A stream of attractive, vibrant, young Jews pours out. An energetic rabbi is leading them on a tour of Jewish sites in Poland. It is good to breathe in their youthful enthusiasm. I read the English translation of the Hebrew words on the backs of their sweatshirts, designed in the form of a candle flame.

> For you promised us
> by your holy name
> That our light would
> never be extinguished.

The Polish guide accompanying the group uses her mobile phone to look for a solution to the problem of the locked gate. All our hopes are dashed as she announces the Chelmno museum will remain closed all day because May 3 is Polish National Day. It is impossible to enter. The rabbi, visibly frustrated, gathers the group, stands with his back to the gate, and gives a short speech, summarizing the history of Chelmno. They all climb back into the bus, and we are left.

We have reached Chelmno on the anniversary of the actual day my parents died. What shall we do? My hands grip the bars of the locked gate; my face is pressed against the metal barrier holding me back from mourning my loss in the spot where my parents took their last breaths. I become aware that I am between Verena from Austria and Jutta from Germany, and the three of us are on our knees at the gate. The sound of weeping breaks my reverie. Verena is pouring out her sorrow in sobs of repentance, coming up from deep within.

Verena was born in 1944. Her father was second in command under the *Gauleiter* (governor) in Salzburg during the Nazi rule in Austria. As a politician, he had helped prepare a landing place for Hitler's invasion of Austria. For the last twenty years, Verena has been in the "school of forgiveness," learning and practicing repentance for family evil and forgiving her father. Jutta prays, broken under the weight of her people's cruelty. A holy moment. The hardness of my own heart over all the years becomes real to me, and I ask God to forgive me.

In the stillness, words came out of my mouth: "Verena, the Lord has heard your tears and confession, and He has forgiven you. And Jutta, the Lord has lifted the guilty burden." What right did I have to speak in that way? As a Jew, how could I say such things? Ancient words spoken by the prophet Isaiah, perhaps 2,700 years ago, become strangely present and alive today:

> *Surely our diseases he did bear,*
> *and our pains he carried;*
> *whereas we did esteem him, stricken,*
> *smitten of God, and afflicted.*

> *But he was wounded because of our transgressions;*
> *he was crushed because of our iniquities:*

the chastisement of our welfare was upon him,
and with his stripes we were healed.

All we like sheep did go astray,
we turned everyone to his own way;
and the LORD hath made to light on him
the iniquity of us all.[10]

And what was the rest of the group doing while Verena, Jutta, and I knelt at the gate? They were kneeling behind us.

We scramble to our feet, take a last look at the vanished Manor House, and re-enter the present. The sound of a cock crowing disturbs the silence.

20

Rzuchowski Forest: "They Burned People Here"

Only a four-kilometer drive from Chelmno and we reach the *Waldlager* (forest camp). We walk into Rzuchowski Forest. From 1941 to 1945, the Waldlager was surrounded by a high, wooden fence with outposts guarded by German SS (an abbreviation for *Schutztaffel*; a literal translation would be "protection squadrons").[1,2] How many bodies were thrown into pits? How many bodies were burned in this place? All reliable data, such as railway records, were deliberately destroyed. Estimated numbers vary: 400,000,[3] 340,000,[4] or at least 152,000.[5] Only seven Jews escaped.

On this fateful Monday in May, as I enter the area of the forest camp, I know I have the freedom to leave, but will I walk out with a wounded soul?

Under the dark, green pines spread high over us, we feel our smallness. What did the oldest, tallest trees see and hear as they stood close together like spectators in a Roman amphitheater? Can they block out the continuous rumble of the grey trucks? Can they ever forget the day when a bolt came loose, the rear doors of the mobile gas chamber opened, and naked bodies fell on the earth?

Do they shudder in the wind?

Can they remember January 19, 1942, when Szlamek Bajler (also known as Yakov Grojanowski)—a youth from Izbica Kujawska, a village 132 kilometers away—made his dramatic escape? He had been pulled out of the crowd arriving in Chelmno and, like other strong young men, was selected to work in the Waldlager, extending his life for perhaps a day . . . a week . . . a month. In the early days of the killing program, before the slave laborers were hobbled by leg irons, Bajler jumped out of the small window of the bus bringing the group of slaves to the forest from Chelmno for the day's labor. He carried his report of carnage in the forest to Warsaw but lived only until April 1942, when he was gassed in Belzec.[6-8]

Fear and Fascination

From ancient times, forests have aroused both fear and fascination in the German imagination. Tribes cleared the trees to develop their settlements. For them, the woods were dangerous, hostile places where wolves and other predators lurked.

My first encounter with the stories collected by the brothers Grimm was in the Köln Jewish hospital just before leaving Germany. I was seven years old, and I remember lying in bed reading and looking at the charming illustrations in a children's book of *Märchen* (folk tales). The stories draw on elemental fears, and the action often takes place in the woods. Two children, Hänsel and Gretel, are lost in a dense forest, abandoned by their stepmother and father during a time of famine. In their hunger, they are tempted by a house made of cake and candy and deceived by an evil witch. The story ends with the witch herself burning in the oven which she has prepared for the innocent children in the depths of the forest. Another child, Little Red Riding Hood, is walking along a forest path taking food to her ailing grandmother who is lying in bed alone in her cottage. This time the deceiver is a wolf, too wily for the child and the old woman whom he has eaten.

Less familiar than Hänsel and Gretel and Little Red Riding Hood is number 110 in Jacob and Wilhelm Grimm's collection of 210 legends in the 1857 edition of *Kinder und Hausmärchen* (Children's and household tales). The title of the story is *"Der Jude im Dorn"* (The Jew in the brambles). Striding through the woods, our hero comes upon an old Jew. Using his newly acquired magic power, he compels the Jew to dance in the brambles, saying, "You've skinned plenty of people; now the brambles can skin you." The torture stops when the Jew hands over a bag of gold. The tale ends in a nearby village, where the hero escapes death by hanging, using his wits and magic to overturn the judgment against him. Instead, guilt is laid on the Jew, and he is hung from the gallows.[9]

The brothers Grimm gathered and recorded the tales people had been telling each other for hundreds of years.[10]

"The Dark Places of the Land Are Full of the Habitations of Violence"[11]

In the Rzuchowski Forest, the story of murder is no folk tale. Cruel and violent death happened on a scale that is unimaginable.

Near the entrance to the forest camp, a massive mausoleum towers over us like a bridge built for a giant. The sculpture was unveiled on September 27, 1964, twenty-five years after the outbreak of World War II. Today it is May 3, 2010, and I tilt my head back, trying to take in the monolith's symbolism. I see echoes of socialist realism towering over me. A procession of children, women, and men staggers across the solid, grey stone. We stand underneath, beside the great pillars raising their heavy burden up to the sky, and feel the crushing weight of the past.

My parents could never tell their story. After July 24, 1939, there was only silence between us. We had no communication, and my engagement with the past began just a few years ago. I am shaken by this sudden, dramatic encounter with their ending, here in the forest.[12]

In front of the enormous mausoleum stands a small monument marking the place where prominent Polish (non-Jewish) intellectuals, professionals, and business leaders were executed in September 1939.[13] We stop and look through the cross-shaped hole cut out of the heart of the small, stone slab, standing upright. We peer through the "window" and see a section of the big, grey monument with the line of doomed Jewish children, women, and men, now framed by the shape of a cross.

We follow the smooth, paved path through empty silence toward our destination. Will we find the location of the pits and incinerators? Without map or guideposts, close together, we stride ahead. We reach another clearing and find a cluster of tombstones, a miniature graveyard. We see the name "Turek" on a signpost. Turek was a *shetl* (Yiddish for village or small town) in the Warthegau region, from where the Jews were plucked from their daily lives—their homes, market, and synagogue—and gassed in the first experimental days of Chelmno. Searching the Internet after our return from Chelmno, I discovered stories and photographs of Jewish families from Turek and the original cemetery before the days of destruction.[14,15]

The names on the tombstones belong to people who had died a natural death, whose bodies had been buried in the Turek Jewish cemetery before 1940. The stones were brought to this site in the forest where the majority of their descendants perished—a mute witness to the disappearance of an entire community.

So many memorials. So many dead. We come to more felled trees and another memorial, this one honoring the 70,000 Jews murdered from the Lodz ghetto.

We continue walking. The tree-lined path under a darkening sky seems endless. Then, we reach the end of the trail. Later, I would write of the experience:

> Our souls encounter disturbed earth . . .
> the wind in the trees lamenting
> dead, naked, emaciated bodies . . .
> dampness in the air.

Into this empty space, the *Sonderwagen* (mobile gas chambers) brought Amalie and Markus Zack.

A Remnant

The genocide in Chelmno took place during two separate periods. Only five Jews escaped in the first stage that lasted from December 7-8, 1941, to April 7, 1943: Szlamek Bajler, Abram Roj, Mordechai Podchlebnik, Yitzhak Justmann, and Yerachmiel Widawski. Szlamek Bajler, described at the beginning of this chapter, did not survive. Abram Roj, the first to escape, eventually emigrated to America, where he died on June 10, 1975. It is believed that Yitzhak Justmann settled in Chicago. Yerachmiel Widawski made his home in Antwerp, Belgium, and died in 1986 at the age of 72.[16,17]

Mordechai Podchlebnik, a leather worker from Kolo, was rounded up in January 1942, when he was thirty-eight years old, as he was doing forced labor in Bugaj, a nearby village.[18] On his arrival in the courtyard of the Manor House, Chelmno, he was selected for slave labor. Three days later, while he was unloading corpses from the gas vans in the forest, he recognized his seven-year-old son, his five-year-old daughter, and his wife. He placed his wife in the pit and pleaded to be shot and join his family. The guard whipped him and said, "You have enough strength; you can work."[19]

Days later, Podchlebnik's *Lebenssucht* (will to live) returned. Early in the morning, the "normal" truck left the Manor House for the forest, filled with slaves for another day's labor. As the truck rattled along the forest road, Podchlebnik asked the SS guard for a cigarette, and when his request was granted, he turned away to light up. When his companions then pressed around the guard begging for a smoke, Podchlebnik swiftly cut the tarpaulin with a small kitchen knife and jumped out of the moving truck. As he ran into the woods, the guard began shooting, but the bullets missed. After hiding in a barn for two days, he came to a cottage where a Polish peasant gave him food, a hat, shaved him, and pointed out the direction to Grabow. A native of Kolo, Podchlebnik was familiar with the area, and he intended to connect with the remaining Jews in Grabow. From there, he made his way beyond the Chelmno region and stayed in hiding.

Podchlebnik's eyewitness account of events in Chelmno was to become critically important because Hitler and his close circle of leaders ordered the total suppression of evidence in the implementation and aftermath of the Final Solution.[20] The Chelmno gassings, burials, and burnings were to be concealed. The German SS officers and police staffing the operation signed documents pledging their secrecy.[21]

After the war, on June 9, 1945, Podchlebnik was called to testify before the Central Commission for Investigation of German Crimes in Poland.[22,23] He was a reluctant witness at the Eichmann trial in Jerusalem on June 5, 1961, Session 65.[24] His 1985 appearance in Claude Lanzmann's film *Shoah* reveals the bitter pain of bringing up his memories.[25] Podchlebnik begins to speak and he is smiling, but as he answers questions about the past, his face crumples, and he weeps.

Podchlebnik's survival and witness to the first phase of mass murder provide a light in the darkness and reveal the truth about the past.[26-29]

The second, shorter phase of operation was from June 23, 1944, to July 14, 1944. By this time, Chelmno was considered to be inefficient, and the last remaining Jews in the Lodz ghetto were taken to Auschwitz.[30]

A group of German *Sonderkommando* (special unit) and forty-seven Jewish slaves remained working in the Rzuchowski Forest. Their assignment was to destroy all the evidence—the Russians were coming. The Germans vainly waited for orders. On the night of January 17-18, 1945, they shot the remaining Jews and fled. Two days later, the Soviet Army reached Chelmno and the Rzuchowski Forest.

Two Jews survived the shooting. One was (Michal) Mordechai Zurawski, a butcher from Wloclawek, who emigrated to Israel in the early 1950s and died there on March 5, 1989.[31] The other was Simon Srebnik (also known as Szymon Srebrnik), whose account would later be immortalized in the film *Shoah*.

Jewish Witnesses to Genocide in Chelmno

The Gassing—Stage I December 7-8, 1941 – April 7, 1943	The Gassing—Stage II June 23, 1944 – July 14, 1944
Three Jewish slave-laborers broke free and testified. There were two other escapees in 1942, Yitzak Justmann and Yerachmiel Widawski, but they are not recorded as witnesses at any trials.	Forty-seven Jewish slave-laborers remained working in the forest until January 17-18, 1945, when they were shot. Two survived.
Abram Roj escaped on January 16, 1942. His story was made known through a published article by his daughter, Sara Roy.	**Mordechai Zurawski** survived and testified: • June 1945 before the Central Commission for Investigation of German Crimes in Poland • June 1961 at the trial of Adolf Eichmann in Jerusalem
Szlamek Bajler (aka **Yakov Grojanowski**) broke free January 19, 1942, and brought his report to the leaders of the Warsaw Ghetto. Gassed April 1942 in Belzec.	**Simon Srebnik** survived and testified: • June 1945 before the Central Commission for Investigation of German Crimes in Poland • June 1961 at the trial of Adolf Eichmann in Jerusalem • 1985 in Claude Lanzmann's film *Shoah*
Mordechai Podchlebnik fled January/February 1942. Survived and testified: • June 9, 1945, before the Central Commission for Investigation of German Crimes in Poland • June 5, 1961, at the trial of Adolf Eichmann in Jerusalem • 1985 in Claude Lanzmann's film *Shoah*	

Sources for this table include the following: District Museum in Konin; Nizkor Project; Montague, *Chelmno and the Holocaust*; Sara Roy's account of her family history; and *Shoah*.[32-36]

Why do I dig so persistently among all the data buried in books and on the Internet? Why do I want to verify the facts—to trace and record the poignant human details? Little is known. Much evidence has been suppressed, destroyed, and denied. Am I gleaning among the stubble for any little stray seed that could connect me with my parents' end? Is this a way of grieving? I want to be a part of telling the truth about Chelmno. I wish to honor each Jew left in the forest. Perhaps I am also delaying the final "goodbye."

Seeing Simon

Back home in Phoenix, the wounded eyes of a small, curly-headed, middle-aged man look at me from the TV screen. I am watching *Shoah*, Claude Lanzmann's film. Simon Srebnik has been brought back to Chelmno from Israel. He stands in the Rzuchowski Forest clearing and says, "It's hard to recognize, but it was here. They burned people here. A lot of people were burned here. Yes, this is the place. No one ever left here again."

The first time Simon Srebnik was brought to Chelmno, he came from the Lodz ghetto. He was thirteen years old. One Sabbath during the summer of 1943, Simon was walking with his father. He heard a shot, and his father fell to the ground. Simon was seized and loaded into a truck. He pleaded with a policeman for permission to go and tell his mother. He knew the policeman. His father had been a hat maker, and Simon was the delivery boy. The policeman was a customer. His request was refused. His mother? She was gassed in the Sonderwagen.

The boy was selected for work. How did he stay alive longer than the other workers? They were all shackled with leg irons, and the Sonderkommando, for their own amusement, organized races and jumping contests using their chained prisoners. Simon won the contests because of his agility.

Then, there was his melodious voice. The Sonderkommando kept rabbits, and several times a week, Simon was sent in a flat-bottomed boat to row up the River Ner, under guard, to the alfalfa fields at the edge of the village to gather food for the rabbits. He sang Polish folk songs, and the guard taught him Prussian military songs. In 1985, older villagers could still remember hearing the beautiful sound of his voice coming from the river.

When the Sonderkommando in their final murderous act aimed a bullet at the head of each remaining Jew, Simon fell and lay wounded among the dead. Somehow the bullet missed his vital brain centers. When he became conscious, he crawled into a pigsty. A Polish farmer found him. He was treated by a Soviet army doctor.

On the screen, Simon Srebnik floats by on a flat bottomed boat singing:

> "A little white house
> lingers in my memory.
> Of that little white house
> I dream each night."

"A Lot of People Were Burned Here"

We come to the end of the road. The ten of us have reached the place where Simon Srebnik stood, looked into the camera in the opening sequence of the film *Shoah,* and said, "They burned people here . . . a lot of people were burned here." Chilled by the vacuum of this forsaken place, we scatter, still searching the ground for signs of pits and incinerators to mark the deaths of my parents.

The wind whips around us, disturbing the weight of death heavy in the air. Rain falls softly. We are shivering in the cold: Hans-Peter, Verena, David, Greetje, Julia, Jutta, Megan, Ryan, George, and I. We find ourselves walking toward a wall at the edge of the clearing.

The 100-foot-long concrete memorial wall near the remains of the largest incinerator was errected in 1990, after the fall of the Berlin Wall and the end of Communism in Poland.[37-39] It is a weather-worn, dejected structure. Could there ever be an adequate memorial for such abhorrent acts? Polish words painted in a single, horizontal, black line span the length of the wall: "In Memory of the Jews Murdered in Chelmno 1941-1945." And, in Hebrew, "The Gate Through Which the Just Will Pass" curves over an open archway in the middle of the wall.

Here, near the foundation of the incinerator, we have found the sacred spot where we will hold a service of remembrance.

21

Friede Eurer Asche
(Peace to Your Ashes)

It is May 3, 2010, and ten of us come together near the foundation of the incinerator in "a land devoured and desolate."[1]

During the first months of the killings, the dead were thrown into pits. The burning of bodies began only in the spring of 1942. The two survivors from the first period of killings described four mass graves more than 100 meters in length. Years later, their testimonies were corroborated by archeological digs.[2-4] Were my parents buried and then further desecrated, pulled out of the pits with the bare hands of Jewish slaves and then burned for fear of typhoid? Or, were they fed to the flames directly from the Sonderwagen? I don't know.

A large family group walks along the wall, peering at the numerous memorial tablets attached to the concrete. We are in a public place. Is it possible to hold a private memorial service here?

The sky gushes water, and the family group scurries away, casting curious looks in our direction. The wind and rain threaten to extinguish the two memorial candles we have lit, one for my mother and the other for my father. Hans-Peter and David bring three concrete slabs from a pile left by the wall and build a shelter to protect the flickering candles.

Jutta pulls a round wooden platter out of her big bag and places it gently on the ground. We move like musicians in an orchestra, responding to an invisible conductor, placing bread, a bottle of wine, a glass, and a bunch of forget-me-nots gathered from the track at Kolo Station on the rustic altar. My parents are looking at us from two black-and-white pictures. Next to them, I lay a letter that I wrote this morning when I first woke up in the Ibis Hotel—a lifetime ago. The letter begins: "*My beloved Mutti und Vati, Here is Hannelore, the little girl you sent away to save her life.*" Carefully I add a small crucifix with Jesus wearing a yellow star. We crown the symbols with a garland of pink and white blossoms—branches cut from the wild apple tree growing between the forgotten, narrow tracks at Kolo. We, too, form a circle with our bodies.

The water splashes down on my parents' pictures. Jutta says, "Heaven is weeping." She takes the white silk scarf from her neck to drape the altar. George covers his head with the blue kippa. We both arrange the white tallit around our heads and shoulders. The last time we wore the tallit we were at the beginning of our journey, praying before the memorial stone in the Jewish cemetery at the edge of Gemünd.

A rustic altar. Photograph by Ryan Thurman.

Today is the anniversary of my parents' death in 1942. A year ago, in the EL-DE-Haus Köln, I heard the word "Chelmno" for the first time. From that moment, the vision to follow their steps developed slowly and gradually. I wanted to honor Markus and Amalie Zack with a remembrance service on the anniversary of their deaths, in the place where they died—to recite a *Yizkor*, ("remember" in Hebrew), a special prayer according to Jewish tradition on behalf of family members who have died.

The day before, when we were in the Jewish cemetery in Lodz and entered the Bait ha Tahara, the funeral house where bodies are prepared for burial, our plan to hold a remembrance ceremony in the Rzuchowski Forest grew to include a symbolic burial. We would combine a funeral service with the ceremony of remembrance.

Kadosh ... Kadosh ... Kadosh
(Holy . . . Holy . . . Holy)

We huddle close together, a *minyan*, ten adults, the number required in Jewish tradition. In the hushed stillness of the clearing, our simple service begins.

With my voice I cry out to the Lord,
with my voice I plead for mercy to the Lord.
I pour out my complaint before him.
I tell my trouble before him.

When my spirit faints within me,
You know my way!
In the path where I walk
they have hidden a trap for me.

Look to the right and see,
there is none who takes notice of me,

FRIEDE EURER ASCHE (PEACE TO YOUR ASHES)

no refuge remains to me,
no one cares for my soul.[5]

My father was a devout Jew. I wonder, "Did such words pour out of his soul as he and my mother stood pressed close with all the other naked bodies, and the steel doors were slammed and bolted shut?"

We open the song books that Verena has prepared for our journey, and ten wavering voices break the repressive silence as we sing in Hebrew *Oseh Shalom* from the Jewish prayer book:

May he who makes peace in the heavens
grant peace to us
and to all our people,
and let us say, Amen.

George never met my parents. On the day they died in Chelmno, Poland, he was a carefree child in Richmond, Virginia, wielding his tiny wooden hammer, pounding brightly colored rods until they disappeared into the holes on his miniature green workbench. I look intently at a photograph from that time and see a nineteen-month-old boy. His face is turned up to the sun, eyes closed tight, mouth open wide with laughter, gleefully pulling away from his mother's hand, eager to explore the wonders of his world.

He has no personal knowledge of the characters or idiosyncrasies of Amalie and Markus Zack, and yet his eulogy for them has an authentic ring. He recounts the testimonies we have heard from Willi Kruff and Lisbet Ernst. He thanks my parents for making the decision that saved my life—for their costly love.

He takes the piece of bread in his hands and breaks it. He asks our Father in Heaven to bless the bread and wine. In this dark death-pit, we give each other the simple food, and our souls are nourished.

Hans-Peter pulls two table forks out of his shirt pocket. This morning he borrowed them with the permission of the Ibis Hotel restaurant. He steps over the low brick wall enclosing the rectangular site of the crematorium. At the corner near the memorial wall, he bends down and easily digs a hole in the soft soil with his improvised tools.

This is the place where ashes mingled. Here my lovely parents were shoveled into the mounds of Semitic dust and shards.

Megan reads the *parashat Bereshit*,[6] the story of Cain and Abel: "And when they were in the field, Cain rose up against his brother Abel and killed him. . . . And the Lord said, 'What have you done? The voice of your brother's blood is crying to Me from the ground.'"

We lift the two, damp tallit from our heads and shoulders, wrap them around the symbols, the blue forget-me-nots, the pictures, the letter, the crucifix with the yellow star, and a few pink and white apple blossoms. We feel the absence of their bodies, the emptiness, as we lower their entwined shrouds into the hole. With tenderness we restore the earth and smooth their grave.

We each hold a sheet of paper. As the child who is mourning the death of my parents, I begin the Mourner's Kaddish:

May His great Name grow exalted and sanctified
(Congregation: ***Amen.***)

in the world that He created as He willed.
May He give reign to His kingship in your lifetimes and in your days,
and in the lifetimes of the entire Family of Israel,
swiftly and soon. Now say:
(Mourners and Congregation: ***Amen. May His great Name be blessed***
forever and ever.)

Blessed, praised, glorified, exalted, extolled,

mighty, upraised, and lauded be the Name of the Holy One. Now say:
(Mourners and Congregation: **Blessed is He.**)

Beyond any blessing and song,
praise and consolation that are uttered in the world. Now say:
(Mourners and Congregation: **Amen.**)

May there be abundant peace from Heaven
and life upon us and upon all Israel. Now say:
(Mourners and Congregation: **Amen.**)

He who makes peace in His heights, may He make peace,
upon us and upon all Israel. Now say:
(Mourners and Congregation: **Amen.**)[7]

I have kept my rain-marked copy of the Kaddish, and now when I hold it in my hands again, I am reminded that our ceremony in the Rzuchowski Forest was no illusion. I was there in the company of a minyan to honor my parents.

We lay the rest of the apple blossoms on the ground within the rectangle. I sprinkle the remaining wine in the corners, and we each leave a stone from Gemünd on the symbolic grave.

We Trust the Flame to Keep Burning

We dismantle the makeshift shelter for our candles and return the concrete slabs to the stack by the memorial wall. What shall we do with the candles? It is the custom to leave them burning for twenty-four hours. During our brief exploration of the area, we discovered a few inches of thick, hollow, metal pipe sticking out from the low, rectangular wall near our grave. Could this be a remnant from the time of fire and smoke? We stand the two lighted candles in the opening and trust the flame to keep burning.

In a final symbolic act, I take off my blue, denim jacket and cut a hole, the expression of mourning at a Jewish funeral, the rending of a garment. On the spur of the moment, I leave the defaced jacket spread out on one of the excavated burial pits.

We turn our backs. Under soft falling rain, we wend our way out of the forest.

A Startling Discovery

Weeks after returning to Phoenix, I continue sorting through the abundant impressions from the time in Poland, assuming I had discovered all I would ever know about my parents' story. I take up the book containing the full text of the film *Shoah* and re-read Simon Srebnik's testimony. According to my understanding, the place of their ending was the incinerator site in the Rzuchowski Forest, where we held the ceremony of remembrance and symbolic burial. Standing at the place in the forest where we gathered, Srebnik says these words,

> *There was a concrete platform some distance away, and the bones that hadn't burned, the big bones of the feet, for example, we took. There was a chest with two handles. We carried the bones there, where others had to crush them. It was very fine, that powdered bone. Then it was put into sacks, and when there were enough sacks, we went to a bridge on the Narew River, and dumped the powder. The current carried it off. It drifted downstream.*[8-10]

I wonder about Mordechai Zurawski, the other slave laborer who escaped at the same time as Srebnik, on January 17, 1945, as the Red Army approached Chelmno. Did he report anything about the secret dumping of Jewish ashes in the river? Online, I search the word "Chelmno" and find the detailed, eyewitness account he gave before a Polish judge, Wladyslaw Bednarz, from the district court of Lodz, in June 1945:

In the forest there were two identical crematoriums [sic]. The tops of the crematoria were at the ground level (they formed a pit). The furnaces were four meters deep, six meters wide, and ten meters long. The sides of the furnace gradually narrowed toward the bottom. . . .

The grate was made of the rails from a narrow-gauge railroad track, the side was made from chamotte brick and concrete. Under the grate there was an ash pit linked with another pit to ensure the proper flow of air to the furnace. A layer of wood was set on fire, on which dead bodies were placed. The corpses had to be arranged in such a way that they did not touch one another. In the lowest level there were twelve people. Their bodies were then covered with another layer of chipped wood and another layer of corpses. In this way the furnace could hold up to 100 bodies at a time. As the corpses burnt down, the free space created at the top was filled with another layer of bodies and wood.

The corpses burned quickly, they turned to ash in more or less fifteen minutes. The ash was then removed from the ash pit with pokers of a special type. These were long iron poles with a forty-centimeter-long iron plate at the end.

Removing the ash was a difficult and hazardous job. No one could keep on with it longer than two or three days, after which the worker was unable to continue and was killed.

The bones and ashes were packed in sacks made of blankets brought by the Jews on transports. But first the bones had to be crushed with wooden stamps on a special cement foundation.

The sacks were driven out of the forest at night to Zawadka Mill and thrown into the River Warta.[11-13]

My passionate desire to find the location of the old mill in the village of Zawadka, the process of finding the ruins by the river, our prayers as we watched the apple blossom twigs swirling in the water before being

247

carried away, all take on a new significance as I read the testimonies of Zurawski and Srebnik. When we stood by the river, I thought we were there to grieve my parents' last night of life. Now I understand. I had been drawn to say goodbye in the place where in the darkness their ashes and crushed bones, mingled with those of so many other burned human beings, were shaken out of a sack, into the water, before drifting away.

Opening the Gift

Did anything happen in Rzuchowski Forest at the end of that six-day journey into the frightening unknown, beyond:

- a few branches missing from a wild apple tree growing between old, narrow tracks at Kolo Railway Station,

- two flowering twigs carried away by the river Ner after circling on the surface next to the ruins of a mill in Zawadka village,

- a virile young tree growing out of the split in a dead tree trunk, embedded at the water's edge,

- some drops of wine mingling with rainwater soaking the soft soil at an excavation site in Rzuchowski Forest,

- ten friends tired after an adventure?

What was the meaning of all those experiences?

Carefully unwrapping those external happenings as if they were intricately printed tissue paper, hesitant to disturb the beauty of their design, I discover a hidden gift. For so many years, I had shuttered my heart, suppressing memories of my mother and father, concealing the loss and grief, fearful of the pain.

My inner isolation began on the evening of July 24, 1939, when my parents helped me to clamber up the frightening, steep, open steps onto the waiting train. I looked down at the holes in the metal grid under my feet. I released their hands. I turned to wave goodbye and saw sorrow in their faces. I crouched in the corner of the carriage. The engine hissed and puffed. Slowly, the train began to move, and unwittingly, I nailed thick bars over the window of my soul.

Gentle, persistent knocking on the barricades has continued throughout the past seventy-one years. Gradually, I have participated in the dismantling of my defenses, leading to this moment.

My parents emerge from the shadows.
They become real.
We embrace.
I release them.
They restore my lost identity.
I am a German, English, Jew.

I hear the words of the prophet Isaiah:

To comfort all that mourn . . .
to give unto them . . .
A Garland for Ashes[14]

. . . and I am strangely consoled.

A Garland for Ashes.
Photograph by Ryan Thurman.

Epilogue

We are a mixed bunch, coming from Phoenix, Austin, Aachen, Oberpleis, Bouderath, and Gemünd, as we hurry down Dreibornerstrasse, our breath blowing little white clouds in the cold evening air. The *Weg der Erinnerung* (Way of Remembrance) ceremony is about to begin.

Here and there, in the lighted shop windows, I catch a glimpse of the same poster hung in a prominent place—a copy of my mother's picture. She is standing in the garden next to a little girl sitting on a swing. My mother and I are on display along Dreibornerstrasse, the street from which we were driven after Kristallnacht.

I have been invited to give a short talk at the beginning of this anniversary of Kristallnacht on November 9, 2011.

The entrance of the small meeting room is crowded with people. The chairs are filled. I stand at the microphone and look at all the eyes focused on me. I see familiar, encouraging faces but also many wary expressions.

What shall I say? I tell about leaving Gemünd, Köln, Germany after Kristallnacht. I share a story or two—the friendship with Willi and Lisbet since my return so many years later. I wonder how the audience is reacting to my presence, a physical reminder of past evil.

I end, saying:

> You may be asking the question, "Why would she return to Gemünd?" *Maria Schmitz-Schumacher asked me the same question in the year*

EPILOGUE

2000 when the four of us, Maria, Dieter, George and I, were sitting around their table drinking coffee and eating cake.

Why would I return to Gemünd?

The question hangs, suspended in a silent moment.

I keep coming back here because the God of Israel has been teaching me about the power of forgiveness. I am still a Jew.

I am a Jew who is a follower of Jesus, our Messiah.

BUNDESREPUBLIK DEUTSCHLAND

Einbürgerungsurkunde

Vorname[n], Familienname, Geburtsname
Johanna Flora MILEY geb. Zack

geboren am	in
18. Februar 1932	Bonn/Deutschland

Wohnort
Phoenix, Arizona / USA

hat mit dem Zeitpunkt der Aushändigung dieser Urkunde die deutsche Staatsangehörigkeit durch Einbürgerung erworben.

Die Einbürgerung hat sich nicht auf Kinder des/der Eingebürgerten erstreckt.

Ort, Datum
Köln, den 26. Februar 2004

Bundesverwaltungsamt

III A 6 - M 76 732

Im Auftrag

Schulz

Ausgehändigt am
APR 1 2 2004

Honorarkonsul
der Bundesrepublik Deutschland
Phoenix

Art.-Nr. 10 001

Bundesdruckerei

Restoration of German citizenship.

Endnotes

Preface

[1] 1 Corinthians 13:8 (English Standard Version).

Part I

[1] To view a photograph of the sculpture see: Great War Forum, "Käthe Kollwitz: 'A Mother and Her Dead Son' (Sculpture): Dragon," November 10, 2008, http://1914-1918.invisionzone.com/forums/index.php?showtopic=110106.

[2] Awad, Peter, "Käthe Kollwitz and The German Expressionists," May 8, 2011, http://perspectiveandstyle.blogspot.com/2011/05/kathe-kollwitz-and-german.html.

[3] Walden, Geoff, "Third Reich Ruins: Ordensburg Vogelsang," July 20, 2000, http://www.thirdreichruins.com/vogelsang.htm.

[4] Heinen, *Gottlos, schamlos, gewissenlos.*

[5] Crossland, David, "World War II: Hitler's Forgotten Castle: Finishing School for Nazis to Become Museum," July 24, 2007, http://www.spiegel.de/international/germany/hitler-s-forgotten-castle-finishing-school-for-nazis-to-become-museum-a-496026-2.html, Part 2.

[6] Crossland, David, "World War II: Hitler's Forgotten Castle: Finishing School for Nazis to Become Museum," July 24, 2007, http://www.spiegel.de/international/germany/hitler-s-forgotten-castle-finishing-school-for-nazis-to-become-museum-a-496026.html.

Chapter 1

[1] Warner Bros, "Into the Arms of Strangers: Stories of the Kindertransport: Study Guide," 2001, http://www2.warnerbros.com/intothearmsofstrangers/.

Chapter 2

[1] Arntz, *Judenverfolgung*, 323.

[2] In a letter dated May 21, 1992, Hans-Dieter Arntz confirmed the year of the expulsion as 1933. He attached a copy of an official letter from the *Gauschützenführer* (Regional Director of the Schützenverein) sent from Köln to all of the Schützenverein in the region, dated May 26, 1937. Number 6 on the list of directives reads, "Members cannot be persons who are not German or of kindred or equal blood." (Translation by George Miley.)

[3] Arntz, *Judenverfolgung*, 352, translation by George Miley.

[4] *Lebensborn* (Wellspring of Life) was a program initiated at the end of 1935. See: Jewish Virtual Library, "The Lebensborn Program," 2012, http://www.jewishvirtuallibrary.org/jsource/Holocaust/Lebensborn.html.

[5] When Willi heard I was writing my story, he sent me copies of several pages from his journal. George has translated the colorful text, laced with phrases used only in the Eifel.

[6] The wooden tapers were frugally cut or split from the blocks used as firewood.

[7] Michiko Kakutani of the *The New York Times* uses the word "memoryscape" in praising W.G. Sebald's book *Austerlitz.* "Books of the Times; In a No Man's Land of Memories and Loss," October 26, 2001, http://www.nytimes.com/2001/10/26/books/books-of-the-times-in-a-no-man-s-land-of-memories-and-loss.html.

Chapter 3

[1] Arntz, *Judenverfolgung,* 363.

[2] *History of Berg Vogelsang,* undated handout distributed at the Ordensburg Vogelsang.

[3] *History of Berg Vogelsang,* undated handout distributed at the Ordensburg Vogelsang.

[4] *History of Berg Vogelsang,* undated handout distributed at the Ordensburg Vogelsang.

[5] NS Documentation Centre, *Cologne during National Socialism,* 152.

[6] Heinen, *Gottlos, schlamos, gewissenlos,* 101.

[7] Universität Hamburg, "The Jewish Community in Hamburg 1860-1943," http://www1.uni-hamburg.de/rz3a035//jew_history4.html.

[8] United States Holocaust Memorial Museum, "Holocaust Encyclopedia: Anti-Jewish Legislation in Prewar Germany," last updated May 11, 2012, http://www.ushmm.org/wlc/en/article.php?ModuleId=10005681.

[9] Arntz, *Judenverfolgung*, 352.

[10] NS Documentation Centre, *Cologne during National Socialism*, 134.

[11] A book written by Martin Davidson, *The Perfect Nazi—Uncovering My SS Grandfather's Secret Past and How Hitler Seduced a Generation*, describes the Brownshirts in vivid detail.

[12] Arntz, *Ordensburg Vogelsang*, 11.

[13] The History Place, "World War II in Europe: The Nuremberg Race Laws," http://www.historyplace.com/worldwar2/timeline/nurem-laws.htm.

[14] United States Holocaust Memorial Museum, "Holocaust Encyclopedia: Anti-Jewish Legislation in Prewar Germany," last updated May 11, 2012, http://www.ushmm.org/wlc/en/article.php?ModuleId=10005681.

[15] United States Holocaust Memorial Museum, "Holocaust Encyclopedia: Examples of Antisemitic Legislation, 1933-1939," last updated May 11, 2012, http://www.ushmm.org/wlc/en/article.php?ModuleId=10007459.

Chapter 4

[1] Arntz, *Reichskristallnacht*, 7-11.

[2] NS-Archiv, "Dokumente zum Nationalsozialismus: Reichspogromnacht, Reichskristallnacht, Fernschreiben Reinhard Heydrich," November 10, 1938, http://www.ns-archiv.de/verfolgung/pogrom/heydrich.php.

[3] Weimarer Republik, "Das NS-Regime," www.dhm.de/lemo/html/nazi.

⁴ Paul, Siegfried, "Die Reichkristallnacht in Hamm," 2011, http://www.polizeihistorischesammlung-paul.de/Reichskristallnacht/reichskristallnacht.htm.

⁵ Arntz, *Reichskristallnacht*, 154-58.

⁶ Arntz, *Reichskristallnacht*, 154.

⁷ Arntz, *Reichskristallnacht*, 163.

⁸ United States Holocaust Memorial Museum, "Holocaust Encyclopedia: Kristallnacht: A Nationwide Pogrom, November 9-10, 1938," last updated May 11, 2012, http://www.ushmm.org/wlc/en/article.php?ModuleId=10005201.

⁹ Arntz, *Reichskristallnacht*, 163.

Chapter 5

¹ *Into the Arms of Strangers* is an Academy Award-winning documentary film that recounts the stories of children who were rescued by the Kindertransport. Harrison, Mark Jonathan (writer and director), 2002, *Into the Arms of Strangers: Stories of the Kindertransport*, Warner Brothers.

² Jewish Virtual Library, "Horst Wessel," 2012, http://www.jewishvirtuallibrary.org/jsource/biography/Wessel.html.

³ Roodenburg, *Social Control in Europe*, 249.

⁴ Schumann, *Hitler and the Nazi Dictatorship*, 368.

[5] Hess, Rudolf, "German Propaganda Archive. The Launching of the Training Ship Horst Wessel," 1998, http://www.calvin.edu/academic/cas/gpa/hess3.htm.

[6] Jewish Virtual Library, "Horst Wessel," 2012, http://www.jewishvirtuallibrary.org/jsource/biography/Wessel.html.

[7] Wikipedia, "Horst-Wessel," last updated August 13, 2012, http://en.wikipedia.org/wiki/Horst_Wessel.

[8] Seder: a ceremonial meal at the beginning of the Jewish Passover held on the 15th of Nisan, either in March or April.

[9] The Sütterlinschrift, created by Ludwig Sütterlin, was taught in German schools from 1915 to 1941. It was banned in 1941 because people in the conquered territories could not understand Nazi commands written in Sütterlin. See: Read Suetterlin/Read Blackletters, "Here you can learn Suetterlin – 'The German Handwritting', "http://www.suetterlinschrift.de/Englisch/Sutterlin.htm.

[10] Bocek, Jonathan, "What is Sütterlin Script," http://www.dererstezug.com/Suetterlin.htm.

[11] Becker-Jakli, *Das jüdische Krankenhaus in Köln,* 163, 168.

[12] United States Holocaust Memorial Museum, "Holocaust Encyclopedia: Anti-Jewish Legislation in Prewar Germany," last updated May 11, 2012, http://www.ushmm.org/wlc/en/article.php?ModuleId=10005681.

[13] Becker-Jakli, *Das jüdische Krankenhaus in Köln*, 254-300.

[14] The History Place, "World War II in Europe: The Nuremberg Race Laws, "http://www.historyplace.com/worldwar2/timeline/nurem-laws.htm.

[15] Corbach, *Die Jawne zu Köln*, 282-86.

[16] Lissner and Reuter, *Andererseits komme ich anfangs nächster Woche*, 90.

[17] Corbach, *Die Jawne zu Köln*.

[18] Corbach, *Die Jawne zu Köln*, 297.

[19] United States Holocaust Memorial Museum, "Holocaust Encyclopedia: Einsatzgruppen and Other SS and Police Units in the Soviet Union," last updated May 11, 2012, http://www.ushmm.org/wlc/en/article.php?ModuleId=10005518.

Chapter 6

[1] Hatchett, *Commentary on the American Prayer Book*, 366.

[2] The Nizkor Project, "My first and foremost task...," http://www.nizkor.org/hweb/people/h/hitler-adolf/hitler-1922.html.

[3] NS Documentation Centre, *Cologne during National Socialism*, 88.

[4] Florida Center for Instructional Technology, "A Teacher's Guide to the Holocaust: The Nazification of Germany," 2005, http://fcit.usf.edu/holocaust/timeline/nazifica.htm.

[5] United States Holocaust Memorial Museum, "Holocaust Encyclopedia: Boycott of Jewish Businesses," last updated May 11, 2012, http://www.ushmm.org/wlc/en/article.php?ModuleId=10005678.

[6] Florida Center for Instructional Technology, "A Teacher's Guide to the Holocaust: The Nazification of Germany," 2005, http://fcit.usf.edu/holocaust/timeline/nazifica.htm.

7 United States Holocaust Memorial Museum, "Holocaust Encyclopedia: Anti-Jewish Legislation in Prewar Germany," last updated May 11, 2012, http://www.ushmm.org/wlc/en/article.php?ModuleId=10005681.

8 Shaw, Annette, "The Evian Conference - Hitler's Green Light for Genocide," 2001, http://www.cdn-friends-icej.ca/antiholo/evian/evian.html, Introduction.

9 There are multiple sources for this information. A detailed history is in Bullock, *Hitler, A Study in Tyranny*, 425-35. See also Wikipedia, "The Anschluss," http://en.wikipedia.org/wiki/Anschluss.

10 Shaw, Annette, "The Evian Conference - Hitler's Green Light for Genocide," 2001, http://www.cdn-friends-icej.ca/antiholo/evian/chapter1.html, Chapters 1-4, Conclusion.

11 Jewish Virtual Library, "The Virtual Jewish History Tour: Switzerland. The Holocaust," 2012, http://www.jewishvirtuallibrary.org/jsource/vjw/swiss.html.

12 United States Holocaust Memorial Museum, "Holocaust Encyclopedia: German Jews during the Holocaust, 1939-1945," last updated May 11, 2012, http://www.ushmm.org/wlc/en/article.php?ModuleId=10005357.

13 Fiddlers Green, "The WWII Nazi DFS-230 Invasion Glider," http://www.fiddlersgreen.net/models/aircraft/DFS-230-glider.html.

14 United States Holocaust Memorial Museum, "German Invasion of Western Europe, May 1940," http://www.ushmm.org/wlc/en/article.php?ModuleId=10005181.

222222222222222222222222222222222ff22222

[15] Wikipedia, "Bombing of Cologne in World War II," last updated September 6, 2012, http://en.wikipedia.org/wiki/Bombing_of_Cologne_in_World_War_II.

[16] Museum of Tolerance, "All Necessary Preparations: 1933-1941," 1997, http://motlc.wiesenthal.com/site/pp.asp?c=gvKVLcMVIuG&b=394917.

[17] United States Holocaust Memorial Museum, "Holocaust Encyclopedia: German Jews during the Holocaust, 1939-1945," last updated May 11, 2012, http://www.ushmm.org/wlc/en/article.php?ModuleId=10005357.

Chapter 7

[1] Corbach, *Departure 6.00 am Messe Köln*, 51, translation from German to English by George Miley.

[2] Corbach, *Departure 6.00 am Messe Köln*, 28, 610.

[3] Corbach, *Departure 6.00 am Messe Köln*, 666, Document 18.

[4] Corbach, *Departure 6.00 am Messe Köln*, 665.

[5] Corbach, *Departure 6.00 am Messe Köln*, 667.

[6] Sterling, *Life in the Ghettos during the Holocaust*, 102.

[7] Kogon, *Nazi Mass Murder*, 73.

[8] Langer, *Art from the Ashes*, 154.

[9] Kogon, *Nazi Mass Murder*, 145.

[10] Kogon, *Nazi Mass Murder*, 76, 77.

[11] Struck, *Chelmno/Kulmhof,* 99-111.

[12] Kogon, *Nazi Mass Murder*, 52.

[13] Kogon, *Nazi Mass Murder*, 77.

[14] Holocaust Education and Archive Research Team, "Chelmno Death Camp," 2007, http://www.holocaustresearchproject.org/othercamps/chelmno.html.

[15] Krakowski, *Das Todeslager Chelmno/Kulmhof,* 72, 73.

[16] Dobroszycki, *The Chronicles of the Lodz Ghetto 1941-1944*, ix.

[17] Krakowski, *Das Todeslager Chelmno/Kulmhof,* 73, translation by George Miley.

[18] Kogon, *Nazi Mass Murder*, 81, 82.

[19] The Holocaust—Lest We Forget, "Chelmno—the perpetrators," http://www.holocaust-lestweforget.com/chelmno-perpetrators.html, and Kogon, *Nazi Mass Murder*, 101.

[20] Kogon, *Nazi Mass Murder*, 276.

[21] Kogon, *Nazi Mass Murder*, 80.

[22] Erhard Michelsohn, a German school teacher who lived in Kulmhof, and Kurt Möbius, a member of the Sonderkommando (special unit) in Kulmhof, described the fate of the victims from the moment they arrived at the castle. See: Kogon, *Nazi Mass Murder*, 80,83.

[23] Montague, *Chelmno and the Holocaust*, 77.

[24] Langer, *Art from the Ashes*, 56.

[25] Kogon, *Nazi Mass Murder*, 83.

[26] Kogon, *Nazi Mass Murder*, 86.

[27] Kogon, *Nazi Mass Murder*, 84.

[28] Kogon, *Nazi Mass Murder*, 84.

[29] Kogon, *Nazi Mass Murder*, 86-87.

[30] Kogon, *Nazi Mass Murder*, 77.

[31] Kogon, *Nazi Mass Murder*, 79.

[32] The History Place, "Biographies of Nazi Leaders: Adolf Eichmann," 1997, http://www.historyplace.com/worldwar2/biographies/eichmann-biography.htm.

[33] "This Day in History December 15, 1961: Architect of the Holocaust Sentenced to Die," http://www.history.com/this-day-in-history/architect-of-the-holocaust-sentenced-to-die.

[34] Langer, *Art from the Ashes*, 57-58.

[35] Aktion Reinhard Camps, "Chelmno," last updated August 26, 2006, http://www.deathcamps.org/occupation/chelmno.html.

[36] Jewish Virtual Library, "Adolf Eichmann," 2012, http://www.jewishvirtuallibrary.org/jsource/Holocaust/eichmann.html.

[37] Kogon, *Nazi Mass Murder*, 89.

[38] Sterling, *Life in the Ghettos during the Holocaust*, 233.

[39] Kogon, *Nazi Mass Murder*, 90.

[40] Gilead, Isaac, Yoram Haimi and Wojciech Mazurek, "Excavating Nazi Extermination Centres," 2009, http://www.presentpasts.info/article/view/pp.12/2.

[41] Habakkuk 1:2 (A Hebrew-English Bible: According to the Masoretic Text and the JPS 1917 Edition), http://www.mechon-mamre.org/p/pt/pt2001.htm.

[42] Habakkuk 3:17-19a (A Hebrew-English Bible: According to the Masoretic Text and the JPS 1917 Edition), http:www.mechon-mamre.org/p/pt/pt2003.htm.

Part II

Chapter 8

[1] Translation by George Miley.

[2] For a concise, objective summary of Christadelphian beliefs see: Zavada, Jack, "Christianity: Christadelphian Beliefs and Practices," 2012, http://christianity.about.com/od/christadelphians/a/christadelphianbeliefs.htm.

[3] Among the papers from my past is a copy of an old British form with my name and personal details. The entry beside the word "GUARANTOR" is hastily handwritten and unevenly squeezed into the small space. It reads: "CASE BEING DEALT WITH BY BIRMINGHAM JEWISH UNITED BENEVOLENT BOARD," thus confirming that my parents sent me without a British sponsor or guarantor. The old form is a testimony to the overwhelmed rescuers and to the terror and faith of my parents.

4 While reviewing this manuscript, I traced Roddy's telephone number and called him. His first words after seventy-three years were, "It's Hannelore!" We talked and talked, and I learned something of the deep pain the Calcotts had experienced in our parting.

5 Adams, Stephen, "Sir Nicholas Winton, the 'British Schindler', meets the Holocaust survivors he helped save," September 4, 2009, http://www.telegraph.co.uk/history/world-war-two/6138441/Sir-Nicholas-Winton-the-British-Schindler-meets-the-Holocaust-survivors-he-helped-save.html.

6 Salzman, L.F., ed., "Parishes: Exhall, A History of the County of Warwick: Volume 6: Knightlow hundred," http://www.british-history.ac.uk/report.aspx?compid=57102.

7 The History Place, "Holocaust Timeline," 1997, http://www.historyplace.com/worldwar2/holocaust/timeline.html.

8 United States Holocaust Memorial Museum, "Holocaust Encyclopedia: Blitzkrieg (Lightening War)," last updated May 11, 2012, http://www.ushmm.org/wlc/en/article.php?ModuleId=10005437.

9 Howard, *Ruined and Rebuilt*, 22.

10 From the wreckage of the Coventry Cathedral, a ministry of reconciliation has sprouted far beyond Coventry, reaching even to the city of Dresden, Germany. Dresden was devastated in a series of Allied bombing raids in February 13-14, 1945, leaving death, destruction, and wounded souls. See: BBC, "Coventry and Warwickshire, The Blitz Stories from Coventry's Twin City of Dresden," http://news.bbc.co.uk/local/coventry/hi/people_and_places/history/newsid_9155000/9155684.stm, and "Coventry and Dresden—A Friendship Spanning Fifty Years," February 13, 2009, http://www.coventry.anglican.org/news/pressreleases/opt/0/download/532.

Chapter 9

[1] "Ol' Man River" is a song of slaves from the 1927 musical *Showboat*, written by Jerome Kern and Oscar Hammerstein II. Translation: I get weary and sick of trying. I'm tired of living and scared of dying. But old man river, he just keeps rolling along!

[2] Horatius Bonar, a Scottish minister, based his 1846 hymn on the text Matthew 11:28-30.

Part III

[1] The Feast of All Saints, "Ever Ancient, Ever New," www.feastofsaints.com/ancientnew.htm.

Chapter 11

[1] Graham, *Just As I Am*, 225.

[2] *In the dark time of the year. Between melting and freezing. The soul's sap quivers.* T. S. Eliot, "Four Quartets. Little Gidding," http://allspirit.co.uk/gidding.html.

[3] Acts 17:30-31 (King James Version).

[4] The Rubicon is a small stream in northern Italy, crossed by Julius Caesar and his army in the year 49 BC. "An ancient Roman law forbade any general from crossing the Rubicon River and entering Italy proper with a standing army. To do so was treason. This tiny stream would reveal Caesar's intentions and mark the point of no return." (See: "Julius Caesar crosses the Rubicon: 49 BC, http://www.eyewitnesstohistory.com/caesar.htm.) Today, the term "crossing the Rubicon" refers to making an irreversible and highly consequential decision.

⁵ Reference to Revelation 7:17 (English Standard Version).

⁶ A hymn by Samuel Crossman, 1664.

⁷ The portrayal of Kate in this paragraph is a mingling of memories, Shirley's and mine.

Chapter 12

¹ "On the Road Again" is a song by Willie Nelson, and is part of the soundtrack to the 1980 movie *Honeysuckle Rose*.

Chapter 13

¹ British Library, "Bombay: History of a City," http://www.bl.uk/learning/histcitizen/trading/bombay/history.html.

² Wikipedia, "History of Mumbai," http://en.wikipedia.org/wiki/History_of_Mumbai.

³ Haub, Carl and O.P. Sharma, "India's Population Reality: Reconciling Change and Tradition. Table 1. Population size and growth, India, 1901-2001," http://www.prb.org/pdf06/61.3IndiaspopulationReality_Eng.pdf.

⁴ Acharya, Arun Kumar and Parveen Nangia, "Population Growth and Changing Land-use Patterns in Mumbai Metropolitan Region of India," December 2003, http://www.google.com/url?sa=t&rct=j&q=&esrc=s&frm=1&source=books&cd=1&cad=rja&ved=0CDQQFjAA&url=http%3A%2F%2Fwww.seer.ufu.br%2Findex.php%2Fcaminhosdegeografia%2Farticle%2Fdownload%2F15332%2F8631&ei=6XU2UO-_L6WO2QXdo4HQCg&usg=AFQjCNGteAVOEQACDjyafVVjBzWQuYiqOQ&sig2=b-WLd5aljsuidcoaDPhnNA.

Part IV

Chapter 14

[1] Arntz, *Judenverfolgung*, 715.

[2] Wikipedia, Torun, http://en.wikipedia.org/wiki/Toru%C5%84#History.

[3] During our stay in Brodnica, I picked up a modest, one-page, folded brochure, written in English and in German, titled "Brodnica," containing a concise overview of my father's home town. It is with me as I write.

[4] International Jewish Cemetery Project, "Brodnica: Torinskie," http://www.iajgsjewishcemeteryproject.org/poland/brodnica-torinskie.html.

[5] I gleaned most of these dates and statistics from the Web a few years after our return from that initial visit to Poland. See: Virtual Shtetl, "Brodnica: History," http://www.sztetl.org.pl/en/article/brodnica/5,history/.

[6] Virtual Shtetl, "Brodnica: History" and "Brodnica: Demography," http://www.sztetl.org.pl/en/article/brodnica/5,history/ and http://www.sztetl.org.pl/en/article/brodnica/6,demography/.

[7] International Jewish Cemetery Project, "Brodnica: Torinskie," http://www.iajgsjewishcemeteryproject.org/poland/brodnica-torinskie.html.

[8] It was permitted to walk within the city, no matter how large, and without the city 2,000 cubits (.596 miles, or 960 meters). See: Jewish Encyclopedia, "Sabbath. Sabbath Journey Limited," http://www.jewishencyclopedia.com/articles/12962-sabbath.

Chapter 15

[1] Nature Preserve Maasberg, "Unique Cultural Heritage: Nahe Valley and Hunsrück," http://www.maasberg.ch/English.html.

[2] "Take us the foxes, the little foxes, that spoil the vineyards; for our vineyards are in blossom." Song of Songs 2:15 (A Hebrew English Bible: According to the Masoretic Text and the JPS 1917 Edition), http://www.mechon-mamre.org./p/pt/pt3002.htm.

[3] Arntz, *Judenverfolgung*, 352.

[4] Alemannia Judaica, "Waldhilbersheim mit Heddesheim. Zur Geschichte der Synagoge," January 2012, http://www.alemannia-judaica.de/waldhilbersheim_synagoge.ht, translation by George Miley.

[5] Alemannia Judaica, "Waldhilbersheim mit Heddesheim. Zur Geschichte der Synagoge," January 2012, http://www.alemannia-judaica.de/waldhilbersheim_synagoge.ht, translation by George Miley.

[6] Zentralarchiv zur Erforschung der Geschichte der Juden in Deutschland. "Jüdische Friedhöfe in Deutschland: Rheinland-Pfalz. Waldhilbersheim," 2006, http://www.zentralarchiv.uni-hd.de/FRIEDHOF/PFALZ/PROJEKTE/f-rlp-nz.htm#Waldhilbersheim.

[7] A good photograph of the cemetery is available at: Alemannia Judaica, "Die jüdischen Friedhöfe im Landkreis Bad Kreuznach (KH, Rheinland-Pfalz). Guldental-Waldhilbersheim (VG Langenlonsheim)," 2011, http://www.alemannia-judaica.de/bad_kreuznach_friedhoefe.htm#Guldental.

[8] James 4:14 (English Standard Version).

9 Foundation for the Preservation of Jewish Heritage in Poland, "News: 2006-11-16 Izbica," November 16, 2006, http://fodz.pl/?d=2&id=290&l=en.

10 Aktion Reinhard Camps, "The Lublin District Transit Ghettos Izbica, Piaski and Rejowiec," last updated September 16, 2006, http://www.deathcamps.org/occupation/transit%20ghettos.html.

11 Mahnmal Koblenz, "Der Güterbahnhof Koblenz-Lützel," http://mahnmal-koblenz.de/index.php/staetten-der-verfolgung/der-gueterbahnhof-luetzel.

12 Holocaust Education Archive and Research Team, "Izbica Ghetto," 2007, http://www.holocaustresearchproject.org/ghettos/izbica/izbica.html, and K. Bielawski, "Izbica," http://www.kirkuty.xip.pl/izbicaang.htm.

13 Translation by George Miley.

14 Corbach, *Departure 6.00 am Messe Köln*, 383.

15 Translation/paraphrase by George Miley.

16 Mama, who are you?

Part V

1 Nouwen, *A Restless Soul*, 134.

Chapter 16

1 A minyan is the minimum number required to recite Kaddish, a prayer for the dead according to Jewish custom.

² Chevra Kadisha: from an Aramaic word meaning "holy society"—in English, "burial society"—a loosely structured, generally closed organization, often associated with a synagogue. See: Tikvat Israel Congregation, "A Guide to Jewish Mourning Practices," July 12, 2010, http://tikvatisrael.org/about/committees/bereave5.pdf.

³ Sierakowiak and Adelson, *The Diary of Dawid Sierakowiak*, 8.

⁴ Arntz, *Judenverfolgung*, 328.

⁵ A modern innovation for girls following the older tradition of *bar mitzvah*, when a boy at the age of thirteen, takes responsibility to follow Jewish law.

⁶ Translation by George Miley.

⁷ Becker-Jakli, *Das jüdische Krankenhaus in Köln*, 325.

⁸ Lebensgeschichten, "Sammellager in Köln," 2009, http://www.lebensgeschichten.net/index1small.asp?typ=L.

Chapter 17

¹ Martin Luther's sympathy toward Jews evaporated when they failed to respond to his invitation to convert. In 1542, three years before his death, he published an essay, "Concerning the Jews and Their Lies." He wrote, "First their synagogues … should be set on fire, and whatever does not burn up should be covered or spread over with dirt …." See: Goldstein, *A Convenient Hatred*, 124.

² There are many sources for this information. See: The History Place, "Holocaust Timeline: The Death of Hitler," 1997, http://www.historyplace.com/worldwar2/holocaust/h-death.htm.

[3] There are many sources for this information. See: Jewish Virtual Library, "Maximilian Kolbe," 2012, http://www.jewishvirtuallibrary. org/jsource/biography/Kolbe.html.

Chapter 18

[1] Translation: "At last, Litzmannstadt." Lodz was known as Litzmannstadt during World War II.

[2] Corbach, *Departure 6.00 am Messe Köln*, 383.

[3] Sierakowiak and Adelson, *The Diary of Dawid Sierakowiak*.

[4] Urzad Miasta, "Litzmannstadt Ghetto," map and information brochure.

[5] Grossman, *With a Camera in the Ghetto*.

[6] Sierakowiak and Adelson, *The Diary of Dawid Sierakowiak*.

[7] Zyskind, *Stolen Years*, 59.

[8] Dobroszycki, *The Chronicles of the Lodz Ghetto*.

[9] Holocaust Education and Archive Research Team, "The Lodz Ghetto. The Beginning of the 'Closed District'," 2007, http://www. holocaustresearchproject.org/ghettos/Lodz/lodzghetto.html.

[10] Fundacja Monumentum Iudaicum Lodzense, "Radegast," http://www. lodzjews.org/root/form/en/radegast/index.asp.

[11] "Litzmannstadt Getto: The Radogoszcz (Radegast) Station, or the loading platform at Marysin Verladebahnhof Getto-Radegast Stalowa Street," http://www.lodz-ghetto.com/the_radegast_station.html,38.

¹² Zyskind, *Stolen Years*, 10.

Chapter 19

¹ Warthegau: the name given to the central region of Poland, including Lodz and the surrounding area, during the Nazi occupation.

² To view photos of the transfer at Kolo Station see: Aktion Reinhard Camps, "From Kolo to Chelmno," last updated May 28, 2006, http://www.deathcamps.org/occupation/kolo.html.

³ Shir Hashirim (Song of Songs) 2:11-13 (A Hebrew-English Bible: According to the Masoretic Text and the JPS 1917 Edition), http://www.mechon-mamre.org/e/et/et3002.htm.

⁴ Aktion Reinhard Camps, "Chelmno," last updated August 26, 2006, http://www.deathcamps.org/occupation/chelmno.html.

⁵ "Chelmno nad Ner Route to Zawadka," YouTube video, 0:25, posted by "alanheath," September 16, 2007, http://www.youtube.com/watch?v=dZtoKxcsvsI.

⁶ Job 14:7-9 (English Standard Version).

⁷ Gilbert, *The Holocaust*, 240.

⁸ The Nizkor Project, "Central Commission for Investigation of German Crimes in Poland: German Crimes in Poland (Warsaw, 1946, 1947): Extermination Camp Chelmno," http://www.nizkor.org/hweb/camps/chelmno/report.html. (Note: The word "Nizkor" is Hebrew for "We will remember.")

[9] Holocaust Education and Archive Research Team, "Chelmo Death Camp," 2007, http://www.holocaustresearchproject.org/othercamps/chelmno.html.

[10] Isaiah 53:4-6 (A Hebrew-English Bible: According to the Masoretic Text and the JPS 1917 Edition), http://www.mechon-mamre.org/e/et/et1053.htm.

Chapter 20

[1] United States Holocaust Memorial Museum, "Holocaust Encyclopedia: SS and the Camp System," last updated May 11, 2012, http:www.ushmm.org/wlc/en/article.php?ModuleId=10007399.

[2] Aktion Reinhard Camps, "Chelmno," last updated August 26, 2006, http://www.deathcamps.org/occupation/chelmno.html.

[3] Lanzmann, *Shoah*.

[4] The Nizkor Project, "Central Commission for Investigation of German Crimes in Poland: German Crimes in Poland (Warsaw, 1946, 1947): Extermination Camp Chelmno," http://www.nizkor.org/hweb/camps/chelmno/report.html.

[5] Aktion Reinhard Camps, "Chelmno," 2006, http://deathcamps.org/occupation/chelmno.html.

[6] His detailed testimony under the name of Yakov Grojanowski is the Jewish Historical Institute in Warsaw (copy in YVA, JM/2713).

[7] Aktion Reinhard Camps, "Szlamek Bajler, also known as Yakov Grojanowski," last updated August 24, 2006, http://www.deathcamps.org/occupation/bajler.html.

[8] Holocaust Education and Archive Research Team, "Belzec: Remember Me," 2007, http://www.holocaustresearchproject.org/ar/belzec/belzecrememberme.html.

[9] Friedman, *A History of the Holocaust*, 1.

[10] Ashliman, D.L., "The Grimm Brothers' Children's and Household Tales (Grimms' Fairy Tales)," last updated September 20, 2011, http://www.pitt.edu/~dash/grimmtales.html.

[11] Psalm 74:20 (A Hebrew-English Bible. According to the Masoretic Text, JPS, 1917 edition), http://www.mechon-mamre.org/e/et/et2674.htm.

[12] In 1961, after years of neglect, a Polish government organization, "Council for the Protection of Monuments of Combat and Martyrdom," turned to the Rzuchowski Forest. Józef Stasiński, a visual artist, was the monolith's designer, and the architect Jerzy Buszkiewicz oversaw construction. See: The District Museum in Konin, "Chelmno: The History of Chelmno Commemoration," http://www.muzeum.com.pl/en/chelmno.htm.

[13] Thaler, Michael, "H-Holocaust: Discussion Logs: Travel in Poland," June 18, 2000, http://h-net.msu.edu/cgi-bin/logbrowse.pl?trx=vx&list=H-Holocaust&month=0006&week=c&msg=km9s8id%2bJjVpcViLVFqagA&user=&pw=.

[14] Seiffe, J., "The History of Turek," last updated December 20, 2005, http://www.jewishgen.org/yizkor/turek/tur459.html.

[15] Pentlin, Susan, Dr., "We Remember Jewish Turek!" last updated November 22, 2007, http://www.zchor.org/turek/turek.

[16] Aktion Reinhard Camps, "Szlamek Bajler, also known as Yakov Grojanowski," last updated August 24, 2006, http://www.deathcamps.org/occupation/bajler.html.

[17] Montague, *Chelmno and the Holocaust*, 128, 148, 196, 219-220, 242.

[18] Holocaust Education and Archive Research Team, "Michal Podchlebnik: Chelmno Survivor Testimony," 2008, http://www.holocaustresearchproject.org/survivor/podchlebnik.html.

[19] Lanzmann, *Shoah*, 7.

[20] Echoes and Reflections, "FAQ about the Holocaust: How did the Nazis try to hide their atrocities?" http://www.echoesandreflections.org/additional_resources/faq.asp.

[21] For the interview of Franz Schalling, a German policeman in Chelmno 1941-42, see Claude Lanzmann's book, *Shoah*, 63.

[22] A variety of documents spanning forty years record his first name as "Mordechai," "Michael," or "Michal" and his last name as "Podchlebnik" or "Podklebnik."

[23] The Nizkor Project, "Central Commission for Investigation of German Crimes in Poland: German Crimes in Poland (Warsaw, 1946, 1947): Extermination Camp Chelmno," http://www.nizkor.org/hweb/camps/chelmno/report.html.

[24] Gilbert, *The Holocaust*, 248, 852.

[25] Lanzmann, *Shoah*, 4, 7, 67, 68.

[26] All three survivors—Podchlebnik from the first killing period, and Zurawski and Srebnik from the second—testified at the district court of Lodz in 1945 and at the Eichmann trial in Jerusalem, April 11, 1961, to May 29 1962. See Montague, *Chelmno and the Holocaust*, 219, and http://www.nizkor.org/ftp.cgi/people/e/eichmann.adolf/transcripts/Sessions, sessions 066-02 (Srebnik), 065.05 (Podchlebnik), and 065-06 (Zurawski).

[27] Holocaust Education and Archive Research Team, "Michal Podchlebnik," 2008, http://www.holocaustresearchproject.org/survivor/podchlebnik.html, and http://resources.ushmm.org/film/display/detail.php?file_num=2280.

[28] Holocaust Education and Archive Research Team, "Szymon Srebrnik," 2008, http://www.holocaustresearchproject.org/survivor/srebrnik.html, and http://resources.ushmm.org/film/display/detail.php?file_num=2282&clip_id=B0665935-9C6E-4F6A-9F47-6166DBE4DF1D.

[29] Holocaust Education and Archive Research Team, "The Trial of Adolf Eichmann," 2007, http://www.holocaustresearchproject.org/trials/eichmanntrial.html.

[30] The District Museum in Konin, "Chelmno," http://www.muzeum.com.pl/en/chelmno.htm.

[31] Montague, *Chelmno and the Holocaust*, 221.

[32] The District Museum in Konin, "Chelmno," http://www.muzeum.com.pl/en/chelmno.htm.

[33] The Nizkor Project, "The Trial of Adolf Eichmann: The District Court Sessions: Session-066-03," 1999, http://nizkor.org/ftp.cgi/people/e/eichmann.adolf/transcripts/ftp.py?people/e/eichmann.adolf/transcripts/Sessions/Session-066-03.

[34] Lanzmann, *Shoah*.

[35] Montague, *Chelmno and the Holocaust*, 110, 218-221.

[36] Roy, "The Journey of a Child of Holocaust Survivors," http://www.palestine-studies.org/journals.aspx?id=4672&jid=1&href=abstract.

[37] In the 1980s, the district museum of nearby Konin began interpreting aerial photographs and excavating the area, discovering remains from the foundation of the incinerator. See: The District Museum in Konin, "Chelmno," http://www.muzeum.com.pl/en/chelmno.htm.

[38] Thaler, Michael, "H-Holocaust: Discussion Logs: Travel in Poland," June 18, 2000, http://h-net.msu.edu/cgi-bin/logbrowse.pl?trx=vx&list=H-Holocaust&month=0006&week=c&msg=km9s8id%2bJjVpcViLVFqagA&user=&pw=.

[39] Gilead, Isaac, Yoram Haimi and Wojciech Mazurek, "Excavating Nazi Extermination Centres," 2009, http://www.presentpasts.info/article/view/pp.12/2.

Chapter 21

[1] Reference to Isaiah 1:7 (English Standard Version).

[2] Aktion Reinhard Camps, "Chelmno," last updated August 26, 2006, http://www.deathcamps.org/occupation/chelmno.html.

[3] The District Museum in Konin, "Chelmno: The History of Chelmno Commemoration," http://www.muzeum.com.pl/en/chelmno.htm.

[4] Gilead, Isaac, Yoram Haimi and Wojciech Mazurek, "Excavating Nazi Extermination Centres," 2009, http://www.presentpasts.info/article/view/pp.12/2.

⁵ Psalm 142:1-4 (English Standard Version).

⁶ Hebrew for "portion of the book of Genesis."

⁷ Judaism 101, "Mourner's Kaddish," http://www.jewfaq.org/kaddishref. htm.

⁸ Lanzmann, *Shoah*, 10-11.

⁹ The German army surrendered on May 7, 1945, and the provisional Polish government set up the Central Commission for the Investigation of German Crimes in Poland, in preparation for the Nuremburg trials, set to begin November 20, 1945. See: Scrapbookpages.com, "Chelmno Death Camp," July 6, 2009, http://www.scrapbookpages.com/Poland/ Chelmno/history.html.

¹⁰ The River Narew (or Ner) is a tributary of the River Warta.

¹¹ The text of the *Testament of the Last Prisoners of the Chelmno Death Camp* was found by the Staff of Yad Vashem Institute in one of the Russian Archives, after the fall of Communism, and made available to the District Museum in Konin. See: The District Museum in Konin, "Chelmno," http://www.muzeum.com.pl/en/chelmno.htm.

¹² Holocaust Education and Archive Research Team, "Szymon Srebrnik: Chelmno Survivor Testimony," June 29, 1945, http://www. holocaustresearchproject.org/survivor/srebrnik.html.

¹³ To view a photograph of the remnants of the mill at Zawadka, indicating where the wooden bridge had stood from which ashes and bone meal were thrown into the Warta River, see: Aktion Reinhard Camps, "Zawadka: Remnants of the Mill," 2006, www.deathcamps.org/ occupation/pic/bigchelmno01.jpg.

[14] Isaiah 61:2b-3 (A Hebrew-English Bible: According to the Masoretic Text and the JPS 1917 Edition), http://www.mechon-mamre.org./p/pt/pt1061.htm.

Bibliography

Arntz, Hans-Dieter. 1990. *Judenverfolgung und Fluchthilfe im deutsch-belgischen Grenzgebiet* [Persecution and flight of Jews in the German-Belgian border region]. Euskirchen: Kümpel, Volksblatt-Druckerei + Verlag.

Arntz, Hans-Dieter. 2007. *Ordensburg Vogelsang....im Wandel der Zeiten.* Aachen: Helios Verlags-und Buchvertriebsgesellschaft.

Arntz, Hans-Dieter. 2008. *Reichskristallnacht.* Aachen: Helios Verlag.

Becker-Jakli, Barbara. 2004. *Das jüdische Krankenhaus in Köln; Die Geschichte des Israelitischen Asyls für Kranke und Altersschwache 1869-1945.* Köln: Emons Verlag.

Bullock, Alan. 1962. *Hitler: A Study in Tyranny. Rev. ed.* New York: Harper Colophon Books.

Corbach, Dieter. 1999. *Departure 6.00 am Messe Köln-Deutz Deportations 1938-1945.* Cologne: Scriba Verlag.

Corbach, Dieter. 1990. *Die Jawne zu Köln.* Köln: Scriba Verlag.

Davidson, Martin. 2010. *The Perfect Nazi: Uncovering My Grandfather's Secret Past.* New York: Penguin Group.

Dobroszycki, Lucjan, ed. 1984. *The Chronicles of the Lodz Ghetto 1941-1944.* Binghamton, NY: Vail-Ballou Press.

Friedman, Saul S. 2004. *A History of the Holocaust.* London: Vallentine Mitchell.

Gilbert, Martin. 1985. *The Holocaust: A History of the Jews of Europe during the Second World War.* New York: Henry Holt.

Gilead, Isaac, Yoram Haimi and Wojciech Mazurek. "Excavating Nazi Extermination Centres." 2009. *Present Pasts (Journal of the Institute of Archeology Heritage Studies Section).* DOI: http://dx.doi.org/10.5334/ pp.12. http://www.presentpasts.info/article/view/pp.12/2.

Goldstein, Phyllis. 2012. *A Convenient Hatred: The History of Antisemitism.* Brookline, MA: Facing History and Ourselves National Foundation.

Graham, Billy. 1997. *Just As I Am: The Autobiography of Billy Graham.* San Francisco: Harper Collins.

Grossman, Mendel. 1977. *With a Camera in the Ghetto.* New York: Schocken Books.

Hatchett, Marion J. 1995. *Commentary on the American Prayer Book.* New York: Harper One.

Heinen, Franz Albert. 2007. *Gottlos, schamlos, gewissenlos: Zum Osteinsatz der Ordensburg-Mannschaften.* Düsseldorf: Gaasterland-Verlag.

Howard, R.T. 1962. *Ruined and Rebuilt: The Story of Coventry Cathedral 1939-1962.* Coventry, UK: The Council of Coventry Cathedral.

Kogon, Eugen, Hermann Langbein and Adalbert Rückerl, eds. 1993. *Nazi Mass Murder: A Documentary History of the Use of Poison Gas.* New Haven: Yale University Press.

Krakowski, Shmuel. 2007. *Das Todeslager Chelmno/Kulmhof: Der Beginn der Endlösung*. Göttingen: Wallstein Verlag.

Langer, Lawrence, ed. 1995. *Art from the Ashes: A Holocaust Anthology.* New York: Oxford University Press.

Lanzmann, Claude. 1995. *Shoah: The Complete Text of the Acclaimed Holocaust Film.* New York: Da Capo Press.

Lissner, Cordula, and Ursula Reuter. 2008. *Andererseits komme ich anfangs nächster Woche—nicht ohne Hoffnungen auf Verlegung meiner Schule nach Cambridge zurück. Gewalt in der Region: Der Novemberpogram 1938 in Rheinland und Westfalen.* Düsseldorf/Münster/Wuppertal: Arbeitskreis der NS-Gedenksstätten Nordrhein-Westfalen.

Montague, Patrick. 2012. *Chelmno and the Holocaust: A History of Hitler's First Death Camp.* London: I.B. Tauris & Co Ltd.

Nouwen, Henri J.M. 2008. *A Restless Soul: Meditations from the Road.* Edited by Michael Ford. Notre Dame, IN: Ave Maria Press.

NS Documentation Centre of the City of Cologne, ed. 2010. *Cologne during National Socialism (A Short Guide through the EL-DE House).* Cologne: Emons Verlag.

Roodenburg, Hermann, ed. 2004. *Social Control in Europe. Vol. 2.* Columbus: Ohio State University Press.

Roy, Sara. 2002. "Living with the Holocaust: The Journey of a Child of Holocaust Survivors." *Journal of Palestine Studies* 32(1), http://www.palestine-studies.org/journals.aspx?id=4672&jid=1&href=abstract.

Schumann, Frederick L. 1935. *Hitler and the Nazi Dictatorship.* London: Robert Hale and Company.

Sierakowiak, Dawid. 1996. *The Diary of Dawid Sierakowiak: Five Notebooks from the Lodz Ghetto*. Edited by Allen Adelson. New York: Oxford.

Sterling, Eric J., ed. 2005. *Life in the Ghettos during the Holocaust*. Syracuse, NY: Syracuse University Press.

Struck, Manfred, ed. 2001. *Chelmo/Kulmhof: Ein vergessener Ort des Holocaust?* Bonn/Berlin: Gegen Vergessen–Für Demokratie.

Zyskind, Sara. 1983. *Stolen Years*. New York: Signet.

CPSIA information can be obtained at www.ICGtesting.com
Printed in the USA
LVOW07s2155020813

346053LV00001B/2/P

9 781478 712817